A Curriculum Design Manual for Theological Education: A Learning Outcomes Focus

A CURRICULUM DESIGN MANUAL for THEOLOGICAL EDUCATION

LEROY FORD

BROADMAN PRESS
NASHVILLE, TENNESSEE

Library of Congress Cataloging-in-Publication Data

Ford, LeRoy.
  A curriculum design manual for theological education : a learning
outcomes focus / LeRoy Ford.
    p.   cm.
  Includes bibliographical references and index.
  ISBN 0-8054-6042-X
  1. Theology—Study and teaching—United States.   2. Theological
seminaries—Curricula.   3. Curriculum planning—United States.
  I. Title.
BV4030.F67   1991
375'.023—dc   90-22062
                                                        CIP

To **Dr. Joe-Davis Heacock,** Dean Emeritus School of Religious Education, Southwestern Baptist Theological Seminary. He first encouraged me as Chairman of the School's Curriculum Committee in the early 1970s to lead the faculty members to express their course descriptions in terms of learning outcomes. As a result, while teaching during sabbatic leave at the National University of Mexico, I wrote a paper entitled "Writing Course Descriptions in Terms of Student Performance." That paper became the basis for faculty training sessions in the School of Religious Education.

Ever the innovative thinker and doer, Dr. Heacock encouraged all the faculty to find new ways to do old things. By the school year 1977-78, each of the ninety-two courses described in what is now *Course Descriptions for the Masters Degree Programs* appeared in terms of learning outcomes at the level of meaningful activity. That edition was probably the first such complete major syllabus of its kind in the history of theological education.

Contents

List of Illustrations

List of Charts

Acknowledgments

Over the years a multitude of persons have contributed to my work in the field of curriculum design. Among the most influential are these:

At the Baptist Sunday School Board of the Southern Baptist Convention, Raymond Rigdon taught me how to plan lesson course outlines and to design units of study. He introduced me to the elements of curriculum design as a framework for curriculum development. He passed on to me the insights he gained as a participant in the Cooperative Curriculum Project of the 1960s.

D. Campbell Wyckoff, professor of Christian Education, Emeritus, Princeton Theological Seminary, challenged me to explore ways to integrate into curriculum design in theological education the affective dimensions of learning. The emphasis on the affective domain of learning incorporated in this manual is a direct result of that challenge.

Justice Anderson, director of the World Mission/Evangelism Center at Southwestern Baptist Theological Seminary, provided over many years valuable insights into theological education in missions. He used in the classroom a previous manual dealing with theological education by extension in missions.

Alfonso Bernal Sahagun, founder of the Faculty of Arts and Sciences at the National University of Mexico opened doors for me to conduct workshops on curriculum design concepts in many universities in Mexico. In 1986 he arranged for me to validate curriculum design concepts in six universities in Mexico—in a cultural environment different from my own.

Ray Buker, long time missions leader among Conservative Baptists, provided my first opportunity to lead what became the first of many design workshops on theological education by extension in missions. These conferences led me to search for cross-cultural common denominators in theological education.

Edgar J. Elliston in The School of World Mission, Fuller Theological Seminary, used validation copies of this manual for two years as a text in theological education in missions with both graduate and undergraduate students. His feedback provided the affirmation I needed in the pre-publication phase of this manual.

Jack Terry, dean of the School of Religious Education, Southwestern Baptist Theological Seminary, provided a supportive environment in which ideas presented in this manual could mature. In that environment, theory became practice and product. Without that support, this manual probably would not have been written.

Several years ago I discovered that Lorin Cranford and I shared many common interests in the field of curriculum design. As associate professor of New Testament and director, Modern Languages Studies at Southwestern, he demonstrated the suitability of the learning outcomes approach in the preparation of course descriptions for New Testament studies and for the teaching of Greek. His work provided helpful insights outside my own field of concentration.

Nearly forty years ago, W. R. Fulton, former deacon in First Baptist Church, Norman, Oklahoma, and professor of education at the University of Oklahoma, taught me how to use the systems approach in the design of units of study.

Every colleague on the faculty in the School of Religious Education took an active role in developing the syllabus *Course Descriptions for the Masters Degree Programs*. In that sense each of them is a co-author.

My colleagues at Southwestern Baptist Theological Seminary—Lorin Cranford, Janis Watkins, John Newport, Pat Clendinning, Bob Brackney, David Kirkpatrick, Daryl Eldridge, William A. (Budd) Smith, Charles Ashby—made possible the course descriptions in Appendix 3.

All cartoons are based on my own stick figure drawings. To add artistic acceptability, Doug Dillard breathed life into those on pages 182, 207, 208, and 263; Joe McCormick did face lifts for those on pages 43, 73, 85, 90, 112, 203-206, 214, 215, 262, 270, 272; Bob Hines improved those on pages 34, 45, 87, 276.

LeRoy Ford
Ridgway, Colorado
1991

Preface

This manual does not consist of a synthesis of the literature on curriculum design in theological education. Rather, it represents a sort of experiential diary of "happenings" which occurred as I worked on curriculum designs and curriculum revisions over a period of about thirty years. During this time I worked on curriculum design at the Baptist Sunday School Board, Nashville, Tennessee, from 1959-1966 and at Southwestern Baptist Theological Seminary, Fort Worth, Texas, from 1966-1984.

While professor of Foundations of Education in the School of Religious Education at Southwestern, I served for many years as chairman of the school's Curriculum Committee and as a member of reaccreditation study teams. For many years I served as editor of *Course Descriptions for the Master's Degree Programs, School of Religious Education.* That syllabus is the first seminary-related publication in which all course descriptions (over one hundred of them) appear in the learning outcomes format.

At Southwestern, I assisted in the development of curriculum designs and instructional and administrative models for use in theological education by extension in missions. Much of what this manual includes comes from experience in leading over seventy curriculum design conferences for missions in fifteen countries in Central and South America, Asia, and the United States. At the university level, the manual reflects insights gained in design conferences at the National University of Mexico, the University of Michoacan, the University of Querétaro, the University of San Luis Potisí, University of Guanajuato, and the Ministry of Public Education in Mexico City.

Many readers will use part 3 of this manual, "Writing the Course Descriptions," apart from parts 1 and 2. For that reason part 3 includes a small amount of material used previously in parts 1 and 2. This I have done in order to avoid as much cross-referencing as possible.

The introductory page to the chapters in this manual, combined with the statement of course goals and objectives, constitutes a course description for a course on curriculum design in theological education.

After this book was almost ready for press, I learned that Winebrenner Theological Seminary in Ohio has revised their curriculum design using a validation copy of my manuscript as a model. They have written institutional goal statements for both the cognitive and affective domains. This is the first real life example of a curriculum design based on the learning outcomes focus.

Goals and Objectives

What goals and objectives should the curriculum designer achieve (at the level of meaningful performance) as a result of study of this manual?

Cognitive goal. As a result of study of this manual, the curriculum designer should demonstrate understanding of the process of developing a curriculum design with the learning outcomes focus.

Affective goal. The curriculum designer demonstrates conviction that persons called by God to Christian ministry ought to have an opportunity to receive theological training regardless of the contextual circumstances in which they live.

Objective. To demonstrate achievement of both these goals, the curriculum designer participates appropriately as a design team member. The team develops or revises a curriculum design with a learning outcomes focus, in keeping with guidelines presented in this manual. The design will include elaborations of all the elements of a design. (Of course, the designer will have to work out his assignment with his colleagues in meeting after meeting in which he makes compromise after compromise!)

In the process of achieving these goals and objectives, the designer should demonstrate understanding of the process of writing course descriptions by designing a course description in the learning outcomes format.

Introduction

This manual assumes that the organizing principle of a curriculum constitutes the primary common denominator among curriculum designs in theological education. The principle operates regardless of cultural orientation or geographical setting. Study of the design approach which this manual presents should benefit curriculum designers in traditional resident operations, extension education operations in missions (such as theological education by extension), Bible schools, correspondence or "distance learning" schools, and the traditional church school.

In its broadest sense theological education includes not only the education and training of persons preparing for Christian ministry as a profession, but also the teaching and training of those who take part in a church's education program.[1] Designers of church curricula should find helpful the insights included here.

The manual elaborates the *learning outcomes* focus in curriculum design. Other designers may choose to use a different focus. Manuals developed with other approaches in mind would form a welcome addition to curriculum design literature. Some designers use the terms *competency-based education* or *performance-based learning* when referring to the learning outcomes focus in curriculum design.

Generally, learning outcomes as used here focus on performance at the "level of meaningful activity." Outcomes refer to things the learner will do in a meaningful way during the entire course of ministry. These meaningful activities result from involvement in all domains of learning—cognitive, affective, and psychomotor.

This manual deals with curriculum design in theological edu-

---

1. A letter from Leon Pacala, executive director of The Association of Theological Schools in the United States and Canada, January 21, 1987.

cation *per se*. It assumes that the many delivery systems (instructional and administrative models) in common use today derive from a comprehensive elaboration of the other elements of curriculum design. Instructional models include the teaching lecture, the case study,[2] instructional systems, and so forth. All result from analysis of the other elements of curriculum design. Administrative models such as the resident institution, the correspondence school, the extension center, the on-the-job training approach, and combinations of these are determined only *after* analysis of instructional models and other elements of the design. In the learning outcomes focus in curriculum design, form follows function. The elements of curriculum design include institutional purpose, institutional educational goals and objectives for learners, scope, multiple contexts, methodology, and instructional and administrative models.

The manual confronts the problem of dealing with the affective dimensions of a design. Little has been done in a practical way to guide designers in making affective learning outcomes an integral part of curriculum design. The approach has problems, but designers cannot allow the problems to serve as excuses for ignoring this rich and essential aspect of curriculum design.

The learning outcomes focus allows designers to identify common learnings which *all* students need to master. These common learnings form a rational basis for determining the "core curriculum." In the learning outcomes curriculum the core consists of a set of meaningful learning outcomes rather than a group of survey courses. The common learnings core is not simply a set of courses all students must take but a set of equipping outcomes which all students need to master in order to function effectively in Christian ministry.

> *In the learning outcomes curriculum the core consists of a set of meaningful learning outcomes rather than a group of survey courses.*

Theological education institutions of whatever kind teach in *everything* they do. This manual brings under the purview of the curriculum design those seemingly noncurriculum-related in-

2. Such as used by the Harvard School of Business

stitutional activities such as chapel services, lecture series, and revivals. It considers them part of a comprehensive curriculum plan. In essence they become purposeful educational strategies. Their use as catchalls for fulfilling political obligations diminishes.

Much of this manual provides guidance in writing course descriptions in terms of learner outcomes. It shows how course descriptions fit into the total design of a curriculum plan. For teachers, the course description is "where the rubber touches the road"—where the design becomes tangible in the design implementation process. For learners, the course description provides the basis for making curriculum decisions.

The procedures outlined in this manual reflect these assumptions:

1. *There already exists an elaboration of theological foundations upon which the curriculum design builds.* In Southern Baptist institutions, for example, the statement adopted by the Southern Baptist Convention in 1963 serves as a guide. Other denominations also have statements which designers may use with little or no alteration.

2. *The learning outcomes focus in curriculum design in theological education constitutes a valid approach.* The learning outcomes focus emphasizes competencies and meaningful performance,[3] but it represents only one approach to curriculum design. The manual should help those designers who have chosen the learning outcomes approach.

3. *The learning outcomes focus forms a logical basis for preparation of course descriptions which provide for criterion-referenced testing and grading.* Criterion-referenced testing measures more accurately the learner's performance than norm-referenced testing and grading (the curve).

4. *Designers are already conversant with some of the taxonomies of objectives.*[4] These taxonomies describe levels of complexity in the teaching-learning process. They give the instructor a scheme for classifying goals and objectives according to complexity, relevance, and practicality. Course descriptions reflect

3. Though meanings are similar, I chose to use the term *learning outcomes* rather than competency-based or performance-based outcomes.

4. Many taxonomies of objectives exist. This manual relies heavily on *Taxonomy of Objectives: Cognitive Domain* by Benjamin S. Bloom, et al. (New York: D. McKay, 1956) and *Taxonomy of Objectives: Affective Domain* by D. R. Krathwohl, et al. (New York: D. McKay, 1964).

these levels. If the teacher desires a high level performance, the goals and objectives for the course reflect high levels. Specification of high levels commits the teacher to keep on teaching until the student achieves. If the instructor settles for lower levels of learning, the goals and objectives reflect those levels.

5. *Curriculum designs ultimately find expression in curriculum plans which in turn find expression in course descriptions.*

6. *Faculty and administration do not feel threatened by a properly developed curriculum design.* A curriculum design, objectively arrived at, may threaten the existence of long-established empires. Teachers should not feel threatened by properly-written course descriptions. If teachers do not understand to some degree the teaching-learning process, their course descriptions may reveal that weakness. Some teachers may fear that others will "steal" their courses if they make their course descriptions public in a published syllabus.

7. *Faculty and administration will face willingly the risks involved when the curriculum design and course descriptions appear in print for all the world to see.* They run the risk of revealing to the curriculum planning forces in the institution and to all others concerned that a course (or parts of it) does not fit into the curriculum plan of the institution. The course may or may not reside legitimately in the institutional purpose and the program and department purposes. It may not fit into the institution's statement of educational goals and objectives for learners. The curriculum forces of the institution may discover duplication of goals and objectives among the courses in the curriculum plan, resulting in waste of financial and personnel resources. Faculty members run the risk of losing courses when the courses do not fit into the curriculum plan. A course in furniture upholstering does not fit into the curriculum plan for training dentists. A given course in theological education may not fit into the curriculum design of a particular institution. Empires may fall. Faculty members run the risk that curriculum forces may discover that some essential goals and objectives do not receive attention.

> *When an institution develops objectively a curriculum design—and implements it—empires may fall!*

8. *It is difficult to revise objectively an existing curriculum design.* Most attempts at curriculum design revision and improvement at best become compromises with history. Tradition and philosophical orientation may prevent full flowering of a learning outcomes focus in curriculum design. However, any faculty member who puts his or her courses under the scrutiny required in developing a course description with a learning outcomes focus will benefit from such a disciplined experience. The exercise forces mastery in the organization of meanings and instructional processes.

> *Most attempts at curriculum design revision and improvement at best become compromises with history and tradition.*

9. *A judgment as to the value of a learning outcomes focus in curriculum design, particularly in writing course descriptions, awaits the judgment of the validity of the instructional processes which ultimately implement the design.* Goals and performance objectives are impotent in and of themselves. Educational goals and objectives require appropriate methods and learning activities to breathe life into them.

10. *Teachers should master the design; the design should not master the teacher.*

11. *There are biblical bases for the learning outcomes approach.* Jesus said, "Why call ye me Lord, Lord, and do not the things which I say?" (Luke 6:46) and "By their fruits ye shall know them" (Matt. 7:20).

I trust that this manual will provide helpful guidance to curriculum designers regardless of where they do the designing—in resident seminaries, Bible schools and colleges, programs of theological education by extension, programs designed for "distance learning," or circumstances which call for a touch of all the approaches.

Synopsis

A curriculum design for theological education is an organized statement and elaboration of the design's elements. The design organizes the institutional purpose, the institutional educational goals and objectives for learners, the scope, the multiple contexts, methodology, and instructional and administrative models in such a way that it ensures appropriate emphasis upon each. The principle which ensures this balance we call the organizing principle.

The organizing principle constitutes the great cross-cultural common denominator among curriculum designs. The organizing principle operates regardless of cultural, geographic, or other contextual settings. It serves as a framework for analyzing the ways in which given contextual settings influence the elaboration of the design elements.

Stated simply, the organizing principle affirms that in all contextual settings . . .

An effective curriculum in theological education involves . . .

Somebody (the learner)

in learning . . .

Something (the scope)

in . . .

Some Way (the methodology
and the instructional and
administrative models)
Somewhere (the multiple contexts)

for . . .

Some Purpose (the educational
goals and objectives)

Designers think first in terms of theological education *per se.* They do not begin by asking: How can we develop a curriculum design for theological education by extension in missions (TEE)?

Instead they ask: What are the elements of curriculum design in theological education? What do the elements include? Which instructional and administrative models would best implement the design in a given context? Theological education by extension may or may not provide the best administrative model. A resident seminary may or may not evolve as the principal administrative model.

A curriculum design possesses definite characteristics:

(a) A curriculum design resides in a document which responsible bodies may adopt, reject, or modify.

(b) A curriculum design draws from such great foundation disciplines as theology, philosophy, sociology, psychology, history, communication arts, and anthropology. Theology serves as the interpreter of the other disciplines.

(c) A curriculum design reflects a deliberate focus such as learning outcomes, social issues, common life experiences, common learnings, interdisciplinary learning, classical disciplines, or a combination of them.

A design which focuses on learning outcomes identifies the institution's educational goals and objectives for learners. The objectives (indicators) express what the learners will do in a meaningful way to indicate achievement of the goals. Designers refer to these "indicators" as learning outcomes or competencies.

Designers derive the learning outcomes from an analysis of the cognitive, affective, and psychomotor learnings desired in theological education.

The design elaborates one by one its elements.

The Institutional Purpose[1]

The institutional purpose for theological education describes *who?* does *what?* for *whom?* For example, "The purpose of the _____ Seminary (who?) is to provide theological education (does what?) for men and women preparing for Christian ministry (for whom?).

The institutional purpose occupies first position in the hierarchy of statements of learning intent included in the design. The hierarchy progresses downward through institutional educational goals and objectives for learners; program and depart-

---

1. It is assumed that a legal instrument such as a charter exists and the institutional purpose is in harmony with it.

ment educational goals and objectives; and on through course, unit, and lesson plan educational goals and objectives.

The Institutional Educational Goals and Objectives for Learners

A goal is a relatively broad statement of learning intent which (a) identifies the kind of learning desired and (b) expresses the subject in a chewable bite.

Educational objectives are the cognitive, affective, and psychomotor indicators of goal achievement. They express the outcomes or competencies which indicate goal achievement. They play a significant role in designs focused on learning outcomes.

The institutional educational goals and objectives provide the raw material from which designers develop programs and departments and courses of study. Designers group together into conceptual families the similar goals and objectives. They give each group (program) a name. For example, the design may (or may not) call for a School of Theology, a School of Religious Education, or a School of Church Music. Each program is legitimized by the existence of many objectively determined educational goals and objectives at the institutional level. Availability of resources affects the number of programs or "groupings" the institution may implement.

Each program has a set of educational goals and objectives lifted from the institutional goals and objectives. In like manner, designers group the *program* goals and objectives together into similar conceptual families or departments and give each a name. For example a School (program) of Theology may include a Department of Missions, a Department of Pastoral Ministry, a Department of Bible Languages, and so forth.

The department educational goals and objectives for learners form the basis for development of individual courses. These goals and objectives harmonize with and reside in all the preceding statements in the hierarchy of educational goals and objectives.

Finally, teachers divide courses into units of study whose goals and objectives reside in all preceding statements. Each unit may have one or more lesson plans which implement the unit and course goals and objectives.

Designers may choose among three approaches to stating institutional educational goals and objectives for learners.

1. *Some designers prefer to express them at a relatively high level of generalization.*—They are broad enough to house all suc-

ceeding statements, yet exclusive enough to provide focus. However, sooner or later designers must elaborate them into specifics for programs and departments.

2. *Some designers identify at the institutional level* all *of the specific operational goals and objectives in the cognitive, affective, and psychomotor domains.*—This approach makes it easier for designers to identify conceptual families for use in determining programs. However, the sheer volume of specifics can cause the "hierarchy" to appear top heavy.

3. *Designers may decide to include at the institutional level both the generalized statements and the specific ones.*—Cognitive goals, focal in nature, lend themselves easily to development of departmentation schemes. Affective goals and objectives, pervasive and permeating in nature, tend to apply in a cross-program, cross-department way and have less influence on development of departmentation schemes. A single affective goal and objective may express the desired outcome for numerous courses. In another vein, each cognitive goal and objective has affective dimensions. Each course which has a cognitive focus primarily will also have an affective (and sometimes a psychomotor) dimension which it may or may not share with other courses.

In expressing affective goals and objectives, designers find it helpful to (a) identify specific attitudinal nouns such as confidence, respect, obedience, commitment, assurance; (b) determine appropriate prepositional connectors such as of, to, for, in, toward; and (c) identify from the design's scope appropriate objects of the prepositions. For example: faithfulness (noun) in (preposition) the exercise of their gifts in ministry (object of the preposition). Other examples include statements like "commitment to lifelong learning" and "dependability in performance of tasks."

With adequate and aggressive curriculum supervision, affective educational goals at the institutional level will find lodging in *all* courses. Such supervision would make spiritual formation part of the warp and woof of the curriculum plan, lessening the need for special courses focusing on development of attitudes and values. Diffusion of learning results in learning in all domains in a single course regardless of its primary focus. While special courses in spiritual formation serve a purpose, a more natural approach makes *every course* a course in spiritual formation through adequate curriculum supervision.

Among other schools, Harvard Business School requires entering MBA students to take a three-week course on business ethics. However, Gary Edwards, executive director of the Washington-based Ethics Resource Center, says, "Ideally, ethics issues ought to be infused throughout an entire business school curriculum."[2]

Could we say that spiritual formation ought to be infused throughout the theological education curriculum—by implementing affective goals in *every* course?

The statement of an institution's educational goals in the affective realm commits the institution to permeate both its curriculum plan and its noncurriculum related activities with experiences which contribute to achievement of its affective goals and objectives. In effect this means bringing under the purview of the curriculum plan those institutional activities which designers normally have considered noncurriculum related (such as chapel services, lectureships, revivals, and so forth). It lifts such activities to curriculum status. They become less oriented toward public relations and fulfillment of political responsibilities.

Curriculum planners and supervisors face difficulties in measuring affective learning outcomes. Many questions call for consideration. How will the student's transcript reflect achievement in the attitudinal dimensions of a course? How will the grading system deal with those delayed-response actions which indicate affective change? Who determines which attitudes and values are desirable? Should teachers make known to the student in advance the affective goals? If so, how can the teacher determine whether the student makes a genuine or faked response? How effective is a simple invitation to make attitudinal change?

> *The illusiveness of affective goals and objectives and the difficulty in evaluating affective performance are not adequate grounds for avoiding them in an institution's curriculum design.*

Educational objectives specify typical actions which indicate goal achievement. For this reason, some designers call them "indicators." Objectives include at least (a) an action verb and (b) an object of the verb. In their more refined state, they indicate stan-

---

2. *The Denver Post,* "Harvard to Require Ethics Class," July 18, 1988, 80.

dards of performance and when necessary the conditions or circumstances under which the action occurs. (For example: The student sight reads musical scores, conducts a business meeting according to Robert's Rules of Order, translates from New Testament Greek into English, or compares biblical and philosophical world views.) Indicators serve as the basis for criterion-referenced testing. Objectives exist because goals exist—expressed or understood.

Scope

The scope of the curriculum design identifies what the curriculum *may* in fact include. The scope derives from the Bible, experience, and all of people's relationships in the light of the gospel. Public schools and universities deal with "people's relationships" but not "in the light of the gospel." This difference spotlights the basic distinctive of theological education.

Designers may express scope in terms of permissible subjects or as desired learning outcomes as used in the learning outcomes focus in curriculum design. Scope consists of Bible-based learning outcomes, experience-based outcomes, and relationship-based outcomes. Each of these sources suggests meaningful performance outcomes, attitudes, and values needed in effective Christian ministry. The ambiguity of some affective outcomes does not excuse designers from including them in scope.

Relationship-based learning outcomes include those growing out of a person's relationship to (a) God, (b) self and others, (c) nature, and (d) history. Designers ask such questions as: Since people have a relationship to God, what do they need to learn to do well in order to function effectively in Christian ministry? What attitudes and values should characterize the relationships of those training for Christian ministry?

A learning outcome or competency growing out of more than one of these sources indicates that it merits serious consideration for inclusion in the scope of the curriculum. Bible-based competencies in and of themselves merit inclusion.

In a real sense, scope consists of all the subjects and learning outcomes specified in the educational goals and objectives for learners. For this reason some designers prefer to develop first the scope. Then they write the educational goals and objectives for learners. This simply illustrates the dynamic nature of curriculum design.

The Multiple Contexts

The multiple contexts within which a curriculum lives shape and form the instructional and administrative models as much or more than any of the other elements. Designers analyze the supportive and nonsupportive (hostile) aspects of the educational, cultural, religious, denominational, familial, geographic, political, developmental, and economic contexts. The developmental context focuses on the learners' readiness to learn in the light of developmental characteristics. In the light of their findings, designers construct a curriculum plan. They develop instructional and administrative models which take advantage of the supporting elements and accommodate appropriately the hostile factors in the contexts.

Instructional and Administrative Models

The multiple contexts, converging upon the other design elements, give clues to the design of appropriate instructional models. Administrative models serve as enabling or facilitating systems for making effective the instructional models. Designers develop instructional models first, then determine appropriate vehicles to administer or to "carry" them. Form (administrative models) follows function (instructional models).

Instructional models include such approaches as instructional systems, case studies,[3] seminars, self-instructional devices, field experiences, the set lecture and the teaching lecture, and various combinations of these and other approaches.

Administrative models which deliver the instructional models include such approaches as the correspondence school (distance learning model), the extension center, the resident institution, the in-service training or on-the-job supervision approach, and other approaches or combinations of them.

Scope and context descriptions and the educational goals and objective for learners provide the bases for development of course descriptions. They serve as a "bank" of ideas from which designers may draw in developing course descriptions.

The Course Descriptions

Course descriptions which focus on learning outcomes include the (a) course title; (b) rationale for the course; (c) course educa-

---

3. Case studies popularized by the Harvard School of Business.

tional goals and objectives; (d) course objectives or indicators of goal achievement; (e) unit titles; (f) unit educational goals and objectives; (g) description of methods and learning activities for use in the course; (h) description of testing and evaluation procedures; (i) mediography; (j) and, if desired, a set of lesson plans for each unit.

Course titles usually take one of two forms: the process title focuses on action; the subject title focuses on identification of the limits of a field of study.

The rationale for the course legitimizes the course within the context of the institutional purpose and the educational goals and objectives for learners expressed for programs and departments.

A course goal identifies the kind of learning expected (knowledge, understanding, attitudes, motor skills) and states the subject in a chewable bite.

A course objective states an observable action which the instructor will accept as valid evidence of goal achievement. The course objective describes the highest level of learning the student should achieve, when possible, at the level of meaningful activity.

A vertical cluster of courses may reserve the high level performance for the last course in the cluster, leaving for prerequisite courses the lower level objectives. For political reasons, even the courses which focus on the lower levels of learning should call attention to the high, meaningful level objectives to add meaning and purpose to what otherwise might appear mundane.

When a curriculum design focuses on learning outcomes, the course goals and objectives should appear *verbatim* as the course description in the institution's catalog.

Sometimes the arrangement and title of units within a course follow the anchor pattern. The first unit introduces the concept; the following units reflect logical breakdowns of the basic concept. The linear pattern consists of several units in logical sequence. Each unit grows out of the preceding one. The "wheel" pattern simply consists of several units of equal weight dealing with a central theme, but they have no logical sequence.

Course designers experience many pitfalls in writing course descriptions. Some tend to express goals in the language of objectives; others do not focus on the primary cognitive, affective, or psychomotor action in the objective but focus on trivia. In the cognitive domain some describe methods instead of cognitive action in the objective; some specify one kind of learning (domain) in the goal but switch to another in the objective; some try to include everything as if to avoid some legal action based on an unintended omission; and so forth.

In the learning outcomes focus in the curriculum, *test* means any activity which indicates the degree to which a learner has achieved a goal. Test items should agree with the objective in subject, form, and level of learning. Teachers should assign the greatest grade weight to performance at the highest level of learning required in the course. The learning outcomes focus in the curriculum assumes that criterion-referenced testing and grading is the desirable approach. Students receive grades based on the degree to which they have achieved goals and objectives. They compete against themselves. In norm-referenced testing and grading, students compete against other students. In institutions which require norm-referenced grading, the teacher should submit both a letter grade and numerical grade in order to represent the student fairly. Norm-referenced grading can easily bear false witness to the student's achievement—as well as to the teacher's proficiency.

The mediography includes all forms of resources available to students in following the learning plan. It includes books, films, audiotapes, videotapes, computer programs, periodicals, and so forth. Because of space limitations, some course designers include only the title and author in the mediography.

Course descriptions may take one of several forms. The long form includes all the items suggested thus far. (See the sample on Greek grammar in Appendix 1.) The short form omits the "lead-up" objectives in each unit of study as well as the description of methods, testing approaches, and mediography. A third form states only the high level outcomes worked on in the course and does not break down the statements into units. This major learning outcome form lists in order of treatment the statements of meaningful level outcomes. The outcomes are not divided into units. (See Appendix 1 for examples.) Each form has its advantages and disadvantages. The long form seems to produce the best results since it requires the teacher to analyze and organize thoroughly the meanings in the course. It also provides a broad basis for developing lesson plans.

Writing goals, objectives, titles, and purposes requires mastery of some of the techniques of generalization. The wording of a statement can express what the statement includes specifically and what it excludes by implication. "Big goals have little goals all clustered up inside 'em; little goals have lesser goals and so on *ad infinitum!*"

Some fortunate curriculum designers have the opportunity to work on curriculum designs *before* the inauguration of a program of theological education. Others must revise existing designs. Their task is much like changing a tire on an eighteen-wheeler as it races down a winding mountain road. In most cases, curriculum revision becomes a series of compromises with history. Designers may take an objective approach, but sooner or later history demands that the new design take on traditional forms.

Catalog descriptions take one of two forms. The subject description elaborates the subject and sets subject boundaries. The process description states the course goal and objectives in performance terms. The process form communicates more readily to students, who, by the way, makes up the target group for the catalog.

Part 1
What Curriculum Means

1
What Does Curriculum Mean?

Goals: A study of this chapter should help curriculum designers understand . . .
   1. the meaning of curriculum, curriculum plan, and curriculum design.
   2. the characteristics of curriculum design.

Objectives: The designer . . .
   1. summarizes the characteristics of a curriculum design as related to form, foundation disciplines, focus, and design elements.
   2. discriminates between curriculum design and curriculum plan.
   3. defines curriculum, curriculum design, and curriculum plan.

Several months ago, I conversed with a friend of mine—a prominent educator in another country. As we drove along the highway he said, "Dr. Ford, if I had had my *curriculum* on the desk of our country's President two weeks earlier, I probably would have been governor of our state." I pondered his use of the term. Then I remembered that in its original meaning, *curriculum* meant "a race." It means what happens. In education, curriculum happens to persons. The happenings occur because somewhere a curriculum design (written or unwritten) exists and persons involved develop a curriculum plan to cause the happenings to take place.

My friend was saying, "If I had had on the President's desk the record of my life's race or the record of the happenings in my life . . ." That's why we sometimes define *curriculum* as "all of life's experiences" or happenings.

1. *What curriculum means.*—The term "curriculum" is from the Latin. It is a noun derived from the verb *currere* which means to run. Literally, a curriculum is a running or a race

course. Curriculum exists only where true learning experiences take place. Accordingly, . . . curriculum may be thought of as the sum of all learning experiences resulting from a curriculum plan . . . directed toward achieving . . . objectives.[1]

A former student of mine once asked a curriculum design authority, "What about those incidental happenings or learnings which occur but not as a result of direct attempts to achieve objectives?"

The professor answered, "Well, I suppose those are in God's curriculum!" In order to enhance the possibility that "happenings" will occur, curriculum planners develop curriculum designs and curriculum plans based upon them.

A curriculum design reflects upon the broad areas of concern which planners must confront in order to develop particular plans for bringing about "happenings" in the life of the learner. A curriculum design describes the parameters within which the curriculum will occur. It enunciates the essential considerations with which designers must deal. These considerations set the bounds and determine factors of limitation designers consider in developing specific plans for translating the curriculum design into action.

2. *What curriculum design means.*—A curriculum design is a statement of and elaboration of the institutional purpose, institutional goals and objectives for learners, scope, contexts, methodology, and instructional and administrative models involved in an educational effort. The design is organized in such a way as to ensure appropriate and balanced emphasis upon each element. A design provides the basis for "blueprinting" a curriculum plan.

3. *What curriculum plan means.*—The difference between a curriculum and curriculum plan is the difference between a race completed and a race planned. Someone said, "The difference between a curriculum and a curriculum plan is the difference between a curriculum 'had' and a curriculum 'planned.'"

A curriculum plan is a detailed blueprint or system for implementing a design. A curriculum plan resides in instructional departments, particularly in course descriptions. In the church school, the curriculum plan resides in instructional periodicals

---

1. Howard P. Colson and Raymond M. Rigdon, *Understanding Your Church's Curriculum* (Nashville: Broadman Press, 1981), 39.

"The Prize is in the Process."

... ROBERT BROWNING .

CURRICULUM IS **ALL** OF LIFE'S
EXPERIENCES RESULTING FROM A
CURRICULUM PLAN — DIRECTED
TOWARD **ACHIEVING OBJECTIVES.**

and the individual "lessons" which incorporate goals and objectives, elaborate the meanings, and describe learning activities and evaluation approaches. In essence, a curriculum plan in theological education resides in course descriptions and lesson plans which finally implement the curriculum design.

Which is more correct?

- What does Trinity's curriculum include?
- What does Trinity's curriculum plan include?

4. *What characterizes a curriculum design?—*

(a) *A curriculum design usually resides in a document.* It consists of pages of print. One can hold it in his hand and wave it! Or he can place it in a file and retrieve it when he needs it. It exists in a communicable form which persons or groups can study, analyze, approve, reject. Professors can use it as a guide for writing course descriptions. Curriculum planners can use it to determine whether or not their plans meet necessary requirements. They can use it to spot duplication in their curriculum plans; to eliminate the irrelevant and to incorporate the essential.

(b) *A curriculum design reflects appropriately the great foundation disciplines.* A foundation discipline is a great field of thought from which designers may derive insight for curriculum planning.

A curriculum design pulls from the Bible and theology those truths which shape the curriculum in keeping with biblical truth, stance, and theological viewpoint. The design screens the insights of the other foundation disciplines through the discipline of theology. Theology "interprets" other disciplines.

A design pulls from educational psychology those truths which make it effective from the viewpoint of how persons learn in given cultural contexts. From developmental psychology, the design reflects insights as to how human development affects how and what persons learn.

In the same vein, a design takes from cultural anthropology those truths which make learning effective within a given cultural context.

In a workshop in Indonesia, I explained how to design a discrimination activity, an activity in which the learner chooses from several possibilities the best or correct answer. A national leader stood and said, "But sir, Indonesians do not like to make choices." The Indonesians have a reason for not liking to make choices. *Takut salah,* they say. ("I'm afraid of being wrong.") In essence he said, "Education within our culture does not place primary emphasis on problem solving."

A design recognizes in communication arts those truths which help communication flow meaningfully and efficiently from sender to receiver. Many principles of communication are universal, but sometimes certain cultural factors determine the means of communication.

> In a conference in Guatemala, with members of a Central American tribe whose adults cannot read, I learned that the adults delight in role playing—as long as men role play in front of men and women role play in front of women. And for some reason the villains in the role play always wear string ties, white shirts, and Panama hats!
> A Wycliffe translator in Guatemala once told me that a K'ekchi child would find it more difficult to locate "hidden" faces or animals in a picture than would the average American child.

In seminaries in the United States, professors usually assume that all students learn in the same way and at the same rate—by listening to a lecture once! One learner in seven has some sort of learning difficulty. Communication arts recognizes the differences and reacts accordingly.

Other foundation disciplines, such as philosophy (especially educational philosophy), sociology, and gerontology make their own contributions in the light of biblical and theological truth.

(c) *A curriculum design reflects a deliberate focus. Focus* means a concentration on a particular principle or concept which serves as an organizing strategy. If asked, "What is the focus of your curriculum design?" the designers can answer. They may answer, "learning outcomes," "social issues," "common learnings," "high level competencies," "interdisciplinary learning," or some combination of these.[2]

(d) *A design relates properly and appropriately all its elements.* The design ensures through the organizing principle that each element receives appropriate attention. A curriculum design includes descriptions of several elements:

---

2. See Ronald T. Hyman, *Approaches in Curriculum* (Englewood Cliffs, N.J.: Prentice Hall, 1973).

- It describes the reasons for which theological education exists (institutional purpose).
- It describes what should happen to the learners (institutional educational goals and objectives for learners).
- It describes appropriate ideas, concepts, meanings, and subject matter for the curriculum and tells which parts should have primary attention in given circumstances (scope).
- It describes ways in which learners learn within given cultures and at given experience levels (methodology).
- It describes various aspects of the environments within which learners learn (contexts).
- It describes how these contexts and other elements influence the structure of the delivery systems which implement the design.
- It analyzes the influence these contexts have on the development of approaches to doing theological education (instructional and administrative models).

A curriculum design helps ensure that "scope" (what we teach) finds expression in teaching methods appropriate for given groups and cultures (how we teach). It sees that educational goals and objectives (why we teach) influence appropriately the determination of what *may be* taught (scope). The design sees that the methods of education reflect learning activity appropriate to learner characteristics and differences (methodology). It sees that the contexts (where we teach and the circumstances surrounding our teaching) influence appropriately all other elements, and that the total design is appropriately tailored to needs in the light of contextual influences.

In a curriculum design, the elements work harmoniously to cause curriculum to happen. These elements receive more detailed attention in the chapters which follow.

2
Curriculum Design in the Real World

Goal: A study of this chapter should help curriculum designers understand the advantages and disadvantages of "free rein" and "revision" approaches to curriculum design.

Objectives: The designer . . .

1. selects the design approach most compatible with the "factors of limitation" within which he operates.
2. explains the advantages and disadvantages of the "free rein" and "revision" approaches to curriculum design.

The elements of curriculum design—institutional purpose, institutional educational goals and objectives for learners, scope, methodology, and particularly the contexts and the instructional and administrative models determine the approaches to doing theological education. The elaboration of the elements reflects appropriate consideration of foundation disciplines such as theology, sociology, communication arts, cultural anthropology, philosophy, educational psychology, and so forth.

A design may or may not call for the traditional resident seminary as the administrative model. It may call for some variation of or some combination with other models such as the extension (TEE) model used frequently in foreign missions.

The elaboration of the elements of a design determines and furnishes the critical data from which designers shape instructional and administrative models.

Curriculum designers for theological education, both at home and in missions, find themselves in one of two circumstances.

The Free Rein Approach

A few designers have the fortunate assignment to develop a design document in advance of the inauguration of an institution. Few designers have this happy opportunity!

Some designers receive an assignment to develop objectively a rational design in an existing institution but have instructions to feel little or no obligation to incorporate existing structures.

Curriculum designs developed from such an objective and rational approach have distinct advantages:

(a) The designers do not have to confront the challenge of established academic empires. They do not have to come to terms with existing structures which reflect tradition more than logic.

(b) Designers feel free to develop a design for theological education *per se*. Decisions about instructional and administrative models come *after* unencumbered elaboration and analysis of the other elements of the design. They do not begin with a resident seminary as a predetermined model. They do not begin with an assumption that theological education by extension (TEE) is the best model for theological education in missions. Designers can view objectively their task. They do not have to develop a design to clothe existing forms.

(c) Designers know that whatever develops in the design has a rational and defensible reason for being. They can provide a logical rationale for including or excluding programs, goals and objectives, departments of instruction, and courses of instruction.

(d) A design ensures that planners will channel toward priorities the available resources of money, time, facilities, and personnel. Planners do not have to sustain preexisting structures.

(e) Designers see in perspective all aspects of theological education. They can perceive the logical sequence of considerations in developing a design. For example, they can see that determination of instructional and administrative models comes *after* the analysis of institutional purposes, educational goals and objectives, scope, contexts, and methodology.

(f) Designers can view as valid any rationally developed implementation model. Many resident seminaries of long standing do not accept transfer of credit for courses completed through theological education by extension. Happily some do. The credits should have equal value if both the resident institution and the extension model evolved from objectively developed curriculum designs and meet other appropriate standards.

Any implementation model developed from an objective analysis of elements should be as valid as any other. For example, the extension model has as much validity as the resident institution model—provided both were based on objective data derived from analysis of elements.

> *The extension model of theological education has as much validity as the resident institution model—provided both are based on objective data derived from analysis of design elements.*

(g) An objectively developed design reveals areas of duplication of effort. The duplication appears for all to see. In one institution, the design revealed that four separate courses taught students how to write educational goals and objectives!

The rational or objective approach has a few seeming disadvantages:

(a) Complete redesign beginning at "point zero" in an existing program of theological education can result in change by revolution! Somebody may get hurt, especially when empires fall! Even when an institution authorizes designers to "begin at point zero," few can follow through.

> *Complete redesign of a curriculum can cause revolution. Somebody may get hurt—especially when empires fall!*

(b) Few persons responsible for creating original designs have the necessary training in curriculum theory and design. Surgeons need training in surgery; curriculum designers need training in curriculum theory and design. Without training, designers may get on a horse and speed off in all directions at the same time.

The Revision Approach

Most designers have the assignment to revise existing structures. They do not have the liberty to create an entirely new design but recommend desirable changes in existing ones. In many cases they must accept existing structures but develop a "design" to legitimize the preexistent structures. They recommend significant changes which improve the overall efficiency and productivity of a design, but they do not alter dramatically the original. They may even develop "prop-up" functions to legitimize long-established forms! This is where most designers live.

I once conducted a workshop on theological education by extension at a mission station in Asia. The existing seminary had already developed a series of extension study books using the programmed instruction format. I asked, "Why did you choose programmed instruction as the instructional model? Why did you choose these particular subjects when preparing the books?" They had done excellent work in developing the courses but could not pinpoint reasons for their decisions.

In later years when asked to conduct workshops, I have insisted that the first week of the workshop deal with the process of developing a curriculum design. Then participants can provide a valid rationale for adopting a particular instructional model. They can establish priorities regarding subjects to offer.

The revision approach has some advantages:

(a) In the revision approach change may come from accretion rather than revolution. Designers take the long look. They keep their eyes on the ultimate result, the "North Star" but realize that change can come step by step.

> *In the revision approach, change comes by accretion rather than revolution.* **Less blood may be shed.**

Through administrative controls they can ensure that what happens *in the future* meets desired standards. Through accretion or accumulation of desirable features sooner or later the designers achieve desired results.

As an administrative control, designers may require that all course descriptions "from this day on" follow the learning outcomes format. A curriculum committee may refuse to consider course descriptions for proposed new courses unless they appear in that format. As another administrative control, those responsible may require that all prospective faculty members receive orientation about the characteristics of the curriculum design. Sooner or later faculty turnover will result in more complete understanding of the design.

(b) In the revision approach, faculty and students face fewer changes at one time. A little confusion spread over a long period

Some designers may try to create a curriculum design without adequate training . . .

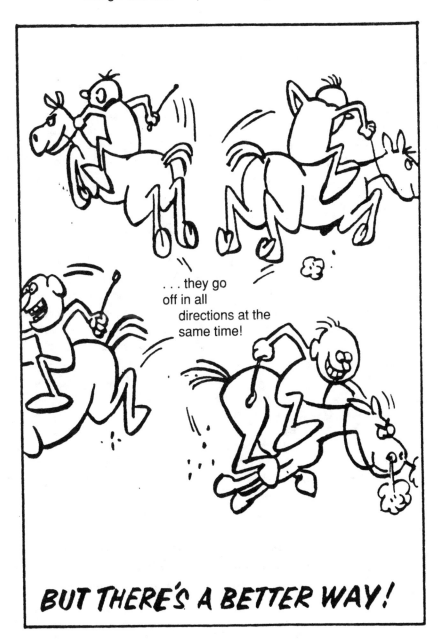

BUT THERE'S A BETTER WAY!

may prove more productive than the greater confusion brought about by sudden revolutionary change.

But the revision approach has disadvantages:

> *In curriculum revision, designers face the frustration of trying to change a tire on a moving vehicle racing down a winding mountain road!*

(a) Designers face the frustration of trying to change a tire on a moving vehicle racing down a winding mountain road! The show must go on! Frequently the designers must keep a curriculum functioning and at the same time develop and implement revisions.

(b) Planners may have to commit resources to programs or structures which do not fit into a rationally determined design. Some seminaries and Bible schools and some programs of theological education by extension have included courses simply because an available teacher had a deep interest in a subject. In some instances, institutions have added courses or even departments of instruction with little consideration of whether they supported the institutional purpose and the educational goals and objectives described in a design.

(c) Often curriculum revisions turn out to be little more than a series of comprises with history. And "history" may turn out to be an account of ill-founded traditions.

Both the "free rein" approach and the "revision" approach have their advantages and disadvantages. Designers involved in either situation can profit from a study of the elements of curriculum design and how to incorporate the elements into the act of doing theological education.

> *Often curriculum revisions turn out to be little more than a series of compromises with history.*

"CURRICULUM REVISERS AT WORK"

Part 2
Developing a Curriculum Design

3
Discover the Common Denominator Among Curriculum Designs

Goals: A study of this chapter should help the curriculum designer understand . . .
1. what organizing principle means.
2. why the organizing principle constitutes the major cross-cultural denominator among curriculum designs.

Objectives: The designer . . .
1. summarizes how the organizing principle (the 5-S principle) can serve as a framework for designing a curriculum regardless of contextual influences.
2. defines organizing principle so as to include references to all the elements of design.

What do all curriculum designs in theological education in the United States have in common? What do they have in common with curriculum designs for theological education in Malaysia? Guatemala? Ethiopia?

Curriculum designers cannot impose upon one culture or subculture a curriculum design created for another. Neither can a denomination impose the same curriculum design upon all its theological training institutions. Design strategies, especially in foreign missions, require more of the designer. What design generalization can apply to theological education in all cultures and at the same time provide enough structure to serve as a basis for development of a particular curriculum design? Which aspects of a design remain constant regardless of contextual differences? Indeed, do such generalizations and constants exist?

The great cross-cultural denominator among curriculum designs in theological education is the *organizing principle*. The principle applies regardless of cultural, developmental, geographic, economic, familial, religious, educational, and political contexts.

> ***The great cross-cultural common denominator among curriculum designs is the organizing principle.***

The organizing principle is that aspect of a design which identifies the design's elements and relates them in such a way that all elements receive appropriate emphasis. In operation the principle guides learners toward achievement of educational goals.

The principle operates in a traditional resident seminary in the United States; an innovative training institution in a pioneer area; a nontraditional, nonresident extension seminary in Indonesia or Brazil; or a "do-the-best-you can" approach among illiterate tribes in Mexico or New Guinea.

The organizing principle reflects all of the elements of curriculum design: the institutional purpose, institutional educational goals and objectives for learners, scope, multiple contexts, methodology, and instructional and administrative implementation models. The principle ensures that the instructional and administrative "carriers" grow out of the interrelationships existing among the other elements of the design.

The simplicity of the organizing principle may make it appear inadequate.

The organizing principle declares that an effective curriculum in theological education involves . . .

Somebody (the learner)

in learning . . .

Something (the scope)

in . . .

Some Way (the methodology
and the instructional
and administrative models)

Somewhere (the multiple contexts)

for . . .

Some purpose (the institutional purpose
and the educational goals
and objectives for learners) . . .
all in the light of the gospel.

We might call this the 5-S principle. It reflects all the elements of curriculum design in theological education.

The curriculum design elaborates the principle by answering questions such as these based on the elements of the organizing principle:

1. *Who are the **"somebodies"**?*—As individual learners, what are they like educationally? ethnically? religiously? developmentally? emotionally? psychologically? culturally? Who *are* the target groups for whom the design is intended?

2. *What are the **somethings** the somebodies need to learn?*— From the viewpoint of theological education, what *may* the curriculum plan include? What does it exclude?

3. *What are the **some ways** in which the somebodies learn the somethings?*—What are the learning styles of the learners? How has culture influenced their learning styles? What kinds of learning activities and methods best suit the subject and learner? What influences the choice of methods? What are the appropriate methods?

4. *What are the **"somewheres"** which influence the shape of the somethings the somebodies learn in some way?*—What are the "contexts" which influence so greatly the implementation of the design? What are the hostile factors in the various contexts which shape the design? What are the supportive factors?

5. *What are the **"some purposes"** for which the somebodies learn something, somewhere, in some way?*—What does the institutional purpose say the learner should learn? What goals and objectives in the cognitive, affective, and psychomotor domains does the learner need to achieve?

As designers answer these questions, the unique input provided by the contextual and cultural influences which affect the design makes the design belong uniquely to that culture in which the curriculum lives.

We may expand the statement of organizing principle so that it says:

An effective curriculum involves unique persons in unique target groups in making cognitive, affective, and psychomotor changes appropriate to theological education. It uses methods which reflect due consideration of principles of learning, especially those related to learning styles within a given culture. The curriculum is implemented through instructional and administrative models shaped by the unique character of the institutional purpose, institutional goals and objectives for learners, the scope, and the multiple contexts within which the curriculum lives. The curriculum involves persons in such a way that they achieve the goals and objectives.[1]

Of all the elements of design, the contexts seem to vary most from one culture to another. Scope has a higher degree of transferability from one culture to another than contexts. In theological education, biblical concepts transfer with equal authority from one culture to another.

Other common denominators exist but have lesser impact than the organizing principle. For example, the structure of institutional purposes forms a common denominator among designs. All institutional purposes tell *who? does what? for whom?*

---

1. Some designers add timing—"at some time" as a part of the organizing principle. History, current events and the church calendar influence the design, especially scope.

4
State the Institutional Purpose for Theological Education

Goal: A study of this chapter should help curriculum designers understand the process for elaborating an institutional purpose statement in curriculum design.

Objectives: The designer . . .

1. elaborates a statement of institutional purpose in keeping with guidelines presented in this chapter.
2. analyzes statements of institutional purpose. Determines what the statements include by specification and what they exclude by implication.
3. explains why an institutional purpose statement answers the questions who? does what? for whom? but does not answer the questions how? and where?

This chapter uses the term *institutional purpose* even though in theory the designers have not as yet decided to establish an "institution" such as a resident seminary or some variation of the extension approach. At this point they think of theological education *per se* and make decisions about implementation (administrative models) later.

When curriculum designers inherit an existing "institution" they may apply the same guidelines for developing or revising statements of institutional purpose. For purposes of convenience, this chapter will use the term *institutional purpose* regardless of whether designers have made a decision about establishing an institution as such.

By purpose, designers mean a statement of theological education's reason for being. The purpose statement draws the parameters within which the curriculum of theological education operates. It draws them broadly enough to allow for essential development and movement within.

Diagram of Elements of Curriculum Design

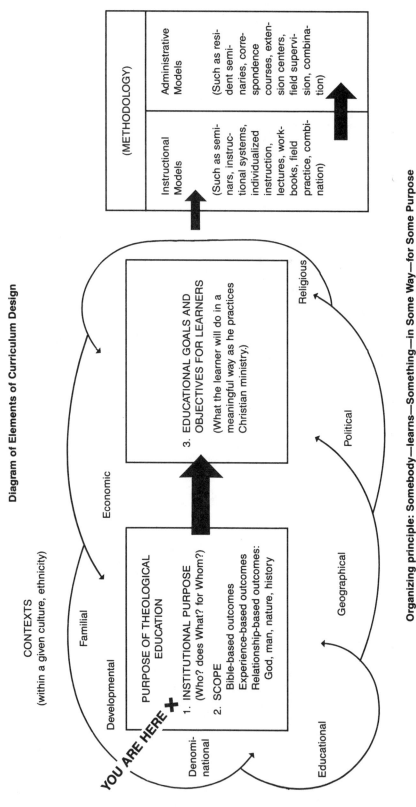

CONTEXTS
(within a given culture, ethnicity)

Developmental

Familial

Economic

Religious

Political

Geographical

Educational

Denomi-
national

YOU ARE HERE ✚

PURPOSE OF THEOLOGICAL
EDUCATION

1. INSTITUTIONAL PURPOSE
   (Who? does What? for Whom?)

2. SCOPE
   Bible-based outcomes
   Experience-based outcomes
   Relationship-based outcomes:
   God, man, nature, history

3. EDUCATIONAL GOALS AND
   OBJECTIVES FOR LEARNERS

   (What the learner will do in a
   meaningful way as he practices
   Christian ministry.)

(METHODOLOGY)

Instructional
Models

(Such as semi-
nars, instruc-
tional systems,
individualized
instruction,
lectures, work-
books, field
practice, combi-
nation)

Administrative
Models

(Such as resi-
dent semi-
naries, corre-
spondence
courses, exten-
sion centers,
field supervi-
sion, combina-
tion)

Organizing principle: Somebody—learns—Something—in Some Way—for Some Purpose

A Model for Curriculum Design Within a Given Cultural Setting

A purpose statement for theological education *per se* might read: The purpose of theological education is to train men and women for Christian ministry. An "institutional purpose" might read: The purpose of _____ Seminary is to provide theological education for men and women preparing for Christian ministry.

The institutional statement includes several things which make it a useful tool for curriculum designers. Simply stated, the purpose statement responds clearly to the questions:

> WHO?
> does WHAT?
> for WHOM?

Note that the questions *how?* and *where?* do not as yet appear. A purpose statement remains open enough to allow responsible persons to develop the means, departmentation schemes, and implementation models later in the design. The instructional and administrative models answer the question *how?* and decisions about them come much later in the design. To specify *how?* at this point would restrict unnecessarily those charged with fulfillment of the purpose. The omission of *how?* is especially important in theological education by extension in missions (TEE). To describe *how?* at this point would specify prematurely an implementation model. Some missions which assumed at the beginning that an extension model would serve best discovered later after preparing a design, that the extension model was not appropriate.

> *The institutional purpose tells*
> *Who?*
> *Does what?*
> *For whom?*

The answer to *where?* properly belongs in descriptions of the administrative model. Answering the question in the institutional purpose statement would place unnecessary restrictions on decisions which designers make later. Omitting *where?* allows a program of theological education to implement its curriculum through resident seminaries, extension centers, or even through correspondence courses in areas where the market and the geographic and other contexts warrant it. Omission of *where?* leaves the door open for a variety of instructional and administrative models.

In the following contrived statement, analyze the restrictions the statement would place on an "institution" in regard to *how* and *where* it would do its work.

> The purpose of the XYZ Seminary is to provide through lectureships in a resident seminary in Kotsebu, Alaska, theological education for men and women preparing for Christian ministry.

The instructional and administrative models in theological education answer the questions
how?
and
where?

What would happen in this case if the analysis in the curriculum design suggested the need for an extension center in Anchorage? What would happen if the analysis revealed that all the prospective students had families, lived in the bush, and could travel only by plane one day a week? What would happen if, by chance, all the students were hearing impaired?

(a) The purpose statement identifies the *who*. For example: The purpose of the program of leadership training in theological education of the Malaysian _____ Convention . . .

Who? The program of leadership training in theological education of the Malaysian _____ Convention. Note that the statement has not yet given a specific name to the program—such as "the purpose of the *Malaysian Theological Institute.*" That awaits a decision about the nature of the program. Of course, if a name already exists, designers use it.

(b) The purpose statement identifies *what* the *who* does. It uses terms which are specific, yet general enough to prevent undue restrictions in developing plans on *how* and *where* to fulfill the purpose. Consider again the example: The purpose of the program of leadership training in theological education of the Malaysian _____ Convention is to provide theological education . . .

What does the *who* provide? The program provides theological education. The broad general phrase "to provide theological education" includes *all* aspects of theological education because it excludes none of them. Designers can read into it both undergraduate and graduate education. (Later the statement of scope in the design will elaborate on what theological education includes.)

(c) The purpose statement specifies for *whom* the program does something. It specifies "for *whom*" in terms general enough to include all the persons the design should include. Consider again this example: The purpose of the leadership training program in theological education of the Malaysian _____ Convention is to provide theological education for men and women preparing for Christian ministry.

The statement includes both men and women but only those men and women who want to prepare for Christian ministry. For whom? Men and women preparing for Christian ministry. The purpose statement for the program of theological education for Baptists in Indonesia at one time broadened the target group to include "all the people of God."

An institutional purpose includes *some things by specification; it excludes some things by implication.*

A purpose statement *includes* certain things by specification; it excludes certain things by implication. At this point "for whom" authorizes the expenditure of financial, physical, and personnel resources in training *both men and women.* If the statement said "theological education for men . . ." and the designer felt that it should include women, then some responsible and accountable persons would authorize the addition of "and women."

The "for whom" phrase in the example makes a further specific limitation. Read again this example: The purpose of the leadership training program of the Malaysian _____ Convention is to provide theological education for men and women preparing for Christian ministry.

The statement includes only those men and women preparing for Christian ministry. A Buddhist could not enroll, since a Buddhist would not prepare for *Christian* ministry. It specifies directly what it includes and excludes certain things by implication. The greater the available resources, the wider the range of "Christian ministry" a curriculum design and plan may include. Unlimited resources could make it possible for theological education to include every aspect of human relationships in the light of the gospel. But the principle of priorities comes into play at this point. So many items of urgent priority need inclusion that purpose statements must exclude some "nice things to know" which have no direct bearing on theological education.

Christian ministry identifies a specific kind of ministry (Christian) but at the institutional level places no limitations on the *kinds* of Christian ministry. The general expression *Christian ministry* allows the curriculum plan to provide training to prepare persons for whatever Christian ministries the institution's resources can afford.

Because it describes the institution as a whole, the purpose statement is broad enough to house all programs of work which the institution must accomplish. In the preceding examples the phrase *Christian ministry* represents a very high level of generalization. It makes legitimate appropriate programs, divisions, departments, and even courses and units of study in the curriculum design and plan.

Designers face the temptation to expand unnecessarily the statement of institutional purpose. Elaboration of the statements remains the function of the descriptions of the other elements of the design. Notice the unnecessary additions to the following statement.

> The purpose of the Southwestern Baptist Theological Seminary is to provide theological education for men and women preparing for Christian ministry. *This means offering both graduate and undergraduate degree programs both on and off campus in extension centers. Christian ministry includes pastoral ministry, education ministry, and music ministry.*

None of the statements in italics belong in the institutional purpose. They belong in the descriptions of program statements and in descriptions of administrative models. By mentioning three branches of ministry, the writer *excluded* all other forms of ministry which the institution might deem necessary later on. The statement includes only those items specified while specifics not mentioned are automatically excluded from the design. Writers do well to follow the archaic principle of journalism: KISS—Keep It Simple, Stupid!

Again the Malaysian statement is inclusive and exclusive. It includes both men and women ("persons" would have been adequate in the statement). It is broad enough to include both graduate and undergraduate education. It includes *all* fields of Christian ministry but excludes training for Buddhist ministry. It includes all fields of Christian ministry simply because it does not exclude any field specifically. It includes pastoral ministry, education ministry, social work ministry, church recreation ministry, church music ministry, and so forth because it does not exclude them. It excludes Moslems but includes Methodists, Presbyterians, Catholics, Nazarenes, members of the Church of Christ, and Mennonites. It includes courses in preaching but excludes courses in dentistry. It provides theological education but excludes courses in biology (unless of course someone can make a case for biology as a Christian ministry). It covers all human relationships to God, people, nature, and history—but it does so "in light of the gospel."

The institutional purpose is broad enough to house both cognitive and affective educational goals for learners. If necessary, it can include psychomotor goals.

The purpose statement is even broad enough to include those noncurriculum-related activities such as student organization activities, chapel programs, and fund-raising projects.

Limitations of financial, physical, and personnel resources determine how comprehensive the curriculum may be in training "ministers" for ministry.

Who? Does what? For whom? A statement which answers these questions appropriately we call the *institutional purpose.*

We have said that purpose statements include certain things by specification; they exclude many things by implication. Study the following purpose statement and answer the questions that follow the statement: The purpose of Southwestern Baptist Theological Seminary is to provide theological education for men and women preparing for Christian ministry.

Answer "Yes" or "No"

If we use this statement of purpose . . .

1. _____ Shall we include courses in biochemistry?
2. _____ May we admit Methodist students?
3. _____ May we teach in languages such as Spanish, French, and Indonesian?
4. _____ May we allow women to participate in training?
5. _____ May we offer studies in religious education?

6. _____ May we locate extension centers in the cities of Caracas, Maracaibo, and Merida if necessary?

7. _____ May we enroll laypersons who do not feel "called" to full-time church-related vocations?

8. _____ May we provide a curriculum for persons who have not completed high school?

9. _____ May we offer courses in preaching?

10. _____ May we establish a school of medicine?

The purpose statement would say *yes* to all questions except 1 and 10. Some would debate the answer to number 7. Now, study the analysis which follows.

As stated, the purpose includes:	*As stated, the purpose excludes:*
Both men and women	Persons preparing for ministry in non-Christian religions
All Christian denominations	Courses *not* supportive of Christian ministry
All kinds of Christian ministry—pastoral, music, education	Vocational training courses
All service programs necessary for conducting theological education	Children
Instruction in all languages	
All courses which contribute to training for Christian ministry	
All persons who have experienced a "divine call" and others who have not	
Persons preparing for full-time church vocation	
Persons preparing for part-time or bivocational Christian ministry	
Teaching and training at multiple locations	

No work is more crucial to development of curriculum designs than development of a precise statement of institutional purpose. The purpose statement authorizes the initiating entity to act—within bounds of the factors of limitation the statement imposes.

If the curriculum designers inherit a purpose statement, they either (a) accept the purpose statement in its original form, or (b) bring about change through appropriate channels.

Building a curriculum design and plan on unauthorized refinements of a purpose statement results in unauthorized use of resources and risks legal complications.

Suppose a purpose statement reads like this: The purpose of XYZ Seminary is to train for the gospel ministry men who have experienced a divine call.

Then suppose curriculum designers change it like this: The purpose of XYZ Seminary is to provide graduate education for men and women preparing for Christian ministry.

What changes appear in the second statement? First, it limits the training to graduate education; the first does not. It includes men *and* women; the first does not. It does not include the phrase, "who have experienced a divine call"; the first does. If the first statement is binding on the planners, they do not have the authority to use resources to achieve the purpose as expressed in the second. If the first statement proves inadequate, then the curriculum designers set in motion the processes necessary to authorize the changes. At times planners spend years changing the directions of institutions by restating the purpose and gaining acceptance of the restatements.

How do designers go about writing a useful statement of institutional purpose? They write a statement which tells who does what, and for whom. The *who* specifies the name of the responsible entity. The *what* tells what the *who* will provide. The *for whom* identifies the target group or groups.

> *Why, it takes a sharpshooter to bring down even such trivial game as snipes and woodcocks; he must take very particular aim, and know what he is aiming at. He would stand a very small chance, if he fired at random into the sky, being told that snipes were flying there.—Henry David Thoreau*

Why begin a curriculum design with a statement of institutional purpose? The purpose delineates the limits for which an initiating entity may use resources provided by supporters who in good faith, through contractual response, created a binding agreement.

The formulation of institutional purposes is a dynamic process. Insights come through the years as individuals and groups search for more precise ways to express exactly what should be expressed.

I once served on a purpose revision committee during a reaccreditation study at Southwestern Baptist Theological Seminary in Fort Worth, Texas. Although the seminary provided theological education principally at the graduate level, the assignment from the Southern Baptist Convention made it necessary that the seminary admit students who did not have an undergraduate degree and were of such an age that it would work a hardship for them to complete an undergraduate degree as a prerequisite for admission. So the seminary developed a plan for admission of such persons to an "associate degree program."

The committee had to come to grips with these two responsibilities in revising the purpose statement. They felt they had to preserve the emphasis on graduate education but could not require it of all students. As a result, the committee formulated this statement: The *primary* purpose of Southwestern Baptist Theological Seminary is to provide *graduate* education for men and women preparing for Christian ministry. I remember that I naively suggested the word *primary* to provide a loophole which would allow us to offer theological education for undergraduates.

The years passed. The next ten-year study came along. By this time those responsible had developed more understanding of the principle of generalization. They eliminated the word *primary* and the word *graduate,* changing the statement to read simply: The purpose of the Southwestern Baptist Theological Seminary is to provide theological education for men and women preparing for Christian ministry.

The committee eliminated the word *primary* because it served no useful purpose. The phrase *provide theological education* is highly generalized and automatically includes theological education for both undergraduate and graduate students. The committee had included the word *primary* in order to "sneak in" authorization of a plan to provide training for undergraduate students. Since the statement does not include the restrictive phrase *called to Christian ministry* the seminary may conduct special classes for persons who simply want training in how to work in the church program organizations.

The seminary can even conduct continuing education workshops and courses because the purpose statement is broad enough to include them—and because it does not specifically exclude them.

The change came over a period of years. In the next study the statement may be changed to say "to provide theological education for *persons*" instead of "for men and women." However, it is not likely because "for men and women" seems to add a bit of literary cadence which has value in writing.

Resident in the institutional purpose are the purposes for all programs, divisions, and departments which may follow in the design. Statements of program purposes come after an analysis of the scope of the curriculum and all the institutional educational goals and objectives for learners. When related goals and objectives are grouped together in conceptual families, that relationship suggests a program purpose. The analysis of the institutional goals and objectives suggests the departmentation scheme—the number of programs of work, for example. The following chart shows a typical hierarchy of purpose statements:

> *Statements of program purposes must await the analysis of the institution's educational goals and objectives for learners.*

Institutional Purpose:
   The purpose of the _____ Seminary is to provide theological education for men and women preparing for Christian ministry.

Program Purposes:
   The purpose of the School of Religious Education of _____ Seminary is to provide theological education for men and women preparing for Christian ministry *through religious education.*
   The purpose of the School of Music of _____ Seminary is to provide theological

education for men and women preparing for Christian ministry *through church music.*

The purpose of the School of Theology of _____ Seminary is to provide theological education for men and women preparing for Christian pastoral ministries.

Division or Department Purposes:

The purpose of the Department of Foundations of Education of the School of Religious Education is to provide theological education for men and women preparing for the Christian ministry of teaching and training.

The statements seem repetitive, but remember these statements do not appear as contiguous items in curriculum designs.

The following chart shows relationships among the several purpose statements.

Hierarchy of Purposes, Goals, and Objectives (Outcomes)

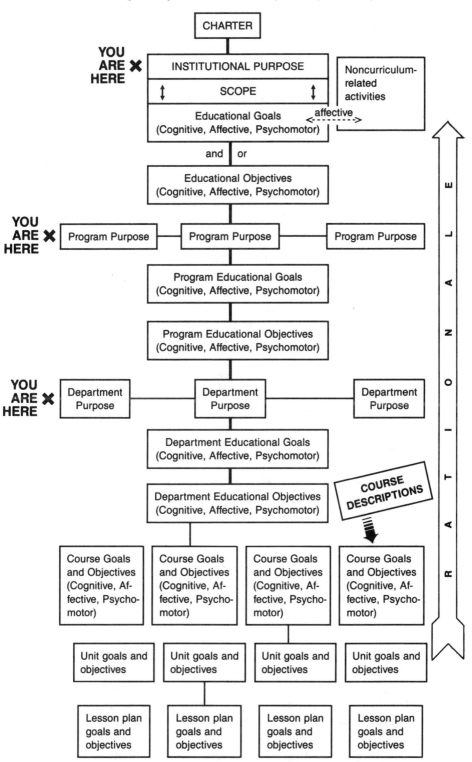

5
Analyze and Describe the Scope

Goal: A study of this chapter should help the curriculum designer understand the process (steps in) for elaborating the scope of curriculum design in theological education.

Objectives: The designer . . .

1. elaborates the legitimate scope of theological education.
2. discriminates among Bible-based, experience-based, and relationship-based learning outcomes.
3. defines scope.

This chapter does not elaborate the scope of the curriculum but describes a process for ensuring comprehensiveness in scope. The chapter on institutional goals and objectives for learners presents listings of possible subjects appropriate for the curriculum.

Because the design elements of scope and institutional educational goals and objectives are inseparably related, designers make an arbitrary decision as to which to elaborate first.

> *Designers make an arbitrary decision as to whether to elaborate first the scope or the educational goals and objectives for the learners.*

This chapter presents a plan for determining a comprehensive way the subject areas and learning outcomes (competencies) which form the focus of a learning outcomes curriculum. A compilation of these subject areas constitutes the scope of the curriculum and serves as a basis for expressing educational goals and objectives for learners.

Scope means all that *may be* dealt with in a curriculum plan.

Scope involves "all of human relationships—in the light of the gospel."

> Scope *means all that* may be *taught within a curriculum plan. The institutional purpose places limits on what the design may or may not include in its scope.*

The educational goals and objectives which appear in chapters 6, 7, and 8 evolved from a systematic analysis of these relationships.

The phrase *in light of the gospel* serves as the added dimension which distinguishes a curriculum design in theological education from other curriculum designs. Public universities and schools deal with most of "human relationships" but not "in the light of the gospel."

In a curriculum design for theological education, designers (a) identify the subject areas appropriate for theological education, and (b) list the tasks or learning outcomes a Christian minister should learn to do well in order to minister effectively. If the institutional purpose includes persons other than church leaders, then designers broaden the scope of goals and tasks to include them.

I once led a design workshop for Baptists in Indonesia. Early in the workshop we discovered that the "for whom" element in the institutional purpose specified "*all* the people of God." It included more than those preparing for Christian ministry as church leaders. That phrase cast the scope of the whole curriculum design in a new light!

A learning outcome identifies a task which a Christian minister should learn to perform well at the level of meaningful activity. For example, "preach the word" is a meaningful activity which modifies the goal "demonstrates understanding of the process of sermon preparation." "Visit the sick" is a learning outcome at the level of meaningful activity. It modifies the goal "demonstrates understanding of principles of hospital visitation." It modifies the affective goal "demonstrates compassion for persons in poor health." "Rightly dividing the word of truth" represents a meaningful outcome or competency. Doing good to "those who despitefully use you" suggests an affective learning outcome based on a goal such as "demonstrates Christian love

Diagram of Elements of Curriculum Design

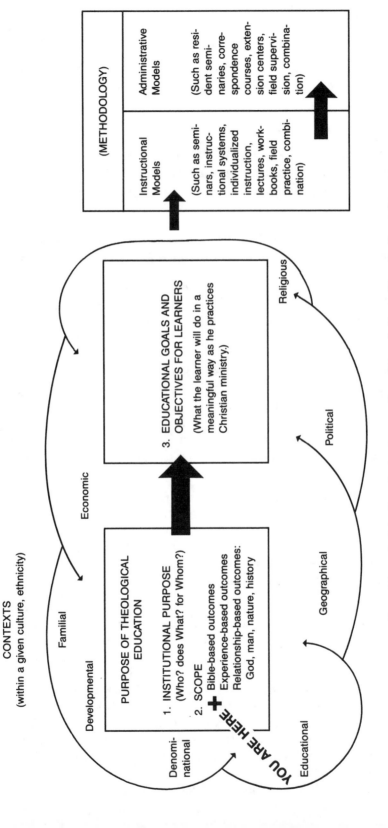

CONTEXTS
(within a given culture, ethnicity)

Denomi-national · Developmental · Familial · Economic · Religious · Political · Geographical · Educational

PURPOSE OF THEOLOGICAL EDUCATION

1. INSTITUTIONAL PURPOSE (Who? does What? for Whom?)

2. SCOPE
Bible-based outcomes
Experience-based outcomes
Relationship-based outcomes:
God, man, nature, history

YOU ARE HERE

3. EDUCATIONAL GOALS AND OBJECTIVES FOR LEARNERS
(What the learner will do in a meaningful way as he practices Christian ministry.)

(METHODOLOGY)

Instructional Models
(Such as seminars, instructional systems, individualized instruction, lectures, workbooks, field practice, combination)

Administrative Models
(Such as resident seminaries, correspondence courses, extension centers, field supervision, combination)

Organizing principle: Somebody—learns—Something—in Some Way—for Some Purpose

A Model for Curriculum Design Within a Given Cultural Setting

for one's enemies." Pairing the goals with representatives indicators or outcomes is a logical action.

> *Meaningful learning outcomes include those outcomes or tasks which learners go around doing in a meaningful way for the rest of their lives.*

This chapter presents three sources from which to identify subjects for inclusion in the curriculum's scope and in the educational goals and objectives for learners.

Some designers prefer to begin by identifying first the competencies or desired learning outcomes. They then write the goals based on the outcomes. Others write first the goals (subjects), then identify the outcomes or performance indicators related to the goals. Either approach works well.

Robert Mager stresses the importance of goals, saying that the outcomes or objectives are simply indicators that the learner has achieved the important goal.[1]

In the field of journalism, journalists verify "news" from two or more independent sources. Usually the story does not go to press without verification from more than one source. Following the same practice, this manual calls for identification of educational goals and learning outcomes for Christian ministry from these three sources: the Bible; human experience; and people's relationships with God, humans, nature, and history.

Each of these sources suggests educational goal subjects and learner outcomes or competencies needed for Christian ministry. Designers determine independently the subjects and outcomes evolving from each category *as if* the other two did not exist. Analysis of the three independently determined lists of goals and outcomes will reveal that many appear in each of the three categories. Subjects form the basis of goals; goals form the basis for objectives. The recurrence of the subjects and outcomes in more than one category suggests that the item should receive high consideration for inclusion in a composite list. Some subjects for goals and some learning outcomes may appear in only

---

1. See Robert Mager's audiotape *Educational Objectives.* Because of the popularity of Mager's *Preparing Instructional Objectives,* many educators associate him only with the specification of performance objectives or indicators.

two of the lists. Conceivably a subject or outcome may appear in only one of the lists but merit consideration. Any Bible-based goal or outcome falls into this category. Any outcome which has its basis in the Bible represents a universal, cross-cultural need.

> *If the Bible says a leader needs to achieve a certain learning outcome, that fact alone provides adequate reason for including that outcome in the curriculum's scope.*

A composite listing of the significant subjects and outcomes derived from these three sources constitutes the "scope" of the objectives for learners dealt with in chapter 6.

When designers choose to express scope in terms of learning outcomes or competencies, they express the outcome in verb form. They ask, "What does the trainee do?" For example, a study of the Bible reveals that the Christian minister does such things as . . .

Preaches sermons	*Ministers* to those in need
Teaches believers and unbelievers (and himself)	*Corrects* the wayward
Counsels those in need	*Prays* without ceasing
Witnesses to the lost	*Disciples* new converts
Communicates the gospel	*Interprets* the Scriptures
Manages well his own household and the church	*Encourages* others

The outcomes as stated identify meaningful activities which the Christian minister needs to do effectively the rest of his life. What designers call "lead-up objectives" or en route competencies or outcomes appear later in course descriptions and unit and lesson plans. (See part 3.) With these instructions in mind, designers determine outcomes based on each source. The chart "Form for Developing a Taxonomy of Relationship Areas of Scope in Curriculum Design" will facilitate a comprehensive analysis of scope.

Designers follow five steps in the process of elaborating scope.

1. *Determine Bible-based learning outcomes or competencies.*—Curriculum planners ask, "What does the Bible say Christian ministers in America, Guatemala, or Malaysia need

to understand? What should they learn to do well? What affective responses do the learners need to make?" Christians believe that the Bible contains truths which apply cross-culturally. The Bible applies universally. A study of the Bible, particularly the New Testament, reveals many learning outcomes which the Christian minister needs to acquire. The Bible states many of them in command form. "*Preach* the word." "*Bear* ye one another's burdens." "*Pray* without ceasing." "*Worship* the Lord in the beauty of holiness." "*Rightly divide* the word of truth," and "*Visit* the sick." These commands suggest needed outcomes. Analysis of what Bible characters did provides clues to other essential outcomes.

A group of nationals and missionaries from the Philippines studied the New Testament, especially Ephesians, 2 Timothy, Titus, Matthew, and 1 Peter. They produced a list of learning outcomes or competencies which included:

Trains and develops leaders	Solves and controls
Prophesies	problems
Evangelizes	Studies
Teaches others	Enlists through outreach
Pastors the flock	Equips the saints
Ministers to others in time	Manages conflict
of need	Disciples others

In their study, they pinpointed Scripture passages from which they had derived the outcomes or competencies. Each major competency includes many "en route" or "enabling" competencies which the designers may want to list. However, this approach tends to get too involved at this point. The "en route" competencies more appropriately belong in course descriptions.

Some outcomes or competencies are related. "Pastors the flock" relates to "ministers to others in time of need." Some very broad statements need breaking down. For example, "pastors the flock" does not pinpoint any *particular thing* leaders do in pastoring the flock. What do they do? They visit the sick, counsel the bereaved, conduct funerals, and so forth as part of the pastoral responsibilities. Other biblically based statements like "perfecting of the saints" need further breakdown for elaborating scope.

In missions settings work groups of *both* nationals and missionaries do a more efficient job of identifying the Bible-based competencies. Work groups consisting of teachers, church staff members, and church members can usually arrive at a more valid list of outcomes than can designers working alone.

Designers compile a list of the Bible-based outcomes and arrange them in order of importance. They set the list aside and proceed to source 2, analysis of experience.

2. *Determine experience-based outcomes or competencies.*—In determining scope, designers ask, "What does *experience* say Christian ministers should learn to do well in the cultural setting where they minister?" In a foreign mission setting, designers ask not only themselves, but practitioners among nationals, "What do you *do* in your role in Christian ministry? What has *experience* taught you that you must do well in order to minister effectively?" Nationals can relate their roles and activities more meaningfully to the culture in which they function. Designers ask the same questions in the United States.

At this point, designers think only of *experience*-related outcomes. For this exercise they set aside the other two sources.[2]

A study group of nationals and missionaries in Malaysia derived from analysis of their own experiences the following learning outcomes.

Preaches and teaches the Bible	Develops training programs for leaders
Works creatively with others	Ministers to individuals and groups
Manages church affairs	Plans and leads worship
Discovers spiritually gifted leaders	Practices personal evangelism
Guides church officers to do their work well	

Already some desirable learning outcomes appear in both the Bible-based and experience-based lists. This is inevitable. It signals validity in the statements.

Job descriptions for church staff members provide a fertile resource for discovering experience-based outcomes. Church personnel committees have already done much of the designer's work.

It bears repeating that in missions, work groups which include nationals with wide experience in ministry and who understand their cultural setting tend to produce a more practical

2. In the final analysis, one discovers considerable similarity between the Bible and experience as sources.

Experience provides data for elaborating scope and writing goals and objectives.

and culturally oriented list of experience-based competencies than groups which include only missionaries.

> *A collection of job descriptions for church staff members provides a ready-made resource for identifying experience-based competencies or outcomes.*

3. *Determine relationships-based outcomes or competencies.*—Curriculum designers ask, "What do human relationships to God, humans, nature, and history say a Christian minister needs to learn to do well?[3] What affective responses should he make in ministry?"

Designers find it helpful to ask study groups to analyze carefully each of the categories of relationships. As in the previous two analyses, designers may list subjects for study or learning outcomes in verb form. The following examples use the second approach. When designers state educational goals and objectives for learners, they will use both the subject (for the goal) and the learning outcomes of competencies.

Observe that many of the outcomes stated indicate achievement of both a cognitive and an affective goal. For example "prays" could indicate that learners understand *how to* pray or that they pray out of conviction that God hears prayer.

(a) Consider the first area of relationships—human and God. Designers ask, "Because church leaders have a relationship to God what subject areas do they need to master? What do they need to learn to do well?" A study group of missionaries and nationals from Thailand submitted these ideas as part of their report:

Prays	Teaches doctrine
Studies the Bible	Interprets the Bible
Worships and leads worship	Preaches
Sings	Teaches the Bible
Proclaims the gospel	Meditates
Testifies	Gives willingly

Some of these outcomes need further breakdown. For example, what competencies do leaders need as they teach the Bible?

---

3. Some would say we need to consider only the God-human, human-God, and person-person relationships.

Form for Developing a Taxonomy of Relationship Areas of Scope in Curriculum Design

	Cognitive Outcomes	Affective Outcomes	Psychomotor Outcomes
Our Relationship to God * * * * * * * * * * God's Relationship to Us			
Our Relationship to Self and Others			
Our Relationship to Nature			
Our Relationship to History			

Breakdowns of these competencies into "subcompetencies" usually takes place when writers develop course descriptions. (See part 3.)

Notice that some outcomes or competencies have appeared in all three lists. Designers may assume a strong need for the competency if it appears in all lists.

(b) Consider the second class of relationships—human to human. Designers ask, "Because persons involved in ministry have relationships with other people, what do they need to do well? What affective responses should characterize their ministry as it relates to others?"

A study group in Thailand submitted these items as a partial list. Note that some, especially the first, have strong affective dimensions.

Forgives and deals patiently with others	Develops organizational aspects of the church so members can accomplish their ministry
Maintains wholesome relationships	
Guides in decision making	Supervises the work of others
Works creatively with others	Makes ethical decisions
Counsels others	

(c) Consider the third class of relationships—human to nature. Designers usually find it difficult to determine outcomes or competencies of this type. Planners ask, "Because humans have relationships to nature, what does the Christian minister need to do well?"

A study group in the Philippines included these in their list: Protects the environment, uses natural resources wisely, and cares for physical health.

(d) Some designers would do well to add a fourth class of relationships—human to history. "Because a person has a relationship to *history*, what does he or she need to do well?" One group stated: Interprets problems and events in their historical context and makes decisions and choices based on insights gained from history.

Determination of the level of meaningful activity in the study of Christian history presents problems. The following quotation provides a clue as to meaningful relationships between persons and history.

What really set [President James] Madison apart, though, was the ability to take a problem in government, no matter how complicated, *examine it in the light of history* [italics added], experience, common sense and some idea of what might justly be done, and then, lucidly, even-handedly explain it better than anyone else could.[4]

Perhaps "analyzing" and "explaining" such complex problems represents the level of meaningful activity because such explanations can serve as prelude to significant decision making. When the student of Christian history examines political, church, and denominational problems in the light of history, he or she analyzes the influences of history on current religious practices and problems and avoids repeating mistakes of the past.

When experience is not retained . . . infancy is perpetual. Those who cannot remember their past are condemned to repeat it.—George Santayana

♦ ♦ ♦

Only one generation separates a heritage remembered from a heritage forgotten.

Explaining calls for performance at the analysis level of response. Recommendation of solutions requires responses at the synthesis and evaluation levels.

4. *In the next step, curriculum designers display side by side the lists from all three sources.*—They pay particular attention to those outcomes which appear in two or three lists. An exercise, such as the following, proves helpful in discovering the most important outcomes. The designers chain together the similar outcomes in the three groups.

When the same outcomes appear repeatedly, one may rest assured of their importance. However, the appearance of a Bible-based outcome in and of itself speaks of its importance and merits inclusion.

---

4. Timothy Foote, "After More Than Two Centuries, This May Be Mr. Madison's Year," *Smithsonian*, September 1987, 80.

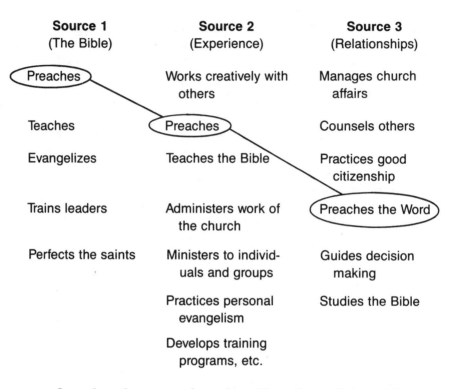

Source 1 (The Bible)	Source 2 (Experience)	Source 3 (Relationships)
Preaches	Works creatively with others	Manages church affairs
Teaches	Preaches	Counsels others
Evangelizes	Teaches the Bible	Practices good citizenship
Trains leaders	Administers work of the church	Preaches the Word
Perfects the saints	Ministers to individuals and groups	Guides decision making
	Practices personal evangelism	Studies the Bible
	Develops training programs, etc.	

One of my former students from Yugoslavia[5] followed the process described and compiled the following list of outcomes or competencies. (This is a verbatim list, unedited for accuracy and style.)

Classify the outcomes according to the primary relationship involved (G=God; M=man; N=nature; H=history).

(____) 1. Conducts a Bible study.
(____) 2. Preaches sermons.
(____) 3. Leads prayer meetings.
(____) 4. Plans and conducts evangelistic meetings.
(____) 5. Plans and conducts worship services.
(____) 6. Leads members in personal witnessing.
(____) 7. Interprets the doctrine of God.
(____) 8. Leads a witnessing team.
(____) 9. Visits sick persons in the hospital.
(____) 10. Counsels effectively a church member.
(____) 11. Organizes a visitation program.
(____) 12. Organizes a mission.

---

5. Ruth Lehotsky, "A Curriculum Design for Theological Education in Yugoslavia," unpublished paper.

(____) 13. Writes a sermon outline.

(____) 14. Gives the reasons for his beliefs.

(____) 15. Interprets Christian principles for moral conduct.

(____) 16. Composes a paper on the Christian view of marriage.

(____) 17. Gives the content of the Gospel according to Matthew.

(____) 18. Conducts wedding and funeral ceremonies.

(____) 19. Conducts baptism and Lord's Supper services.

(____) 20. Explains problems in human behavior from the psychological viewpoint.

(____) 21. Relates correctly science and Christian religion.

(____) 22. Explains the beliefs of a Muslim.

(____) 23. Traces the "church" back to the first century A.D.

(____) 24. Conducts a new member orientation program.

(____) 25. Teaches an adult Bible study class (Sunday School).

(____) 26. Teaches a Bible teaching class for children (Sunday School).

(____) 27. Teaches a Bible teaching class for young people (Sunday School).

(____) 28. Sets up conference programs.

(____) 29. Conducts a Vacation Bible School.

(____) 30. Organizes a retreat.

(____) 31. Conducts a teacher training clinic.

(____) 32. Performs effectively church administration.

(____) 33. Keeps the membership records up to date.

(____) 34. Organizes a youth club.

(____) 35. Organizes and leads a summer camp.

(____) 36. Performs duties of a host/hostess.

(____) 37. Leads a church business meeting.

(____) 38. Performs effectively responsibilities of a deacon.

(____) 39. Writes a Sunday School lesson.

(____) 40. Conducts a membership analysis in his or her local church.

(____) 41. Writes the history of his or her church.

(____) 42. Writes a program for Christmas or Easter celebration.

(____) 43. Composes a paper on the psychological development of children and young people.

(____) 44. Uses appropriate methods in teaching children.

(____) 45. Uses appropriate methods in teaching young people and adults.

(____) 46. Explains principles in the teaching process.
(____) 47. Handles effectively the church finances.
(____) 48. Uses audiovisual materials in religious education.
(____) 49. Conducts recreational activities in the church.
(____) 50. Sets up a church library.
(____) 51. Dramatizes a Bible story.
(____) 52. Plays the pump organ.
(____) 53. Teaches songs in the Sunday School.
(____) 54. Translates from the Greek New Testament.
(____) 55. Interprets properly free church theology.
(____) 56. Writes an article or a report for the Union magazine.
(____) 57. Represents the church to government authorities.[6]

Note that number 57 grows out of the political context, but represents a necessary competency in Yugoslavia. The same competency would have less importance in some other countries.

5. *Next, curriculum designers arrange the outcomes or competencies in order of priority and group the similar ones together into conceptual families.*—They then have a comprehensive description of scope—items which designs *may* include in the curriculum as subject matter or learning outcomes.

A more comprehensive list of goals and learning outcomes appears in chapter 6. Designers who prefer to begin with subject items in scope (from which they construct educational goals) will produce lists similar to those in chapter 6. The following chart is used in compiling a list of outcomes or competencies.

Designers who prefer to state the items as learning outcomes or competencies may follow the format shown in the example from the curriculum design for Yugoslavia.

Designers who prefer to state the scope items as subjects only may follow the format used in chapter 6 and in the following chart.

In review, scope means all that *may be* dealt with in theological education. Designers determine scope by analyzing what the Bible, experience, and human's relationship to God, other persons, nature, and history say that Christian ministers should do well in the performance of ministry.

---

6. With appropriate alterations, the Mexican Baptist Bible Institute in San Antonio, Texas, once included this list in its curriculum design. Changes were necessary because of the different geographic, economic, political, and educational contexts.

Scope
(Meaningful level competencies growing out of the Bible,
experience, and "all of human relationships in the light of the gospel)

Sources

I. *Bible* (cognitive, affective, psychomotor)

1. _____
2. _____
3. _____
4. _____
5. _____
6. _____
7. _____
8. _____
9. _____
10. _____
11. Other

II. *Experience* (cognitive, affective, psychomotor)

1. _____
2. _____
3. _____
4. _____
5. _____
6. _____
7. _____
8. _____
9. _____
10. _____
11. Other

III. *Human Relationships* (cognitive, affective, psychomotor)

To God:

1. _____
2. _____
3. _____
4. Other

To Experience:

1. _____
2. _____
3. _____
4. Other

To Nature:

1. _____
2. _____
3. _____
4. Other

To History:

1. _____
2. _____
3. _____

6

Establish the Institution's Educational Goals and Objectives for Learners

Goals: A study of this chapter should help the curriculum designer understand . . .
1. the meaning of goal and objective.
2. the process for elaborating at the institutional level a statement of educational goals and objectives for learners.
3. the characteristics and values of educational goals and objectives for learners.

Objectives: The designer . . .
1. elaborates at the institutional level a statement of the cognitive, affective, and psychomotor educational goals and objectives.
2. writes at the level of meaningful activity educational goals and objectives in the learning outcomes format.
3. discriminates between goals and objectives.

It is not worth the while to go round the world to count the cats in Zanzibar.—Henry David Thoreau

---

Sometimes institutions move the target to where the arrow went! They find it easier to shoot without aiming. A cartoon character once boasted, "I don't know where I'm going, but I'm making great time!"

Curriculum designers fix targets. They develop at the institutional level the educational goals and objectives for learners.

> *Designers may arbitrarily choose to develop the scope of the curriculum first. Scope identifies either subject areas or outcomes. They use the subjects as a basis for stating educational goals. Chapter 5 deals with the process for determining scope.*

This chapter deals with the upper echelon of the hierarchy of educational goals and objectives. Later chapters trace the educational goals and objectives from the institutional level through program and department levels. Educational goals and objectives at the individual course and unit of instruction level receive attention in part 3, "Writing the Course Descriptions."

> *The most significant omission from many curriculum designs in theological education is the absence of a comprehensive statement of meaningful educational goals and objectives for the learners.*

Some designers may prefer to develop the curriculum's scope description before developing institutional educational goals and objectives for learners. Chapter 5 presents the process for developing the scope description.

Defining the Terms

Goal means a relatively broad statement of learning intent which specifies the *kind of learning* desired and expresses the subject in a meaningful but chewable bite.[1]

> *A goal is a relatively broad statement of learning intent which specifies a kind of learning desired and expresses the subject in a meaningful but chewable bite.*

---

1. In the world of business, goal and objective have opposite meanings from the meanings in education. In business, *goal* means a measurable step toward achievement of a broad objective.

Diagram of Elements of Curriculum Design

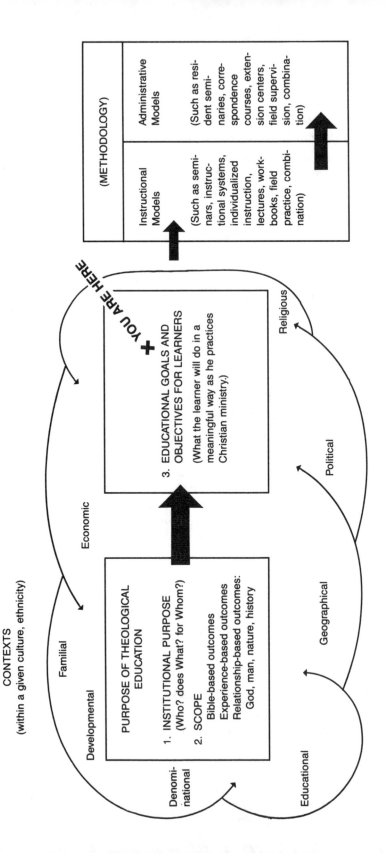

CONTEXTS
(within a given culture, ethnicity)

Developmental   Familial   Economic   Religious

Denominational   Geographical   Political   Educational

(METHODOLOGY)

Instructional Models	Administrative Models
(Such as seminars, instructional systems, individualized instruction, lectures, workbooks, field practice, combination)	(Such as resident seminaries, correspondence courses, extension centers, field supervision, combination)

+ YOU ARE HERE

3. EDUCATIONAL GOALS AND OBJECTIVES FOR LEARNERS

(What the learner will do in a meaningful way as he practices Christian ministry.)

PURPOSE OF THEOLOGICAL EDUCATION

1. INSTITUTIONAL PURPOSE (Who? does What? for Whom?)

2. SCOPE
Bible-based outcomes
Experience-based outcomes
Relationship-based outcomes: God, man, nature, history

Organizing principle: Somebody—learns—Something—in Some Way—for Some Purpose

A Model for Curriculum Design Within a Given Cultural Setting

SOMETIMES WE TEACH WITHOUT A TARGET! THEN WE RACE TO MOVE THE TARGET TO WHERE THE ARROW WENT!

Goals do at least two things:

1. *The goal says learners will demonstrate the kind of learning.*—They will demonstrate an understanding of something, an attitude toward or about something, or a skill in doing something. In public education, designers usually classify these goals as cognitive, affective, or psychomotor in nature. This manual uses the term *understanding* to refer to the cognitive domain (both knowledge of facts and information and understanding of concepts and relationships). At times it uses the terms *attitudes* and *values* to refer to affective learning. *Skill* refers to psychomotor skill.

2. *A goal expresses the subject in a chewable bite.*—*Chewable bite* is a relative term. A goal for an entire course would require an entire semester for "chewing." A goal for a single class session would specify a much smaller chewable bit. Part 3, "Writing the Course Descriptions," provides more detail about this concept. A goal *does not specify* what the teacher will accept as valid evidence that the learner has achieved the goal. That function remains for the objective.

In the following examples of educational goals, find (a) the kind of learning, and (b) the chewable bite of the subject.

• The student demonstrates understanding of the steps in sermon preparation.

• The student demonstrates an attitude of compassion for unsaved college students.

• The student demonstrates skill in choral conducting.

Are the subjects "chewable" in a semester? a unit of study? a single class session?

Each of these statements could well appear in the institution's list of educational goals for learners. They reflect a relatively high level of generalization and all of them reside in the statement of institutional purpose which legitimizes them.

An objective (outcome) serves a unique function.

> ***An objective tells what learners will do in a meaningful way to indicate achievement of a goal.***

An objective tells what learners will do in a meaningful way to prove or indicate achievement of a goal. In this manual objective and learning outcome mean the same thing. Notice the objective in the following example: The student demonstrates an attitude

of compassion for the unsaved by *doing such things as witnessing consistently as a life-style.*

At the institutional level designers try to state the objectives for learners in terms of meaningful activity and at a relatively high level of generalization.

Learners do not go around the rest of their lives saying, "Look, I can name the eight steps in preparing a sermon!" So what? They, however, can use the steps to plan and deliver a sermon—the level of meaningful activity. As a rule, statements representing the lower levels of learning belong in unit descriptions and lesson plans.

Goals and objectives are closely related. For that reason, designers and teachers should see them in close contiguity. The following example shows how an educational goal and an educational objective relate one to the other: The learner demonstrates understanding of the process of family financial planning (goal) by developing a family financial plan for his or her own family (objective).

Characteristics of Educational Goals

At the higher levels in the hierarchy of educational goals and objectives a goal has several characteristics.

1. *A goal at the institutional level reflects a relatively high level of generalization.*[2]—The statements are broad and comprehensive enough to house all the subgoals and objectives which may follow at lower levels in programs, departments of instruction, course descriptions, and lesson plans. Notice the high level of generalization in the following goal: The goal for learners is that they understand the history and tenets of the Christian faith and other world religions.

The statement is general enough to legitimize a Church History Department and include studies in Christianity, Buddhism, Taoism, Hinduism, and Islam. It is broad enough to legitimize in the curriculum plan not only a study of the tenets of world religions but also their history. Designers could even read into the goal a study of a more narrowly focused subject such as "A History of Baptists in Early America."

Goals do not imply the level of performance required to prove achievement. That belongs to the statement of objectives or indicators of goal achievement.

---

2. See chapter 20 for guidelines on arriving at statements which reflect a high level of generalization.

The word *understanding* as used in this manual encompasses learnings at *all* the levels of cognitive learning, including knowledge of facts and information. The *objective* indicates which level of learning. *Understanding* includes comprehension; the ability to transfer learning to new situations; the ability to analyze and solve problems; the ability to create new and original documents such as sermons, music compositions, and lesson plans; and the ability to discern the relative worth of these documents.

2. *A goal reflects an appropriate degree of comprehensiveness.*—Since *scope* means "all of human relationships (to God, others, nature, history) in the light of the gospel," the institution's education goals and objectives result from an analysis of these relationships.

Designers can ensure comprehensiveness by following the guidelines for describing scope. (See chapter 5.)

3. *Goals provide the basis for determining departmentation schemes.*—An institution's educational goals are comprehensive enough to make it possible for programs of work in the institution to choose those which relate primarily to the program. Curriculum designers use the statements as a basis for developing a departmentation scheme for the institution. They group related goals (conceptual families) together and give them a name (like "program of leadership training in church music," and "program of leadership training in religious education"). Designers may decide that certain items in the list constitute "common learnings" or "core learnings" which *all* graduates should master. These common learnings provide the basis for a "core curriculum" or a "common learnings" curriculum.

Statements of educational goals at the institutional level provide the basic raw materials from which departmentation schemes evolve. Formulation of goals should precede decisions about departmentation schemes. The goals should reflect comprehensiveness in both subject matter and in attention to all the domains of learning. The statements include goals related to the cognitive domain (knowledge and understanding), the affective domain (attitudes and values), and psychomotor domain (skills).[3]

---

3. The writer recognizes that persons use the term *skill* to identify certain high-level cognitive actions. For example, persons say, "He is a skillful teacher." In this case the skill is a "perceptual skill" and not a motor skill. This manual uses the term *skill* to refer only to psychomotor skills.

Designers <u>can</u> carry too far the concept of generalization!

4. *Institutional educational goals reflect the affective dimensions of learning intent.*—An analysis of course descriptions reveals that few give attention to affective goals. Perhaps because of their illusiveness, the course descriptions do not include goals and objectives related to developing viewpoints toward persons, places, and things. Designers who perceive curriculum as all of life's experiences will not omit the affective realm. The Bible focuses on affective change in persons. Affective change does occur when teachers focus on the cognitive domain. However, much more affective learning would occur if teachers deliberately focused on attitudes and values.

> *One of the greatest weaknesses in curriculum design is the failure of designers to include the affective domain in designs and in the curriculum plans which follow.*

The teachers themselves appropriate from educational psychology the principles of teaching for attitudinal change as they develop lesson plans or teaching materials.

Affective educational goals are pervasive and penetrative in nature. They resist efforts to focus them into departmentation schemes or programs. Cognitive and psychomotor educational goals are focal in nature and lend themselves to logical departmentation.

The essentiality of affective educational goals at the institutional level demands that designers incorporate and deal with them energetically in the curriculum plan. Their use in the curriculum plan needs to be supervised as expectantly as cognitive and psychomotor goals.

Implementation of institutional affective educational goals tends to erase the line of demarcation between curriculum designs and plans and those institutional activities not generally considered part of the plan. For example, institutional activities such as chapel programs contribute significantly to the achievement of affective goals.

5. *The goals are idealistic.*—Designers accept the fact that not all learners will learn all that a goal may include, but an idealistic goal forms a "North Star" toward which learners may make progress.

6. *Purposes, goals, and objectives form a hierarchy in the curriculum's design.*—Purposes and educational goals and objec-

tives for learners form a hierarchy. As shown in the following chart "Hierarchy of Goals and Objectives" these statements appear at several levels. (See charts "Hierarchy of Purposes, Goals, and Objectives" and "A Flow Chart of Educational Goals and Objectives.)

The institutional level
The program level
The department level
The individual course level
The unit of instruction level and
The lesson plan level.

The curriculum design elaborates the goals and objectives at each level.

Values of Educational Goals and Objectives

This manual considers the institution's statement of educational goals and objectives for learners as a distinct element of curriculum design. Goals and objectives have several values.

1. *They serve as a constant reminder of all that the curriculum may include.*—The comprehensive statement of educational goals and objectives serves as a "bank" from which designers draw to develop departmentation schemes and curriculum plans. The subjects of the goals are synonymous with the scope of the curriculum.

Designers sometimes focus so intently on traditional subjects that they forget to consider other legitimate ones. They need a comprehensive list to remind them of what they may include.

2. *The institution's educational goals and objectives for learners serve as a sounding board for determining whether courses belong in the curriculum.*—They provide standards for making curriculum decisions. Only those subjects and learning outcomes (competencies) which reside in the goals and objectives should become part of a curriculum plan.

Some who work in curriculum planning tend to emphasize their own specialties and interests. An adopted statement of goals and objectives calls them back to basics. The statements prevent the imbalance created by special interests. The curriculum "consumer" participates in a relevant "race."

As a rule the curriculum of theological education does not include courses which another institution could better handle. For example, a school of religious education offered courses in type-

Hierarchy of Purposes, Goals, and Objectives (Outcomes)

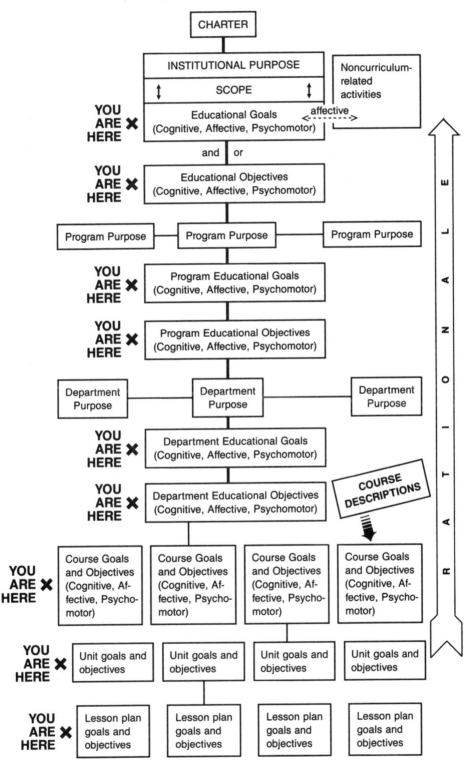

A Flow Chart of Educational Goals and Objectives

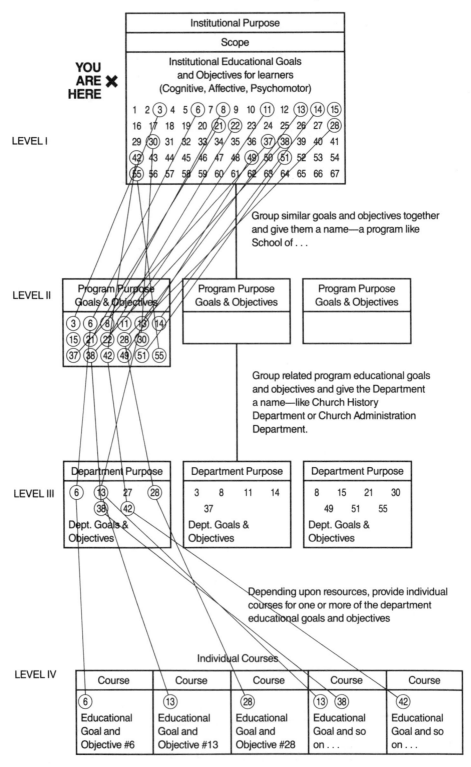

writing, shorthand, and bookkeeping as part of the requirements for church secretaries. A full-time professor offered the courses. Then planners realized that an outstanding junior college two miles away offered all of the courses and provided state of the art equipment. The school dropped the courses from its curriculum plan. The institution's educational goals and objectives serve as a basis for developing a rationale for inclusion or exclusion of given courses in the curriculum.

3. *Educational goals and objectives for learners serve as a basis for determining priorities in implementing the curriculum's scope.*—Some courses obviously facilitate achievement of the institution's educational goals and objectives for learners; others do so but only peripherally. Designers can determine through research which goals and objectives have greatest priority in Christian ministry. Few institutions have the resources to give extensive attention to *all* goals and objectives.

A research project conducted by the School of Religious Education at Southwestern Baptist Theological Seminary, Fort Worth, Texas, revealed the following order of priorities in outcomes or competencies needed by graduates. Graduates need the ability to:
- function as team members,
- communicate effectively,
- train leaders,
- teach,
- enable others,
- plan for evangelism and outreach,
- develop curriculum plans,
- develop special ministries, and
- counsel others.

4. *Educational goals and objectives for learners help ensure proper expenditure of time, money, and personnel resources.*—Some courses represent "nice things to know and do" but in no way lead toward achievement of the educational goals and objectives. Stewardship responsibilities of theological institutions demand that the institutions use resources efficiently.

Many courses represent "nice things to know and do" but in no way lead toward achievement of the educational goals and objectives.

5. *Educational goals and objectives serve as reminders that a design should deal appropriately with all domains of learning (cognitive, affective, psychomotor).*—If the design includes them, then the curriculum plan will include them. Curriculum forces implement them through adequate and aggressive curriculum supervision.

6. *An institution's educational goals for learners provide the basic rationale for the development of programs, departments, courses, and units of study.*—Each course, department, and program goal should reside in the "parent statement" of the institution's educational goals. Otherwise the subgoals have no reason for being. Institutions have no authority to include in their hierarchy of intentions subgoals which do not reside in the institution's educational goals.

Developing Institutional Educational Goals

Goals and objectives are closely related, but for purposes of convenience this chapter separates them.

Rare is the institution which can produce on demand a logically arrived-at set of the institution's educational goals for learners. In view of the scarcity of actual models, this manual cannot quote educational goals and objectives from existing designs. The examples of goals which follow have been developed by the writer to illustrate what such a statement would look like. It has not been tested for comprehensiveness, but it should give designers a point of reference. Such a set of goals forms a "bank" from which designers can select in setting up programs, departments, and courses of instruction in the curriculum plan.

> *Few institutions can produce on demand a set of learning outcomes (goals and objectives) which form the heart of an effective curriculum design. Why? They do not as yet realize that the whole curriculum plan must be built upon them.*

The examples on the following pages show the kinds of goals a design might include in the cognitive, affective, and psychomotor domains. Since these statements are part of the institution's goals for learners, note the relatively high degree of generalization involved in many of them.

> *An institution which does not have a statement of educational goals and objectives for learners is like a ship without a rudder. It may have a lot of "sail" but no sense of direction.*

Cognitive Educational Goals
(Knowledge and Understanding)

The cognitive goals for learners include those which relate to knowledge (facts and information) and understanding (ability to interpret, translate into new forms, analyze, synthesize, and evaluate). Designers follow the process for development of scope in order to identify the subjects the statements include. (See chapter 5.) Designers use different approaches to developing cognitive goals at the institutional level.

1. *Some institutions of theological education prefer to state several highly generalized goals which are broad enough to house all the more specific ones which appear later in program, department, and course statements.*—The International Correspondence Institute's (ICI) college division degree program has stated quite clearly its institutional purpose (called "overarching objective") and the institutional goals (called "general objectives") in highly generalized terms.[4] The statement differs from the learning outcomes design in that the document states the goals in terms of what the institution will do rather than what the student will understand, feel, and do. Thus they are outcomes or objectives and not goals.

The overarching curriculum objective of ICI is to train leaders for the various ministries of the church.[5] These leaders will include pastors, evangelists, educators, missionaries, and others. A strong spiritual commitment will be encouraged throughout the educational program.

ICI stated the following general objectives with the future ministries of the students in view and developed a curriculum

---

4. *ICI Format and Instructional Design Manual, College Division Degree Program,* 3rd International Correspondence Institute, Chausée de Waterloo, 45, 1640 Rhode-St. Genèse, Belgium.

5. I would call this the institutional purpose.

plan leading to the achievement of each of these objectives. Their design manual states that:

> The general objectives are for the student to:
> 1. Acquire a knowledge of the Bible content.
> 2. Understand the Christian message and how to communicate it.
> 3. Obtain the means for personal spiritual growth and development.
> 4. Gain an understanding of the church and its ministries.
> 5. Develop leadership and ministry skills.
> 6. Understand people, their cultures, and the natural world.
> 7. Develop study, thought, and communication skills.

Notice the stem of the statements, "The general objectives are for the *student* to:"

Designers can easily change the statements into the format used in this manual for stating goals. For example, number 2 could read: "The student demonstrates understanding of the Christian message and how to communicate it." Number 5 could read: "The student demonstrates understanding of the principles of leadership and ministry." Whether to leave the statements as they are or to change to "the student demonstrates understanding . . ." is a matter of preference. Either form communicates the ideas.

The Seminary Extension of the Southern Baptist Seminaries states six competencies in generalized terms.[6] Though stated in terms different from those used in this manual, they serve as a valid example. They are stated as examples of "competencies which many extension education programs seek to develop." These statements could also appear as goals. Number 2, for example, could read: "The student demonstrates understanding of the guidelines for preparing and delivering sermons."

1. A growing understanding of the Bible and ability to use Bible study skills.
2. Skill in preparing and delivering sermons.
3. Ability to interpret accurately and lovingly the plan of salvation and other great realities of the Christian faith.
4. Ability to minister to persons and families in crisis.

---

6. Raymond M. Rigdon, *Resource Guide, Developing Church Leaders Through Extension Education*, Seminary External Education Division, the Southern Baptist Convention.

5. Ability to plan church work.
6. Ability to motivate and lead people.

Institutions which use the highly generalized approach probably induced the statements *after* analyzing and classifying a much more extensive list of more specific statements. Such general statements would require elaboration later in order to facilitate the formation of programs, departments, and course descriptions.

The following list of typical institutional educational goals for learners appears in the format recommended in this manual. Each of these goals has an affective dimension, but this list does not identify it. (See guidelines later in this chapter.) Note that the level of generalization leaves room for identification of many more *specific* ones. As stated they do not suggest priorities.

The institution's (seminary, Bible college, correspondence school, and so forth) cognitive educational goals for learners include the following:

1. The learner demonstrates understanding of the nature of the biblical revelation.

2. The learner demonstrates understanding of the background, history, and major teachings of the books of the Bible.

3. The learner demonstrates understanding of the history and tenets of the Christian faith and other world religions.

4. The learner demonstrates understanding of theological method.

5. The learner demonstrates understanding of the principles of Bible interpretation.

6. The learner demonstrates understanding of the original languages of the Bible.

7. The learner demonstrates understanding of approaches to witnessing and evangelism.

8. The learner demonstrates understanding of approaches to effective communication of the gospel through worship, witness, education, ministry, and application.

9. The learner demonstrates understanding of the process of sermon preparation.

10. The learner understands the principles of teaching and training.

11. The learner demonstrates understanding of ap-

proaches to equipping church members for service in the church, denomination, and world.

12. The learner demonstrates understanding of church and denominational polity.

13. The learner demonstrates understanding of principles of administration, management, and leadership in the church and denomination.

14. The learner demonstrates understanding of the guidelines for Christian family living.

15. The learner demonstrates understanding of principles and approaches to care for and counsel persons who have special needs.

16. The learner demonstrates understanding of approaches to fulfilling a church's missions responsibilities.

17. The learner demonstrates understanding of guidelines for developing creative interpersonal relationships.

18. The learner demonstrates understanding of the ethical dimensions of Christian ministry in all the relationships of life.

19. The learner demonstrates understanding of the principles and methods for age-group education.

20. The learner demonstrates understanding of guidelines for developing special ministries in the church (church social ministry, church recreation, and so forth).

21. The learner demonstrates understanding of guidelines for developing a personal physical wellness program.

22. The learner demonstrates understanding of the role of music in worship, witness, education, and ministry.

23. The learner demonstrates understanding of music theory.

24. The learner demonstrates understanding of the history, geography, and archeology of the biblical world.

25. The learner demonstrates understanding of the nature of biblical authority.

26. The learner demonstrates understanding of the background, history, contents, and major teachings of Psalms (and other books of the Bible).

27. The learner demonstrates understanding of the theology of the Old Testament and New Testament.

28. The learner demonstrates understanding of the missionary message of the Bible.

29. The learner demonstrates understanding of the biblical and theological foundation of Christian missions.

30. The learner demonstrates understanding of the ethical teachings of the Bible.

31. The learner demonstrates understanding of the relationship between philosophy and the Christian faith.

32. The learner demonstrates understanding of the nature, sources, and scope of systematic theology.

33. The learner demonstrates understanding of the biblical basis of evangelism.

34. The learner demonstrates understanding of the nature of the church and its ministry.

35. The learner demonstrates understanding of principles of biblical preaching.

36. The learner demonstrates understanding of the nature and conditions of learning.

Not every student is expected to achieve all of these goals, but he or she achieves that portion considered appropriate to the area of Christian ministry involved, plus any common learnings expected of *all* students.

Note that these goals reflect a high level of generalization. The list is not comprehensive. Institutions should analyze learning needs of students and devise a list which they consider comprehensive.

The goal statement "understands the nature of the biblical revelation" does not at that point break biblical revelation into its parts. Designers make an arbitrary decision as to when to break the items into their parts. They may choose to break them down at the institutional level, in which case they would consider individually each of the general statements just shown and ask, "What 'subunderstandings' should a learner acquire?" They may choose to reserve the specific statements for the programs and departments of instruction.

2. *Designers may deliberately choose at this time to develop both the general educational goals for the institution and the specific, refined, enabling goals which course designers may "lift out" and use as program, departmental, and course goal statements much further in the curriculum design.*—Because designers make an arbitrary decision as to where to place the more specific goals, this manual includes them in this chapter. Discussions of program, department, and course goals will cross-reference back to this list of specific statements.

A rather extensive list but by no means comprehensive list of examples of educational goals appears below. Work groups in an institution should elaborate the list and test it for comprehensiveness. The list covers a wide scope of subjects common to theological education. Some relate to theology, some to church music, and some to religious education, and so forth.

The list is divided into groups without names. Analyze each "conceptual family" and give each a name. For example, several relate to the role of the church in education.

Under which of the general statements on pages 99-101 would you place the more specific statements in this list? At this point remember that even these more specific statements will require further elaboration when designing units of study with a course description.

The student demonstrates understanding of . . .
- the contexts in which historical events of the Bible occurred.
- the techniques and methods of archeological exploration.
- the bearing of geography, history, and archeology on preaching from the Old Testament and New Testament.
- the different types of biblical criticism.

The student demonstrates understanding of . . .
- the contributions of John Calvin to the progress of Christianity.
- the causes and results of the Reformation.
- the influence of major Reformers on the English Reformation.
- the role of Baptists in the development of separation of church and state in America.
- the role of Baptists in securing religious liberty in America.
- the American pattern of church-state relations.
- the concepts of the relation between religious and political authority in the West.
- the contemporary patterns of church-state relations outside the United States.
- the forces, movements, and personalities which have shaped Christianity in the United States.

The student demonstrates understanding of . . .
- the biblical theology of mission.
- the philosophy and strategy of missions.

- the sociopolitical and religious contexts of world missions.
- the history and beliefs of Islam.
- the anthropology of cross-cultural evangelism.
- the strategies for starting churches.
- the approaches to theological education on the mission field.
- the principles of church growth.
- the influence of cultural anthropology on communication of the gospel.
- the current problems in world missions.

The student demonstrates understanding of . . .
- the biblical principles of Christian living and decision making.
- the principles of Christian decision making.
- the biblical teachings and strategies concerning social action.
- the guidelines for dealing with controversial issues.
- the ethical applications of the gospel.
- the biblical and sociological perspectives of contemporary moral issues.
- the place of Christian ethics in the legal system of the nation.
- the approaches to meeting family needs in the church.
- the ethics and politics of health care and health care delivery systems.

The student demonstrates understanding of . . .
- the influence of philosophical developments upon biblical and theological studies.
- the approaches to Christian apologetics.
- the evidences for the validity of the Christian faith.
- the philosophical, theological, and historical significance of the major art forms.
- the types of American philosophical and theological thought.
- the relationship between the biblical world view and science.
- the models for understanding the authority and inspiration of the Bible.

The student demonstrates understanding of . . .
- the person and work of Christ.
- the nature of the Holy Spirit.

- the nature of the church.
- the biblical sources of the doctrines of God and humans.
- the theology of the intertestamental period.
- the Pauline metaphors expressing salvation.
- the psychological and sociological roots of the thoughts of the Reformers.
- the doctrine, worship, traditions, and polity of Roman Catholics.
- the theology of American cults.

The student demonstrates understanding of . . .

- the methods of personal witnessing.
- the strategies of Jesus in personal evangelism.
- the theological basis and methods for involving laity in evangelism and church growth.
- the role of media in evangelism and church growth.
- the methods of personal witnessing.
- the strategies of Jesus in personal evangelism.
- the theological basis and methods for involving laity in evangelism and church growth.
- the role of media in evangelism and church growth.

The student demonstrates understanding of . . .

- the pastor's responsibility for the management of ministry.
- the minister's role in today's society.
- the issues in the church's ministry to persons in urban areas.
- the responsibility of the pastor in planning and leading in worship.
- the pastor's role in ministry to the aging.
- the theological and psychological perspectives of ministry.
- the approaches to using the Bible in pastoral care.
- the methods of pastoral counseling.
- the approaches to family life education and counseling in crises.

The student demonstrates understanding of . . .

- the principles of basic sermon preparation.
- the fundamentals of sermon construction.
- the guidelines for preaching the biographical sermon.
- the varieties of biblical preaching.
- the guidelines for preaching on contemporary issues.
- the process of preparing an evangelistic sermon.

- the theory of oral communication.
- the relationship between proclamation and culture.

The student demonstrates understanding of ...

- the forms of church polity.
- the principles of administrative leadership and supervision.
- the functional elements of long-range planning.
- the guidelines for family financial planning.
- the biblical basis for mission education.
- the principles of church office management.

The student demonstrates understanding of ...

- the methods of counseling in courtship and marriage.
- the theories of personality.
- the major classifications of abnormal behavior in psychopathology.
- the dynamics of group work.
- the techniques of vocational counseling.

The student demonstrates understanding of ...

- the lesson planning process.
- the influence of modern philosophies of education on educational practice in the church.
- the theory and design of Christian education curriculum.
- the process of developing a church curriculum plan.
- the steps in preparing a course description.
- the principles of research methodology.
- the process of designing instructional systems for theological education by extension.
- the influence of culture on learning styles.
- the process of developing a prospectus for a dissertation.

The student demonstrates understanding of ...

- the principles of directive writing in the church curriculum.
- the principles, techniques, and philosophies involved in production of Christian radio and television.
- the basic forms of creative drama.
- the techniques of public speaking.

The student demonstrates understanding of ...

- the developmental needs of single adults.
- the characteristics of adult learners.
- the approaches to activity programming for youth in the church.

- the guidelines for developing a campus ministry.
- the approaches to developing creativity in children.
- the steps in establishing and maintaining a church recreation program.
- the curriculum, methods, and facility requirements for use with preschoolers.
- the design and equipment requirements for a weekday center for young children.
- the influence of the physical, emotional, social, cognitive, and spiritual development of children on methods of teaching children in the church.
- the problems of the visually handicapped and hearing impaired child.

The student demonstrates understanding of . . .

- the community resources available in church social ministry.
- the family system as the primary transmission agent of cultural behavior.
- the methods of social work and practice.
- the theoretical approaches to social casework practice.
- the problems of social work administration.
- the patterns and causes of juvenile delinquency.

The student demonstrates understanding of . . .

- music form and analysis.
- music theory.
- the process of voice production.
- the principles of church music education.
- the role of music in missions.
- the theological and biblical content of hymns.
- the philosophy and practices of church music in historical perspective.
- the philosophy and psychology of church music.
- the process of music composition.
- the process of writing and arranging for vocal and instrumental media.

Curriculum design groups may want to assign to a task force the job of compiling a comprehensive list of general and specific educational goals at the institutional level.

The following guidelines should help designers develop a comprehensive statement. With adaptation they apply equally well to developing goals in the affective and psychomotor domains.

1. Ask, "What 'understandings' do the Bible; experience; and human relationships to God, humans, nature, and history require of the minister?"
2. Combine similar statements. Eliminate statements which can be generalized under another.
3. Ask, "Would elimination of a given statement create an obvious void in the educational goal statement?"
4. Ask, "What obvious voids exist?"
5. Using a list of essential courses now offered, identify the course in which the goal statement now resides.
6. Ask practitioners to evaluate the statements for comprehensiveness and relevance. SME's (subject matter experts) can help greatly at this point.

With a relatively high degree of generalization, an institution's educational goals for learners describe what learners should experience as they "run the race" in the curriculum.

In stating cognitive educational goals, designers find it helpful to make a list of nouns which answer the question "understand what?" For example, the goal may call for understanding of principles, forms, guidelines, processes, steps, concepts, elements, relationships, causes, effects, similarities and differences, consequences, roles, influences, techniques, theories, and so forth.

Affective Educational Goals
(Attitudes and Values)

The expression of an institution's affective educational goals for learners is one of the most neglected parts of curriculum design in theological education. In many school bulletins they are dispersed here and there. If compiled, they would constitute a statement. The Bible, experience, and all human relationships provide examples of affective learning needs. Designers ask, "What attitudes and values do persons need because they have relationships with God, other persons, nature, and history? What attitudes and values does the Bible require of persons engaged in Christian ministry? What does experience reveal about necessary attitudes and values?" The biblical revelation points toward change in attitudes and values. The word *repent* means to rethink.

> *What we have loved, others will love; and we will teach them how.—Wordsworth,* Prelude

> *The expression of an institution's affective educational goals for learners is the most neglected part of curriculum design in theological education.*

The neglect of a tangible focus on the affective domain may exist because affective goals are pervasive and permeating in nature. They permeate *all* the curriculum. When designers specify goals related to attitudes and values, they discover that many apply equally well to multiple facets of an institution's curriculum plan. Experience shows that affective goals have wide cross-program and cross-department application, but some of them tend to relate rather clearly to given programs and departments.

Cognitive goals are more focal in nature. Designers find it easier to use them in developing and implementing curriculum plans. The illusiveness of many affective goals causes many designers to focus attention on the more tangible, more easily evaluated cognitive domain. Cognitive goals lend themselves more easily to division into conceptual families.

> *Dealing with the affective domain in curriculum design requires a greater tolerance for ambiguity than many designers possess!*

The affective educational goal (and/or objectives) for learners grows out of the institutional purpose (along with the cognitive and psychomotor goals). It expresses at a relatively high level of generalization the affective results desired in learners. It describes the affective characteristics desired of those engaged in Christian ministry. (For example, "The student demonstrates assurance of his call to salvation and Christian ministry" and so forth.)

The affective educational goal for learners expressed at the institutional level includes (a) those affective characteristics which the Bible specifies, (b) those affective characteristics which experience proves desirable, and (c) those affective characteristics which evolve out of human relationships to God, humans, nature, and history. And all is in the light of the gospel.

The affective goals, along with the cognitive and psychomotor goals, constitute the raw material out of which departmentation schemes, institutional programs, program and department purposes, and goals evolve. Designers group the related goals and/or objectives together into conceptual families and give them a name (institutional programs). These groupings become the educational goals for learners expressed at the program level and ultimately at the department and course level. Because cognitive and psychomotor goals seem to be more focal in nature than affective goals, programs seem to evolve more directly from them. Because affective goals seem to be more pervasive and permeating then cognitive and psychomotor goals, they seem to resist confinement in "blocks" in a departmentation scheme.

When an institution adopts affective institutional educational goals for learners, it commits itself to provide resources, organization, and energetic curriculum supervision for implementing them. This commitment applies as well to the cognitive and psychomotor goals.

Once stated and adopted the institution decides upon strategies for implementing the affective goals. Two approaches seem worthy of attention:

1. *State the affective dimension for every course.*—Because of the pervasive nature of affective educational goals, the institution may choose to require course designers to state clearly those affective outcomes which seem especially relevant to a given course. Once these outcomes are included in the course description, instructors are obligated to include them in the instructional design (lesson plans). For example, a course in "Church and Denominational Polity" might include as an affective goal: "The student demonstrates *loyalty* to the church and denomination." Learning strategies would include listening to testimonies, discovering what *loyalty* means, and what authoritative sources like the Bible say about loyalty to the church. In this approach the affective goals become part of the warp and woof of the institution's curriculum plan as opposed to becoming the basis for creation of a special department or course.

Some items in the statement of affective educational goals

may be of such global importance that they permeate *every* course and become "common learnings." Others may have special relevance to specific courses. That course then becomes the institution's primary vehicle for implementing that aspect of the goal. Many designers prefer focusing on the affective dimensions of *every* course to developing a special course in spiritual formation.

2. *Provide special courses for dealing with attitudes and values*.—Because of the extreme importance of affective educational goals at all levels of the curriculum design hierarchy, some institutions may choose to implement the goals primarily through a special organizational entity. It may choose to create a Department of Spiritual Formation for example, along with other departments such as Department of Psychology and Counseling. This approach, however, does not eliminate the necessity for dealing with the affective dimensions of learning in all courses. It simply focuses or spotlights affective educational goals.

Institutions find it easier to state affective educational goals and to design learning strategies for accomplishing them than to *evaluate the results* of teaching for affective outcomes. It is axiomatic that transcripts reflect learner achievement. Many instructors lack the tolerance for ambiguity which is involved in evaluation of affective learning. Institutions must come to grips with those troublesome questions related to evaluation of affective outcomes.

Affective educational goals are so pervasive that they reach beyond the institution's curriculum design and plan *per se*. Traditionally we have separated curriculum designs and plans from those other institutional activities which have supportive or facilitative roles. However, the pervasive nature of affective educational goals *invites* deliberate use of those activities as learning strategies. For example, designers must consider this question: Were the affective outcomes the result of something which happened in a given course, or the result of some activity not directly course related? The affective change desired in persons enrolled in a course may have occurred not from participation in the course but from attending chapel or participating in a student organization. Thus an institution's affective educational goals for learners should become a guiding force in planning those seemingly noncurriculum related activities such as chapel programs.

> *An institution's affective educational goals for learners*
> *should become a guiding force in planning those*
> *seemingly noncurriculum related activities*
> *such as chapel programs.*

Institutions should consider adding a second evaluation record to a student's transcript. This record of affective change of status would consist of a list of significant indicators of affective change. Designers would consider each affective goal in the institution's educational goal statements and ask, "What are some acceptable *indicators* of goal achievement?" This list, representative in nature, would be refined by a task force and used by both student and teacher as an evaluation instrument. The design of such an instrument would be time-consuming and perhaps frustrating, but intelligent designers with the aid of God's Spirit could arrive at a beneficial instrument.

A list of affective goals could consist of priority items selected from the institution's affective objectives. An affective goal may state: "The student demonstrates compassion for the lost and others in spiritual need." Designers would ask, "What are some valid indicators that a student has compassion for the lost?" The indicators (objectives) might include statements like: Witnesses consistently. Indicators are to goals what windows are to a house. Often the goal lacks meaning when considered apart from the indicators.

> *Indicators are to goals what windows are to a house.*

The following examples of affective goals may serve as a pattern for designers. At the institutional level, affective goals, like cognitive goals, may have a relatively high level of generalization. Notice the "affective noun" which precedes each goal.

The institution's (seminary, Bible college, and so forth) affective goals for learners is that they demonstrate such attitudes and values as . . .
  • assurance of their call to salvation and Christian ministry.

An analysis of experience can help designers pinpoint affective goals.

OR "Daddy, get your value system organized!"

- confidence in the authority and relevance of the Bible in every relationship of life.
- faithfulness in the exercise of their gifts in ministry.
- commitment to the development of the spiritual life.
- obedience to the demands of the gospel.
- dependence on the Holy Spirit as Teacher, Counselor, and Guide.
- commitment to life-long learning.
- dependability in performance of task assignments.
- commitment to equipping the saints.
- compassion for the lost and unenlisted.
- commitment to excellence in personal and group endeavors.
- pride in the denominational heritage.
- confidence and patience in the democratic process.
- trustworthiness in interpersonal relationships.
- generosity in meeting human needs.
- forgiveness in all of life's relationships.
- honesty in all of life's relationships.
- loyalty to the church and denomination.
- commitment to cleanliness of person and surroundings.
- commitment to careful planning and management of personal and church affairs.
- commitment to efficient management of time.
- respect for the integrity and worth of persons.
- respect for individual differences in persons.
- respect for the priesthood of the believer.
- honesty and punctuality in handling financial obligations.
- respect for law and order.
- openness toward new ideas.
- sensitivity to needs for ego support in others.
- sympathy toward others in times of bereavement.
- steadfastness in prayer.
- impartiality in personal relationships.
- commitment to ministry to the total person.
- persistence in leading the church to teach in all that it does.
- others . . .

The affective noun should convey a degree of action imagery. For example, the word *obedience* projects the image of a person following instructions regardless of personal desires and consequences. Some words like *commitment* and *loyalty* are stronger in action imagery than words like *appreciation*. *Appreciation*, while a good word, conveys a sort of generic fuzziness when compared to words like *faithfulness* and *confidence*. The word *commitment* describes persons who set aside their personal agenda in order to achieve a much desired end. The word *loyalty* calls up images of unwavering devotion in the presence of oppressing forces. Designers would find it helpful to elaborate precise definitions of the affective words.

Study again the preceding list of affective goals. Look for goals which seem to apply to all of theological education. Which seem to apply more specifically to a given program? For example, which seem to apply more specifically to church administration? to pastoral ministry? to evangelism and missions? to interpersonal relationships?

As with cognitive goals, curriculum designers may want to condense the affective goals into a much shorter list of statements, but the "summary" list should include all the essential items.

Institutions which are serious about the development of a curriculum design may form task forces to develop comprehensive, validated lists of affective educational goals for learners. The validity of course descriptions developed later depends upon their relationship to these educational goals.

> *The specification and implementation of the affective dimension of all courses in a curriculum plan would significantly lessen the need for special courses in spiritual formation.*

The difficulty in measuring achievement of affective goals does not provide adequate grounds for neglecting them in curriculum design in theological education. Often teachers must be satisfied simply to *invite* students to make an affective response. The invitation at the end of a sermon "invites." More easily evaluated are the teacher's methods of teaching for affective change.

The statement of an institution's educational goals in the affective domain commits all programs of the institution to permeate their curriculum plans with experiences which contribute to achievement of the goals.

> *The difficulty in measuring achievement of affective goals does not provide adequate grounds for neglecting them in curriculum design in theological education.*

Inclusion of affective educational goals for learners indicates commitment on the part of the institution to implement them. The institution agrees to use its resources and curriculum plan to facilitate achievement of the goals. This means these aspects of the educational goal *must be dealt with* somewhere in the courses in the curriculum plan. Thus the phrase *curriculum supervisor* evolves.

Special courses related to change in attitudes and values have a place in the curriculum plan; however, designers should make sure that inclusion of such courses does not represent efforts to pick up "dropped stitches" which should have been part of the fabric of the curriculum but were not.

When an institution formulates an affective educational goal, it should ask, "Does the statement *omit* any essential goals? Does each phrase reflect a high degree of generalization which leaves room for less comprehensive goals appropriate for programs, departments, and courses?" For example, if in the example shown, the designers omitted "faithfulness in the exercise of their gifts in Christian ministry" a glaring gap would become evident. These broad comprehensive statements have resident within them the more limited goals which make up the institution's program goals, department goals, and course and unit goals. Designers may test statements by listing less comprehensive statements and attempting to find the phrase in the general statement under which they would be subsumed.

Like cognitive educational goals, affective goals are comprehensive enough to allow programs of the institution to select those which have special bearing upon that program. In a larger sense, *all* affective educational goals relate to *all* programs, departments, and courses of instruction.

Affective goals include the same elements that appear in cognitive and psychomotor goals. They specify the kind of learning and state a subject. The goals may say, "The learner will demonstrate an *attitude of concern* . . ." or the goal may simply say, "The student will demonstrate concern for . . ." The goal may omit the word *attitude* and simply say, ". . . will demonstrate concern for, respect for, loyalty to" and so forth.

Another useful approach calls for beginning the statement with words such as *views* or *values*. For example, an affective goal may state: "The student views systematic theology as a dynamic process rather than a static discipline," or "The student values the educational benefits which derive from the democratic process."

> *In a larger sense,* all *affective educational goals for learners relate to* all *programs, departments, and courses.*

Many curriculum designers experience difficulty in finding the precise words to express kinds of attitudes. In stating affective goals, designers have found it helpful to develop a chart similar to the one which follows. It can serve as an idea starter. Generally, teachers and designers find it difficult to think of *kinds* of attitudes.

The chart first lists attitudinal nouns (kinds of learning), then appropriate prepositions. Possible objects of the prepositions follow (subject). The Bible itself suggests attitudinal nouns (compassion, love, constancy, and so forth). Books on professional ethics suggest others. A study of the basic areas of concern in Christian ethics would prove helpful in the discovery of words which describe desirable viewpoints toward persons, ideas, and concepts.

In essence the chart constitutes a taxonomy of possible statements of affective goals for learners. To vary the approach used in the chart, teachers may use verbs in the statements. For example, a goal may state: "The student should *resolve* to conduct family worship."

A third approach to elaborating a taxonomy of attitudes and values is to ask, "What are the attitudes and values involved in the social, political, religious, aesthetic, economic and theoretical spheres of life?"

Developing Affective Goals[7]

Attitudinal Nouns	Preposition	Possible objects of prepositions
1. Assurance	of	salvation, victory
2. Commitment	to	lifelong learning
3. Commitment	to	the Bible, prayer, building up others, long-range planning
4. Compassion	for	a neighbor in need, the unchurched, prisoners, those who suffer bodily pain, orphans, the divorced, those who hunger
5. Confidence	in	God's *promises* in times of need, intercessory prayer, God's *provisions* in times of need, God's leadership, administrative leadership
6. Contentment	in	life's circumstances, one's work
7. Contrition	for	wrongdoing, sins, maltreatment of others, complacency
8. Control	of	thoughts, feelings, actions
9. Conviction	that	every person called of God has a right to theological education regardless of contextual circumstances
10. Cooperation	with	fellow staff members, the denomination
	in	developing plans
11. Dedication	to	effective teaching wholesome family living, Bible reading, personal health care
12. Fairness	in	interpersonal relationships, busines dealings, dealing with children
13. Faith	in	times of doubt, times of insecurity
14. Faithfulness	in	stewardship of life
15. Forgiveness	toward	accusers, one's self, others
16. Generosity	toward	persons in need, enemies
	in	support of missions, praising others, affirming others
17. Gratitude	for	the service of others, material blessings, opportunities to serve, good health, simple things
	toward	family members, church members

7. Designers may want to add a fourth column in which they add a biblical source or example. For example, number 15 could read " . . . as evidenced in Jesus' prayer in Luke 23:34."

Attitudinal Nouns	Preposition	Possible objects of prepositions
18. Helpfulness	in	times of grief, times of sickness
	toward	the discouraged
19. Impartiality	toward	children in the family, fellow workers
	in	decision making
20. Impartiality	toward	races, employees, staff members
21. Honesty	in	all of life's relationships
22. Hope	during	times of despair, during times when doors seem closed
23. Hospitality	toward	friends, strangers, less fortunate
24. Humility	in	handling power, serving others
25. Love	for	the unlovely, the lovely, friends, enemies
26. Loyalty	to	the church, the denomination, the institution, the leadership of the institution, one's convictions, one's friends
27. Modesty	during	times when others praise you
	in	speech, dress
28. Obedience	toward	God, one's calling
29. Openness	toward	ideas of others, personal criticism, new ideas, conflicting opinions
30. Patience	during	times of stress, times when things move slowly, periods of opposition
31. Persistence	in	working toward goals, fighting evil, doing good, enlisting workers, witnessing
32. Respect	for	priesthood of believers, dignity of persons, civil law, rights of others, other races
33. Restraint	in	criticism of others
34. Reverence	for	the dignity of humanity
	toward	God
	in	worship, daily living
35. Sensitivity	to	unspoken needs, needs for ego support, personal desires, needs for self-respect
36. Steadfastness	during	times when things go wrong, times when opposition comes, the world falls in
37. Submission	to	God's leadership, God's will, legal authorities

Attitudinal Nouns	Preposition	Possible objects of prepositions
38. Sympathy	toward	the bereaved, the unemployed, the handicapped
39. Thankfulness	for	service opportunities, God's leadership, what others have contributed, answered prayer, God's love
40. Thoughtfulness	on	special occasions
	toward	the undeserving
	in	manner of life
41. Tolerance	toward	new ideas, renegades, unfaithful stewards
42. Trustworthiness	in	confidential counseling, business dealings
43. Willingness	to	sacrifice time, help those in need, refrain from seeking one's own way
44. Others . . .		

Designers may judge the clarity and practicality of affective goals by attempting to identify precise representative indicators which would prove achievement of the affective goals.

After analyzing and accepting the lists of affective goals, designers combine them with the lists of cognitive and psychomotor goals. (See the form at the end of this chapter.) The compilation constitutes the institution's educational goals for learners.

Psychomotor Educational Goals (Skills)

Designers include the psychomotor (skills) goals[8] in the compilation of institutional goals for learners. Programs of theological education which focus primarily on the performing arts and church and denominational programs which focus on church camping, recreation, and certain other facets of theological education place much emphasis on the psychomotor domain of

---

8. The psychomotor (skills) domain does not include what designers sometimes call perceptual skills which in reality belong in the cognitive domain at the higher levels of learning. For example, in evangelism persons might say, "He's a skilled witness." Witnessing is not a motor skill like riding a bicycle. It is a perceptual skill which represents achievement at a high level of understanding.

learning. Relatively few learners are involved except in programs like church music.

Some large institutions have multiple programs, departments, and courses which require a high degree of motor skill. The following short list shows the kinds of skills which might appear in an institution's statement of motor skills goals.

> The institution's (seminary, Bible college, and so forth) skills goals for learners is that they demonstrate competency in the performance of those motor skills necessary in the field of church music.
> - Skill in choral conducting
> - Skill in sight reading musical scores
> - Skill in instrumental performance
> - Skill in vocal performance
> - Other . . .

A motor skill such as "skill in performing the ordinance of baptism" belongs in the institution's educational goal statements but in another "conceptual family."

After completing the statements of psychomotor goals, designers compile them along with the cognitive and affective goals. The comprehensive list of educational goals at the institutional level provides the raw materials from which designers make decisions about which programs the institution should included in its departmentation scheme.

Many performance skills require understanding (cognitive learning) of theoretical foundations and historical antecedents. For this reason the institution's statement of cognitive goals should include them. For example, a school of music treats such understandings as theory of music, form and analysis, and music composition. The understandings may or may not result in motor skill development, but they provide essential prerequisite learnings associated with performance skills.

A compilation of goals from the three domains might be similar to the chart on page 121. The list constitutes the element of design called "The Institution's Educational Goals for Learners."

As in the cognitive and affective domains, the skills goals do not describe indicators (objectives) which the instructor will accept as valid evidence that the learner has achieved the goals. These indicators, along with necessary conditions and standards of performance appear in the objectives.

The composite list of the institution's educational goals

The Institution's Educational Goals for Learners, All Domains

Cognitive Goals	Affective Goals	Psychomotor Skills Goals

should specify what all students would achieve in all domains of learning if they should live long enough to achieve all of them. Obviously, they cannot. But all goals appear in the "goal bank" and provide the raw material for making decisions about departmentation schemes.

Designers now take the next step in developing a curriculum design—identifying and selecting high level learning outcomes or *objectives* which teachers will accept as valid evidence that learners have achieved the goals.

Developing Institutional Educational Objectives (Indicators of Goal Achievement)

Thus far this chapter has dealt with the institution's educational *goals* for learners. At this point the chapter begins a treatment of the institution's objectives (indicators of goal achievement) for learners which state in relatively generalized terms what the student will *do* to demonstrate in a meaningful way achievement of the goal. These are the statements which constitute a learning outcomes focus in curriculum design.

To develop educational objectives at the institutional level, designers analyze one by one the goals for learners. They ask, What will the student do at the level of meaningful activity to indicate or prove that he or she has achieved the goal? The answers to this question give this curriculum design approach its name—learning outcomes.

At the institutional level, an objective or outcome tells what the learner will do in a meaningful way to indicate achievement of the goal.

The following goal appears in the list given previously in this chapter: The learner demonstrates understanding of the process of sermon preparation . . .

Designers ask, "What will students do at the level of meaningful activity which will prove to themselves and to the teacher that they understand the sermon preparation process?" Which of the following would prove achievement of that learning goal at a high level of learning?

The student demonstrates understanding of the sermon preparation process . . .

_____ 1. by naming the ten steps in sermon preparation.
_____ 2. by writing a properly stated sermon objective.
_____ 3. by planning and preaching a sermon on an assigned Bible passage.

The chart on the next page presents the "up-the-stairs" technique for determining the level of meaningful activity.

Some designers prefer to identify first the objectives or the learning outcomes. Then they construct the goal which precedes it. Designers should record whichever item comes to mind first—the goal or the objective. When they have one of the statements, they can construct the other. Designers have found either approach workable.

Because designers need to think of objectives in close contiguity with goals, the following example shows an objective in the context of the goal: The student demonstrates an attitude of compassion for the unsaved by witnessing consistently as a lifestyle.

The teacher observes the proof and says, "I know the student has achieved the goal because I observed his performance." In this example, the teacher or others observed the student as he witnessed.

Objectives form the most visible expression of learning outcomes. Many designers like to think of objectives as "indicators" of goal achievement. This term accurately describes the function of objectives. They represent learner competencies, performance, and outcomes which enable ministers to perform effectively their task.

The teacher may observe performance by evaluating a paper, observing a demonstration, or watching some other activity which gives valid evidence that the learner has achieved the goal.

In these examples find the objective or the "indicator" of goal achievement. Note the three different formats.

(a) By voluntarily doing *such things as* as enlisting persons in a Sunday School class, the student will demonstrate compassion for the unsaved.

(b) The student will demonstrate understanding of the lesson planning process by planning and conducting a Sunday School teaching session.

(c) The student demonstrates skill in directing congregational singing. To demonstrate this skill he will lead a congregation in singing a randomly selected hymn.

The "Up-the-Stairs" Technique
for Identifying the Meaningful Level of Activity for a Course in "Basic Sermon Preparation"

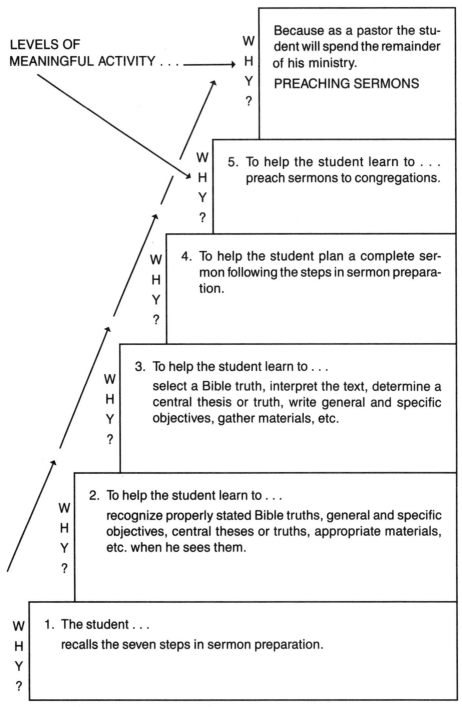

LEVELS OF MEANINGFUL ACTIVITY . . . ⟶

W H Y ? Because as a pastor the student will spend the remainder of his ministry.
PREACHING SERMONS

W H Y ? 5. To help the student learn to . . . preach sermons to congregations.

W H Y ? 4. To help the student plan a complete sermon following the steps in sermon preparation.

W H Y ? 3. To help the student learn to . . . select a Bible truth, interpret the text, determine a central thesis or truth, write general and specific objectives, gather materials, etc.

W H Y ? 2. To help the student learn to . . . recognize properly stated Bible truths, general and specific objectives, central theses or truths, appropriate materials, etc. when he sees them.

W H Y ? 1. The student . . . recalls the seven steps in sermon preparation.

The preacher does not go around the rest of his life saying, "Look! I can recite the seven steps in sermon preparation!!"

> *Course objectives at the level of meaningful activity*
> *should become the stuff from which field education*
> *programs are made.*

These are the kinds of goals and objectives which taken together form the comprehensive list of the institution's educational goals and objectives for learners. The scope of the curriculum and the educational goals and objectives for learners are inseparably linked. An accumulation of the subjects expressed in the goals and the actions expressed in the objectives actually constitute the scope of the design. The process described in chapter 5 focuses on the process for ensuring comprehensiveness and relevance.

As with educational goals, the objectives should reflect as high a level of generalization as possible when stated at the institutional level. If the designer can think of several subobjectives or performances which together constitute the general one, then in all probability the objective is broad enough.

Cognitive Objectives for the Institution (Knowledge and Understanding)

Cognitive objectives at the institutional level represent usually the analysis, synthesis, and evaluation levels of cognitive learning.[9]

The following compilation of institutional objectives for learners pair easily with some of the cognitive goals shown earlier in this chapter. Analyze each and reconstruct the goal which probably precedes it. For example the objective "plans and preaches sermons" implies the goal "understands the process of sermon preparation" (goal 9). Then match the objectives with the appropriate goals given on pages 99-101. These statements assume that the leader either leads others to do the job or does it himself.

---

9. For a treatment of what these levels mean see *Design for Teaching and Training* by LeRoy Ford or *A Taxonomy of Objectives: Cognitive Domain* by Benjamin Bloom.

> *An interesting thing happens when specifying*
> *educational objectives or learning outcomes. A given*
> *objective may indicate achievement of goals in* both *the*
> *cognitive and affective domains. Often the voluntariness*
> *of the action classifies it as affective.*

Note that each objective (learning outcome) begins with a verb in present tense form.

To demonstrate achievement of the institution's educational goals for learners (cognitive), the student . . .

- trains church members to perform the functions of a church: worship, witness, proclamation, education, and ministry. (8, 10)
- plans and preaches sermons. (9)
- counsels individuals and groups. (15)
- counsels persons preparing for marriage. (15)
- baptizes new Christians.
- functions creatively with other professional staff and church members.
- communicates effectively.
- interprets Scripture.
- teaches individuals and groups.
- plans and conducts outreach programs.
- ministers in areas of human need.
- manages church and education programs.
- equips church members for ministry and service.
- models the role of an effective teacher and leader.
- organizes the church for ministry and service.
- supervises the church staff.
- guides in long-range planning.
- witnesses to the unsaved.
- disciples fellow Christians.
- follows a personal and family plan for spiritual development.
- leads democratically.
- plans physical facilities for the church.
- plans and conducts visitation programs.
- develops and follows a plan for lifelong learning.
- interprets plans and strategies for fulfilling a church's mission responsibilities.

- translates New Testament Greek into English.
- others . . .

A rather extensive list of possible specific cognitive objectives or learning outcomes developed by a school of religious education is given in the following pages. A work group in an institution could develop such a list for a given program and test it for comprehensiveness.

For many years the School of Religious Education at Southwestern Baptist Theological Seminary has pioneered in the development of a learning outcomes curriculum. The major portion of this list consists of items condensed from *Course Descriptions for Masters Degree Programs*.[10] Each item represents an attempt to describe an objective at the level of meaningful activity. Notice that each statement begins with a verb. Because no other similar statements have been located as of this date, the list is included almost in its entirety. The objectives appear in "conceptual families" along with the course titles. In actual practice, designers would arrange into conceptual families a list of randomly ordered objectives.

One advantage of a comprehensive listing of course objectives (outcomes) is that designers can spot readily areas of duplication. As you read the following lists, watch for items which appear in more than one course.

Competency Statements
School of Religious Education[11]

Church and Education Administration
Church and Denomination Administration
    Writes a church constitution and by-laws.
    Develops purpose and objectives statements for a church.
    Designs church programs to assist a church in achieving
        its purposes and objectives.
    Develops model for selection and ordination of deacons.
    Trains officers, committee members, and deacons.

---

10. In 1984, LeRoy Ford condensed the course descriptions in *Course Descriptions for the Masters Degree Programs* so that the descriptions included only objectives stated at the level of meaningful activity. No other similar lists have been located as of this date.

11. Designers may wait to elaborate these statements at the program or division level.

Enlists and trains church leaders.
Identifies physical resources needed for an organization.
Develops plans for providing physical resources.
Develops administrative control instruments.
Evaluates sample church constitutions and by-laws.

The Church Staff
Writes job descriptions for church staff positions.
Organizes or reorganizes a church staff.
Writes job qualification requirements.
Determines staff needs of a church.
Interviews prospective church staff members.
Inducts and orients new staff members.
Conducts staff meetings.
Supervises a church staff.
Guides employee development.
Terminates staff members.

Church Publicity
Produces a publicity program for a church.
Evaluates a church's publicity program.
Chooses printing processes for church publicity.
Writes news stories.
Selects publicity pictures.
Designs and does layout for a church newspaper.

Management for Ministry in Religious Education
"Salvages" unsatisfactory workers.
Administers positive discipline.
Guides the decision-making process.
Delegates responsibility properly.
Manages meetings.
Uses telephone properly.

Church Financial Planning
Develops a financial plan for own family.
Develops a church program of family financial planning.
Assists families in financial planning.

Stewardship and Church Finance
Gives personal stewardship testimony.
Designs plans for budget support.
Develops approaches to special funding.
Develops church financial policies.
Makes purchases for a church.
Develops plans for handling church funds.

Church Business Administration
Administers church financial plans.

Manages church office.
Supervises building and equipment maintenance.
Develops plan for church parking.
Manages church kitchen and food services.
Supervises use of building.
Develops fire protection plans.
Develops insurance plans.
Develops employee benefit plans.
Administers church weekday ministries.
Develops plans for capital improvement funding.
Administers salary plans.
Develops public relations plans.
Develops purchase order systems.
Develops property security plans.
Develops policies for use of facilities.
Handles legal matters.
Church Office Management
Develops office management and control procedures.
Develops procedures for purchase of supplies.
Designs office layouts.
Guides interviews with personnel committees.
Writes office policies and procedures.
Survey of Education Administration
Designs leadership training programs.
Develops procedures for nominating committee.
Administrative Leadership and Supervision
Analyzes a church's training needs and procedures.
Conducts a talent survey.
Develops a leadership training program.[12]
Evaluates leadership training progress.
Missions Education in the Church
Determines mission education needs for a church.
Designs a strategy for missions education in a church.
Determines goals, objectives, and action plans for mission education in a church.
Creates missions awareness in a church.
Educational Evangelism
Conducts a prospect analysis of church and Sunday School rolls.
Prepares a calendar of educational evangelism activities.

---

12. Notice duplication in Survey of Education Administration. Such duplication does not come to light until designers prepare a document such as this.

Religious Education and Missions
    Designs a religious education model for use in another culture.
    Develops leadership training guidelines for another culture.

Behavioral Sciences

Personality Development and Introduction to Behavior Modification
    Applies principles of behavior modification in counseling.
Practicum in Marriage Counseling
    Conducts marriage counseling sessions in groups.
    Conducts individual marriage counseling sessions.
    Gives and interprets psychological tests.
The Psychology of Human Relations in the Home
    Designs a training course in human relations in a home.
Psychology of Human Relations in a Church
    Functions (relates) creatively with professional staff and other church members.
The Art of Counseling
    Guides and counsels individuals and groups.
    Listens during counseling process.
    Leads a therapy group.
    Writes referral letters for counselees.
    Communicates effectively.
Counseling Methods in Courtship and Marriage
    Counsels persons anticipating marriage.
    Counsels married persons.
Abnormal Psychology
    Guides and counsels persons who have deviant and inappropriate behaviors.
Group Dynamics
    Guides and counsels persons in a group setting.
Educational Programming for Family Life Ministries
    Designs family enrichment activities.
    Plans and conducts family life conferences.
    Plans and conducts marriage enrichment retreats.
    Plans and conducts parenting workshops.
    Plans and conducts sex education seminars.
    Trains church leaders to meet crisis needs.
    Produces a calendar of family ministry activities.
    Conducts a family needs survey.

Foundations of Education

Educational Psychology[13]
  Evaluates the schools of educational psychology.
  Determines learning goals (cognitive and affective).
  Selects appropriate media and methods for instruction.
  Designs tests for assessment of learning.
Philosophy of Education
  Develops a personal philosophy of education in the
     church.
Research and Statistics in Ministry
  Researches given projects.
  Solves given statistical research problems.
  Designs *direct observation study*.
  Develops questionnaires.
  Conducts *formal interviews*.
  Writes test items.
Principles of Teaching
  Writes learning goals and objectives.
  Designs learning activities.
  Writes lesson plans for church program organizations.
  Evaluates learning.
  Conducts teaching-training sessions.
  Develops a philosophy of teaching and training in the
     church.
Building a Church Curriculum Plan
  Develops a curriculum plan to help a church achieve its
     goals and objective.
  Interprets denominational literature.
  Evaluates curriculum materials from other
     denominations.
  Writes church goals.
Modern Philosophies of Education
  Writes teaching-learning plans which reflect given
     philosophies of education.
Research and Statistics
  Writes a prospectus for a research project.

---

13. Many courses such as Educational Psychology may include only "lead-up" or "en route" objectives. The course serves as a foundation course in a vertical cluster. The "meaningful activity" appears later in courses at the top end of the cluster. In this case, the meaningful activity appears in the course which calls for planning and leading teaching-training sessions.

Designs simple research experiments of various types.
Solves research problems using appropriate techniques.
Christian Education in Deaf Ministry
Develops a proposal for a deaf ministry in a church.
Signs short stories.
Developing Teaching and Training Systems
Develops multimedia self-instructional materials for
theological education by extension using the systems
approach.

Social Service

Introduction to Social Ministries
Refers persons in need to appropriate community
agencies.
Determines helping needs in given cases.
Designs a social ministry program or proposal for age
groups.
Designs a program of church and community weekday
ministries.
The Church and Community Intervention
Analyzes a community's social needs and resources.
Develops intervention strategies for a church and
community.
Human Behavior and Psychotherapy
Counsels persons exhibiting severe deviant behavior.
Counsels alcoholics.
Counsels drug and narcotic addicts.
Counsels those who exhibit violently aggressive behavior.
Human Behavior and Culture
Develops a proposal for a church ministry to cultural
groups.
Social Services Methods and Practice
Develops a strategy of intervention with persons who
desire help.
Diagnoses a client's functioning level and suggests a plan
of intervention.
Social Casework
Interviews (clients) and assesses social problems involved.
Social Group Work
Does social group work in settings like hospitals,
children's homes, detention centers, and so forth.
Social Services Administration, Supervision, and
Consultation

Develops planning, supervision, and consultation
strategies for a social ministry program in a church.
Writes a job description for a social ministry position in
the church or denomination.
Supervises a church social service ministry.
Enlists, trains, and supervises volunteers in a church
social service ministry.
Consults churches in regard to social ministry programs.
Field Instruction (Social Services)
Guides therapy groups of persons with personal
problems.
Serves as a staff member in a social service agency.
Works in a social service agency.
Juvenile Delinquency and the Church
Develops a church or associational ministry program for
dealing with juvenile delinquents using
denominational and community resources.
Determines referral sources for given persons.
Child Welfare
Establishes a comprehensive child welfare program in a
church or the denomination using support services,
supplemental services, and substitution services.

Communication Arts

Communication Strategies for Church Ministry
Designs a communication model for a church to use in
reaching internal and external audiences.
Broadcast Writing: Radio
Writes original or adaptive promotional materials for
radio (commercials, sermons, news items, dramas,
features, documentaries, and children's programs).
Writes continuity for various types of radio broadcasting
(religious, music, country and Western music, and so
forth).
Broadcast Writing: Television
Writes for religious television original or adaptive
commercials, news items, features, continuity,
documentaries, children's programs, sermons, and
dramas.
Uses effectively body language and other visual support.
Writing Lesson Materials for Pupils
Writes topical lessons for church curriculum (Sunday
School lessons and so forth).

Writes expository lessons for church curriculum (Sunday
School lessons and so forth).
Writing Lesson Procedures (Teaching Plans) for Teachers
and Leaders
Writes teaching-training plans for use by teachers and
leaders in the church.
Writes resource units for the church curriculum.
Writes leadership training (how-to) articles for church
curriculum.
Ministry, Media, and Marketing
Analyzes a given "market" for a video production.
Plans a promotional campaign for a video production.
Public Relations for Churches
Produces a public relations program for a church.
Writes a public relations script for electronic media
production.
Identifies a church's publics.
Writes church goals and objectives.
Advertising for Church and Media
Plans and evaluates an advertising campaign for a
church.
Designs advertising campaign for specific church
activities.
Church Publicity
Designs, produces, and evaluates publicity pieces for
specific church activities and programs.
Evaluates an overall promotion and publicity program for
a church.
Does layout and design for church publications.
Writes news stories.
Uses pictures in layout and design.
Chooses printing processes for church publications.
Acting for Church and Media
Performs a monologue.
Performs a duet scene.
Rehearses camera positions.
Performs a scene for religious radio and television.
Stage and Television Lighting for Church Production
Designs light plots for stage and television production.
Designs lighting for stage and television.
Religious Radio and Television
Writes script format for religious radio or television
program package.

Produces a script format for radio or television.
Religious Radio Production
Plans and directs a religious production for radio.
Operates properly the equipment used in productions for radio.
Religious Television Production
Plans and directs a production for religious television.
Operates properly the equipment used in television production.
Media-Produced Counseling
Devises appropriate responses to persons who respond to media productions.
Counsels by telephone.
Counsels by mail.
Nonprojected Visuals in Religious Education
Creates nonprojected aids for teaching and training.
Selects teaching pictures.
Writes lesson plans calling for use of pictures.
Designs posters.
Designs maps.
Uses objects, models, exhibits, and displays.
Designs charts, graphs, and diagrams.
Plans observation trips.
Graphic Design
Designs graphic aids for use in the church and denomination.
Designs layout for printed media.
Designs graphic art for religious television.
Speech for Christian Workers
Writes speeches for various occasions in the church.
Speaks at various church functions.
Guides a problem-solving discussion.
Delivers a persuasive speech.
Platform Leadership
Delivers a message which achieves a goal.
Does interviews, personal investigation, and library research for a speech.
Produces a multimedia presentation for a church.
Develops a personal program for improvement in platform leadership.
Writes messages in personal and direct language.
Oral Interpretation
Reads orally a Scripture passage.

Reads orally poetry and prose.
Reads orally a selection of church literature for children.
Religious Drama
Writes and produces original religious drama for the church.
Performs in a religious drama group.
Directs a religious play (casts parts, selects staff, conducts rehearsals, and so forth).
Performs a monologue.
Does "duet acting."[14]
Production of Religious Drama
Plays a major role in a religious drama.
Performs a religious monologue.
Performs duet scenes.
Outlines working schedules for production staff members in a religious drama.
Plans rehearsal schedules.
Directs a religious drama.
Creative Arts in Teaching Children in the Church
Designs a teacher training program for teaching children in the church.
Uses creative arts in teaching children in the church.
Writes children's stories.
Tells a children's story.
Collects teaching pictures for children.
Paints friezes.
Makes mobiles, charts, and dioramas.
Writes choral readings.
Writes songs and poems.
Develops dramas with children.
Makes and demonstrates the use of puppets.
Plans field trips.

Adult Education

The Church's Educational Ministry with Single Adults
Designs programs and ministries which reflect the needs of single adults in and out of the church.
Evaluates church programs with single adults.

---

14. Notice duplication in "Acting for Church Media" and in "Production of Religious Drama." A document such as this reveals such duplication.

The Church's Ministry with Older Persons
  Designs church programs with older persons.
  Establishes cooperative commitments with secular and
    community programs with older adults (when
    appropriate).
  Establishes relationships with older adults in health care
    facilities.
  Evaluates church and denominational programs with
    older adults.
  Trains laypersons to minister to older adults in the
    church.
  Counsels with terminally ill.
Survey of Adult Education in the Church
  Develops a philosophy for adult education in a church.
  Designs an adult education program for a church.
  Evaluates the church's program of adult education.
  Leads adult learning groups in the church.
  Interprets curriculum materials for adults.
Adult Developmental Psychology
  Evaluates church and secular curriculum materials for
    adults from the viewpoint of developmental
    psychology.
Campus Ministry
  Designs programs of campus ministries.
  Evaluates national campus ministry movements.
  Develops a model of church-sponsored ministries with
    students.
  Develops a calendar of activities for campus ministry
  Trains student leaders.
  Designs staff relationship patterns.
  Supervises and manages student centers.
  Writes job descriptions for directors of campus
    ministry.
The Church's Ministry with College and University Students
  Designs a model for a church's total ministry with its
    students.
  Designs a student internship program emphasizing
    selected phases of a church's total ministry.
  Develops guidelines for determining a church's student
    ministries needs.
  Evaluates direct church-to-campus ministries.
  Trains volunteer workers with students.

Childhood Education

Survey of Childhood Education in the Church

Evaluates equipment and learning environments for preschoolers and children.

Interprets preschool curriculum for preschoolers.

Plans units of study for preschoolers and children.

Designs ministries to parents and families of preschoolers and children.

Weekday Centers for Young Children

Writes goals for church weekday centers for children.

Writes job descriptions for staff members of church weekday centers for children.

Draws floor plans for a church weekday center.

Selects suitable equipment and materials for a church weekday center for children.

Plans operations policies and procedures for church weekday centers for children.

Prepares guidelines for food services for weekday center for children.

Studies in Childhood Education

Evaluates and selects appropriate toys and playground equipment for children in the church.

Handles socialization and emotional problems with children.

Designs learning experiences for children in the church.

Guides appropriately the spiritual development of children.

Parent-Child Relations

Guides in the solution of problems in parent-child relations.

Plans and conducts meetings with parents.

Curriculum for Weekday Centers

Develops curriculum units for use in church weekday centers for children.

Creates learning centers appropriate for young children in the church.

Evaluates and selects learning materials for children.

Selects for children appropriate learning activities in language arts, sciences, math, and so forth for use with children in church weekday centers.

Creates a learning activity file.

Religious Education in Early Childhood
    Plans units of study for preschoolers in the church.
    Designs floor plans for preschool departments in the
        church.
    Equips preschool departments.
    Chooses curriculum materials for preschoolers in a
        church.
    Teaches preschoolers.
    Designs a program of ministry to parents for a calendar
        year.
Religious Education in Middle and Later Childhood
    Plans units of study for children in middle and later
        childhood.
    Designs floor plans for children's division (middle and
        later childhood).
    Chooses and interprets children's curriculum for middle
        and later childhood.
    Designs a program of ministry to parents of children
        ages six through eleven.
The Director of Children's Work
    Designs a calendar of activities for parents, children,
        and teachers in children's departments in the
        church.
    Writes job descriptions for directors of children's work.
    Communicates effectively with children, parents, staff,
        and teachers.
    Plans and conducts a parent-teacher meeting.
    Designs seminars for parents of children in the church.
    Conducts department planning meetings.
    Plans and conducts teacher-training courses for teachers
        of children in the church.
    Plans and conducts a children's fellowship.
    Plans and conducts a Vacation Bible School.
    Plans and conducts reading clubs, camps, and retreats for
        children.
Religious Education for Exceptional Children
    Develops a church program ministry for exceptional
        children (hearing impaired, visually impaired,
        mentally retarded, gifted, learning disabled, and
        speech handicapped).
    Signs for hearing impaired.
    Plans curriculum for exceptional children in the church.

Directed Teaching in Early Childhood
Writes teaching plans for early childhood.,
Develops and supervises a leadership training program for early childhood.
Plans and conducts teaching sessions for early childhood.
Plans learning activities for learning centers.
Plans learning activities for group situations.
Teaches songs and music activities.
Conducts Bible activities with young children.
Plays the Autoharp.
Selects resource materials for teaching young children.
Designs teaching aids for teaching young children.
Designs bulletin boards for teaching young children.
Maintains discipline with young children.

Church Recreation

Church Recreation: Philosophical Foundations
Elaborates the theological basis for church recreation.
Develops personal philosophy of church recreation.
Survey of Church Recreation
Develops and organizes a church recreation program.
Plans age-group activities for a selected recreation program area.
Develops recreation programs for the handicapped.
Designs and administers a church recreation interest survey.
Writes job descriptions for a minister of recreation.
Trains church recreation leaders.
Plans facilities for church recreation.
Social Recreation
Enlists prospects through social recreation.
Plans a social recreation leadership training program for a church.
Guides group activities in social recreation.
Plans and directs social recreation events.
Plans and publicizes social recreation events.
Plans a calendar of events for social recreation.
Camp Administration
Plans and directs a day camp for a church.
Plans and directs a resident camp for a church.
Plans and directs a retreat for a church or association.
Writes job descriptions for camp personnel.
Trains camp personnel.

Develops plans for a campsite.
Prepares budgets for a church camp.
Develops food service for a church camp.
Plans for camp safety and health according to standards.
Develops an insurance plan for a church camp.
Church Recreation: Administration
Develops a master plan for church recreation.
Develops curriculum plans for church recreation.
Writes job descriptions for ministers of recreation.
Manages time effectively.
Enlists, trains, and supervises church recreation
    volunteers.
Plans a budget for church recreation.
Manages and controls use of church recreation facilities.
Church Recreation Facilities
Adapts church facilities for church recreation.
Makes agreements with other agencies for use of
    recreation facilities.
Develops manuals for recreation facility management.
Plans church recreation facilities.
Trains and assigns volunteer church recreation workers.
Manages a church recreation facility.
Selects church recreation equipment.
Schedules building maintenance.
Sports and Games
Plans and directs sports events for a church.
Enlists and trains sports leadership for a church.
Writes job descriptions for sports leaders.
Organizes team sports within the church and with other
    churches.
Organizes special interest groups in sports.
Determines insurance needs for a sports program.
Purchases and cares for sports equipment and uniforms.
Develops a budget for a sports league.
Aerobics Fitness
Follows a personal program of aerobics fitness.
Tests for physical wellness.[15]
Prescribes programs for physical wellness.
Administers and interprets physical wellness tests.
Designs a physical wellness program for a church.

---

15. The term *physical wellness* is becoming vogue today.

Arts and Crafts
Conducts interest surveys for arts and crafts.
Teaches arts and crafts.
Trains arts and crafts leaders.
Designs an arts and crafts facility for a church.
Adapts existing facilities for use in arts and crafts.
Develops policies for an arts and crafts program in a
church.

Youth Education

Survey of Youth Education in the Church
Designs a youth ministry model for the church.
Designs a Bible study ministry for youth.
Designs Discipleship Training ministry for youth.
Designs mission education ministry for youth.
Guides and counsels youth.
Youth Issues
Develops a ministry model for dealing with youth issues.
Ministry to Youth
Develops a personal philosophy for youth ministry in a
church.
Prepares a ministry model for the minister to youth.
Develops curriculum plans for a youth ministry.

Affective Objectives for the Institution
(Attitudes and Values)

Jesus said: "By their fruits ye shall know them" (Matt. 7:20).
He specified some indicators (objectives) of affective learning
when He said, "Love your enemies; do good to them, . . . that
despitefully use you" (Luke 6:27-28). Designers make interesting discoveries when specifying affective objectives or learning
outcomes.

1. *They discover that a given indicator of affective change may
at the same time serves as an indicator of achievement in the cognitive domain.*—Whether a given objective (indicator) relates to

> *Jesus revealed His understanding of the role of
> educational goals and objectives in curriculum design
> when He said, "By their fruits ye shall
> know them" (Matt. 7:20).*

a cognitive goal or an attitudinal goal is largely a matter of viewpoint. For example, a cognitive objective (indicator) might state that the trainee "visits the sick." This could mean that he comprehends and applies the *principles* for making a meaningful visit to the sick. The cognitive dimension of an effective visit *indicates* mastery of the competency. He demonstrates understanding of the principles of visitation.

> *A given indicator of achievement of an affective goal may at the same time serve as an indicator of achievement in the cognitive domain.*

On the other hand "visits the sick" may indicate achievement of an *attitudinal* goal. If the trainee voluntarily visits because his life-style reflects a deep sense of concern for the welfare of the patient and the family, if he has a deep sense that as he visits the person he visits Christ (Matt. 25:40), then "visits the sick" indicates achievement of an attitudinal goal. In this case he demonstrates an attitude of concern for the physically or emotionally ill person by visiting consistently, without prompting, without a sense of obligation.

> *To be a philosopher . . . is to solve some of the problems of life, not only theoretically, but practically.—Henry David Thoreau*

The following example is more generalized than the previous illustration and would more nearly represent an objective at the institutional level.

For example, notice the similarity of the objectives in the following statements.

Affective—The student demonstrates an attitude of *commitment* to lifelong learning by developing and following a personal plan for lifelong learning.

Cognitive—The student demonstrates understanding of the *process* of developing a plan for lifelong learning by developing and following a personal plan for lifelong learning.

Observe that the indicators are the same but the goals (the stems of the statements) cast the learning in different domains.

2. *Designers discover that they must consider each affective objective as a representative response.*—The learner may not respond in the exact way the designer specified in the objective, but the response may be as valid as the specified one. In view of this possibility, many designers insert in the goal-objective statement the phrase *"by doing such things as . . ."*

3. *Designers also discover that the degree of voluntariness of a response determines the degree to which the response is an affective one.*—Educational psychologists use the phrase *approach response* to describe these significant unsolicited responses. The learner voluntarily, without prompting, does something which indicates achievement of an affective goal. Objectives specify "representative" responses only.

Paul says, "But it has been my wish to do nothing about it without first consulting you *and* getting your consent, *in order that your benevolence might not seem to be the result of your compulsion or of pressure but might be voluntary [on your part]"* (Philem. 14, AMP, author's italics).

How do designers determine indicators of attitudinal learning? The elaboration of indicators of attitudinal change does not come easily. The following suggestions may help.

Some designers use the "projection in time" technique to determine representative objectives or indicators. A goal may read, "The learner demonstrates an attitude of concern for the emotional needs of learning impaired children." Using the projection in time technique, the designer assumes that he could observe in real life a person whose life-style shows commitment to meeting the emotional needs of learning impaired children. He assumes, also, that he could follow such a person around during an entire day or week keeping a log of the things he saw the committed person doing with learning impaired children. What would the designer write in the log?

The log might include observations like these: "I saw John enrolling in a college course in special education. I saw John sharing with parents of retarded children a new book on *Living with Special Children.*" Such observations can serve as representative or typical indicators. They tell typical things the learner does to show that he has the attitude.

The following guidelines have helped designers in identifying outcomes related to attitude and values.

1. *Identify the attitude and state it in an attitudinal goal.*—By way of review, these statements (a) specify in broad terms the attitude or value, and (b) state the subject. One planning group included the following:

Goal
- The trainee demonstrates an attitude of confidence in intercessory prayer by voluntarily doing such as . . . (attitude: *confidence;* subject: *intercessory prayer*)
- The trainees demonstrate an attitude of concern for the salvation of the lost by doing such things as . . . (attitude: *concern;* subject: *salvation of the lost*)

2. *List specific but "typical" indicators.*—We say typical because designers find it impossible to *list all* the possible valid indicators of achievement of attitudinal goals. The planning group mentioned above listed the following indicators of achievement of the attitudinal goals shown:

Goal	*Indicators*
• The trainee demonstrates an attitude of confidence in intercessory prayer by voluntarily doing such as . . . (attitude: *confidence;* subject: *intercessory prayer*)	1. Maintaining a prayer list 2. Interceding for others 3. Studying what the New Testament says 4. Confessing needs 5. Encouraging others to pray 6. Others . . .
• The trainees demonstrate an attitude of concern for the salvation of the lost by doing such things as . . . (attitude: *concern;* subject: *salvation of the lost*)	1. Teaching a home Bible study group 2. Distributing helpful tracts 3. Witnessing to family members 4. Witnessing on the street 5. Attending training sessions on witnessing 6. Others . . .

Designers could then generalize the indicators in the second example and say, "Witnessing consistently as a life-style." This statement would more nearly fit into a list of the institution's affective educational goals.

3. *Decide whether or not to publish the list of attitudinal indicators.*—In either case the indicators may become the basis for courses or units of study.

In curriculum design the question arises: Should designers *specify* and communicate to *the learners* the attitudinal objectives? Or should the designers use the objectives only as resources for design?

The *pro* argument says "yes"—communicate the indicators to learners, otherwise they will not visualize the kind of persons they should become. Designers can find biblical support: Jesus said, "One thing thou lackest: go thy way, sell [all your goods]" (Mark 10:21). Jesus *told* the learner—and the telling suggested that selling goods and giving to the poor were valid indicators of a desirable attitude and value system. Communicating affective objectives at the institutional level is not as questionable as at the department or course level.

The *con* argument says develop the objectives but do not communicate them to the learners. This argument says learners may simply *mimic* the indicators. They may perform not because they have developed the attitude but because they want to please the authority figure. The argument says teach, but *wait* until the learner of his or her own volition *does* what the indicator describes (or makes an analogous response). Jesus said, "By their fruits ye shall know them" (Matt. 7:20).

A decision about whether to inform the student of the affective objectives is not pertinent to the development of curriculum design *per se*. The design should include them in order to provide a basis for making curriculum decisions later.

In either case, designers identify the attitudinal objectives. They develop attitudinal indicators using the same process used for identifying cognitive competence. Both identify (a) the kind of learning, and (b) the subject. For example, the attitudinal goal says "an attitude of confidence in prayer" as opposed to a cognitive goal which says "an understanding of what intercessory prayer means." The indicators of attitudinal achievement reflect the same cadence as those stated for cognitive outcomes.

Affective goals function differently. Learners make the response *of their own volition* under the guidance of the Holy Spirit. Designers find it difficult to devise accurate measuring instruments. They design ways to teach and train for the outcomes but observe patiently to determine whether the learner has reached the goal.

Designers identify (a) those areas of scope which call for affective learning as the primary outcome, and (b) the attitudinal dimensions of given cognitive and psychomotor goals. Then they state the *representative* indicators (objectives) which provide a basis for making judgments as to whether the learner possesses the attitudes and values.

As a rule, objectives or outcomes at the institutional level appear at a higher level of generalization than objectives for departments and courses. In the following example note the generalization process in operation.

> *Affective goal:* The learner demonstrates compassion for the unsaved. To demonstrate achievement of this goal, the learner . . .
>
> • A generalized objective *at the institutional level* . . . witnesses consistently as a life-style.
>
> • A specific enabling objective *at the department or course level* . . . witnesses to college students; . . . conducts a church census to discover unsaved in the community.

Few institutions have at the institutional level an organized statement of affective educational objectives. This unfortunate situation effectively blocks the systematic incorporation of the affective learning outcomes at the program, department, and course level. Of course, individual teachers may incorporate them in courses, but the absence of such a statement at the institutional level makes aggressive supervision of the curriculum difficult.

As with other kinds of objectives, designers should analyze one by one the general affective goals to arrive at more specific ones. They ask, "What responses would indicate that the learner has achieved the goals? What action indicators would give evidence that the learner possesses a given attitude? What affective responses should he make because he has a relationship to God, humans, nature, and history? What affective actions should he take because of what he has learned from experience? What affective actions should he take because the Bible commands it?"

It is interesting that items on the forms used by church personnel committees to evaluate prospective staff members consist almost entirely of indicators of affective learning.

The following statements may serve as a pattern to follow in developing the institution's statement of affective educational objectives for learners.

To demonstrate achievement of the institution's *affective* educational goals for learners, the learner makes such responses as:

- witnesses consistently as a life-style.
- develops and follows a plan for lifelong learning.
- develops and follows a physical wellness program.
- gives regularly and proportionately to the support of the church.
- serves in a local church in appropriate ways.
- handles financial obligations honestly and promptly.
- practices cleanliness of person and surroundings.
- develops and follows a plan for personal and family spiritual growth.
- ministers to persons in Jesus' name.
- leads through the democratic process.
- disciples new converts.
- manages well his own household.
- practices hospitality in the home.
- avoids gossip and talebearing.
- seeks the welfare of others above his own.
- manages time efficiently.
- obeys laws and regulations.
- participates appropriately in missions.
- models the role of a good parent.
- moves church membership promptly when relocating.
- keeps confidences in counseling.
- others . . .

These randomly arranged statements of affective educational objectives reflect a relatively high level of generalization. Designers can break most of them down into more specific ones. For example, "ministers to persons in Jesus' name" houses specific objectives like "visits the sick and bereaved." The more specific ones surface in course descriptions.

> *A refined statement of affective objectives could serve as a valuable transcript supplement to reflect a student's status in the realm of affective learning.*

As a helpful activity, pair affective objectives shown above with appropriate affective goals shown on pages 111 and 113.

Analyze each of the objectives shown above and construct the goal which probably precedes it. Would a refined list of affective indicators or objectives as shown have value as a "transcript supplement"? Analyze the list and organize the objectives into groupings of related or similar ones. For example, which would you classify under the caption "Christian ethics"?

Designers should ponder questions like these when considering the role of affective goals and objectives in the curriculum:

• Do the attitudinal goals relate to attitudes toward the course itself or to attitudes toward that larger body of concerns which, taken together, characterize the learner's philosophy of life?

• When and how should the instructor make known to the student the affective goals and objectives? In advance? In a published document? What are the pros and cons of informing the student at all?

• How will the student's transcript reflect the attitudinal dimensions of the course? What part of the grade should reflect affective change in the learner?

• How will the grading system view those delayed response actions which indicate affective change? The lapse of time between the "stimulus"—the course—and a voluntary response may be one, ten, or thirty years! And grades are due next week!

• How do instructors determine whether the affective change occurred as a result of the student's participation in a course or as a result of some extracurricular or noncurriculum related activity, such as attending a chapel service? For example, affective change desired in a course may have occurred not in the course but as a result of listening to a performance of *Messiah*.

• Who determines which attitudes are desirable? How does one determine attitudinal *standards*?

• To what extent and how directly does the institution's charter and institutional purpose call for attention to attitudinal dimensions in learning? What should designers do when neither the charter nor the institutional purpose deal with desired affective results?

• Which levels of learning in the affective domain may a teacher expect of a student in a given course? How can one make adequate judgments regarding indicators of affective change at higher levels such as "characterization" in the Krathwohl taxonomy? For example, at the highest levels, the learners would exemplify not only a specific attitude but would have integrated it with a multitude of others to form a philosophy of life.

- How can an instructor discriminate between genuine affective responses and "faked" responses made to "please" the teacher?
- How effective is it in teaching to issue an "invitation" to respond and then to leave the matter at that point? How may an instructor go *beyond* the *invitation* to affective response?
- Should an institution develop an hierarchy of affective goals in which goals filter down from an institutional purpose to a unit description in a course? Should each affective goal at the lower levels of the hierarchy reside in and be legitimized by statements above it in the hierarchy?
- In the cognitive and psychomotor domains, instructors inform learners periodically about progress or lack of it. Can instructors do the same in regard to affective goals? How?
- If evaluation of affective change comes primarily from direct observation of unsolicited responses, what difficulties does this create for the instructor who must terminate the course within an artificially assigned time limit? The semester system imposes an artificial standard of performance—the learner will achieve the goal in four months!
- Do most instructors have sufficient "tolerance for ambiguity" to deal creatively with affective educational goals and objectives?
- What problems arise when instructors wait for *specific* indicators of affective change? How does the instructor handle those "representative responses" which are valid but which he did not specify previously?
- To what extent can instructors include standards of performance in affective goals and objectives?
- What form should affective goals take in the curriculum plan? In a course? In a unit of study? How does one combine them with cognitive goals? How can instructors deal with both cognitive and affective (and perhaps psychomotor) goals in the same lesson plan? How can teachers determine the affective dimension of cognitive goals? What influence would such a situation have on selection of methods and learning activities.
- How can designers arrive at a comprehensive list of possible attitudinal terms for use in writing goals? (For example, confidence, compassion, loyalty, patience, forgiveness, and generosity.) Many designers discover this to be a major problem.
- When a student makes an affective response, to what extent does it represent *permanent* change?
- If instructors must watch for voluntary affective responses

in a learner, how does he "watch" twenty, thirty, or fifty class members?

Psychomotor Objectives for the Institution (Skills)

Curriculum designers generally express the institution's skills objectives at the level of complex overt response. The learner performs a complex activity with a high degree of skill. A lower level habit would find expression in course descriptions which break complex overt responses down into their parts. At this level a learner masters to the point of habit a part of a complex skills.[16]

The following short compilation of the institution's psychomotor objectives for learners pairs easily with some of the psychomotor educational goals given on page 120. Analyze each of the objectives or indicators and reconstruct the psychomotor goal which probably precedes it. Then match the objectives with the appropriate goals.

To demonstrate achievement of the institution's psychomotor goals for learners, the student . . .
- conducts choral groups,
- sight reads given musical scores,
- plays given instruments,
- sings in recitals,
- composes music compositions (does this belong also in the statement of *cognitive* objectives?),
- directs congregational singing, and
- others . . .

After designers have compiled the statements of educational objectives in all three domains for the institution, they combine them into one document. The document which lists the institution's educational objectives for learners represents the learning outcomes which serve as the focus for this approach to curriculum design.

Next, the designers group the institution's educational goals and objectives for learners into family groups (conceptual families). They group related ones together. The resulting groupings

---

16. From Elizabeth Simpson, *Taxonomy of Objectives: Psychomotor Domain* (unpublished paper, University of Illinois, Urbana, 1968). See LeRoy Ford, *Design for Teaching and Training* (Nashville: Broadman Press, 1976), units 10 and 11.

we generally call "programs." The nature of the groupings gives clues as to what name the program should receive.

> *The compilation of the institution's objectives in the cognitive, affective, and psychomotor domains identifies the "learning outcomes" upon which the curriculum design focuses.*

Revisions of curriculum sometimes come to a screeching halt at this point. History and tradition knock on the door. They say, "Fit those goals and objectives into this preexisting mold." True curriculum revision demands that designers derive programs of work from an objective analysis of the institution's educational goals and objectives. The decisions may or may not satisfy tradition and history.

The following chart should prove helpful in compiling the educational objectives in all three domains. Designers combine the list of objectives with the list of goals. This compilation represents the elaboration of the second element of curriculum design—institutional educational goals and objectives.

> *At the point of designation of programs of work based on the analysis of the institution's educational goals and objectives for learners, curriculum revision often comes to a screeching halt. History and tradition close the door and say, "No admittance!"*

The Institution's Educational Objectives for Learners, All Domains

Cognitive Objectives	Affective Objectives	Psychomotor Objectives

7
Develop Program Purpose, Educational Goals, and Objectives for Learners

Goals: A study of this chapter should help the curriculum designer understand the process of elaborating . . .
1. program purposes.
2. program goals and objectives for learners.

Objectives: The curriculum designer . . .
1. elaborates program purposes which are in harmony with the institutional purpose.
2. elaborates educational goals and objectives in harmony with the program and institutional goals and objectives for learners.
3. identifies "conceptual families" among the institutional goals and objectives for learners.

The Program Purpose *Mission Statement*

At this point the institutional purpose and the educational goals and objectives for learners already exist; therefore, designers have the raw materials from which to state a program purpose. Designers cannot complete the program statement until they have determined the conceptual families of goals and objectives resident in the institutional statements. However, they can begin with a generic statement similar to this one:

The purpose of _____(program name)_____ is to provide theological education for men and women preparing for Christian ministry in _____(conceptual family name)_____ .

An existing program purpose statement at Southwestern Baptist Theological Seminary is:

The purpose of the *School of Religious Education* is to provide theological education for men and women preparing for Christian ministry in *religious education.*

In this example, "religious education" is a legitimate form of "Christian ministry."

The program purpose introduces the first "limitation" imposed upon the institutional purpose. It divides the institutional statement into major subgroupings. It represents the institution's first attempt to establish and implement a departmentation scheme. The combination of all program purpose statements equals the statement of institutional purpose.

As in the institutional purpose, the program purpose tells *who* (the School of Religious Education), *does what* (provides theological education), and *for whom* (men and women preparing for Christian ministry in religious education).

The Program Educational Goals and Objectives for Learners

If designers have done a thorough and objective job of identifying the institution's educational goals and objectives, they should experience less difficulty in stating the *program* purpose, goals, and objectives. The task is primarily one of establishment of categories or conceptual families. At this point designers discover and analyze not only the conceptual families but the common learnings and cross-program educational goals and objectives—those outcomes which *all* students should master. (See chart on page 156.)

Curriculum designers and revisers should attempt to put out of their minds any existing curriculum design structures. They should set aside existing names of programs, departments, and courses. At a later time they may have to use them as they face the necessity of compromising with history and tradition. At this point they should do an objective study.

Designers find it difficult to set aside the language of the trade and refrain from automatically and unconsciously fitting the findings into familiar patterns. If an existing institution already has named its programs "theology," "education," and "church music," designers will tend to group educational goals and objectives according to that preexisting pattern. At this point many curriculum design studies go awry. This is the point at which curriculum studies are most vulnerable to the pressures of tradition.

A Flow Chart of Educational Goals and Objectives

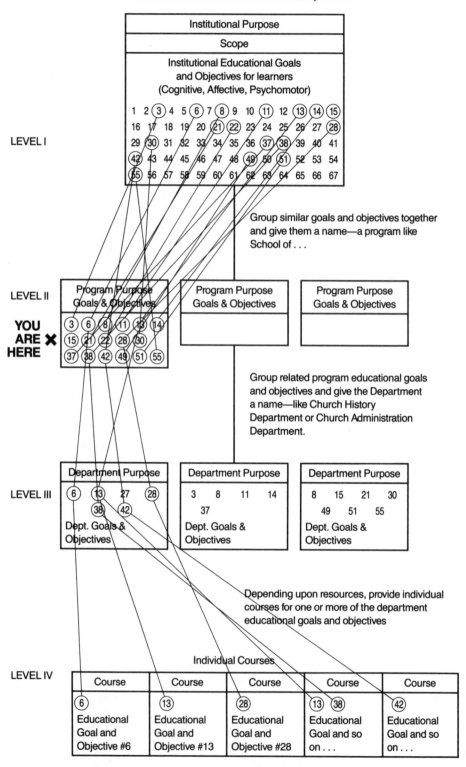

A road sign in Kansas in the early part of this century read, "Don't get in the rut, you may be in it for the next twenty-five miles!" Designers find it difficult to escape the confining influence of established norms.

The educational goals and objectives for programs come directly out of the institution's statements. Designers simply classify them into conceptual families or programs to make it easier to implement the design. Dividing the goals and objectives into programs provides a means for dividing the work load and creating a climate for specialized research and creative exploration within a more limited area of the design's total scope.

State the Program Educational Goals: Cognitive

Where do designers begin in classifying the institution's goals and objectives into conceptual families? They *do not* begin by asking, "Which of these belong to the School of Social Work? Theology? Church Music?"

The following approaches may serve as a starting point:

1. *Select at random one of the institution's educational goals.*— (See pages 99-101.) Then determine which of the remaining goals seem "family" related.[1] For example, the first cognitive goal listed in the examples on page 99 states "understanding the nature of the biblical revelation." Proceeding down the list it seems fairly evident that among others, the following fit into the conceptual family of "nature of biblical revelation":

- the nature of the biblical revelation
- theological method
- the principles of Bible interpretation
- others

What "name" would fit these statements?

If designers select as a point of reference in the institution's educational goals and objectives the statement "understands principles of effective teaching and training," they would discover several other items which relate to the same conceptual family:

- principles of effective teaching and training
- principles of Bible interpretation (Notice that this one also appears in the previous example.)
- principles and methods of age-group education

---

1. Designers may reverse the process and decide which statements *do not seem to fit* into the immediate conceptual family under consideration.

- theory and design of the church curriculum
- others

What "name" would fit these statements?

2. *Practice classification by arranging the cognitive goals according to a set of theologically sound classifiers.*—"All human relationships" (to God, humans, nature, and history) as described in scope determination may serve as classifiers. (See chapter 5.) For example, which items relate to human relationships to God? God's relationship to humans? Human relationships to others and themselves? Human relationships to nature? Nature's relationship to humans? Human relationships to history?

Development of this taxonomy may not constitute the final "conceptual family" decision, but it can serve as a stimulator in the classification process.

The functions of a church constitute another set of possible classifiers. Designers ask, "Which of the institution's goal statements relate to worship? to proclamation? to education? to ministry?"

These exercises may induce some "ah-ha" moments regarding the establishment of meaningful and workable conceptual families or programs.

After classifying the goals and objectives into conceptual families, designers give each a name. The name should immediately convey the nature of the program. The number of separate programs decided upon depends upon available resources. If factors of limitation such as resources prohibit implementation of the ideal number of programs, designers set about reducing the number to accommodate the limitations. They combine into one statement what they may prefer to separate into two. Then they revise the program statement to include both. Research to determine priority goals proves helpful at this point.

3. *Arrange in order of priority the conceptual families of the institution's educational goals for learners.*—Designers validate the priority assumptions through research among practitioners, scholars, and others.

As suggested in chapter 6, designers discover that a great many of the goals appear in several or even all of the groupings. For example, goals related to principles of teaching and training would probably appear very often in different groupings. If a given goal seems to play a significant role in multiple groupings, designers consider this phenomenon as significant and classify that goal as a "common learning." Common learnings outcomes consist of those outcomes considered appropriate and essential for *all* students regardless of the program in which a student concentrates. The compilation of all the common learnings serves as the basis for a "core curriculum," in this case a core of learning outcomes or competencies.

In a learning outcomes curriculum design, designers do not think of a core curriculum as a collection of survey courses designed to ensure that all students get a smattering of everything, but as a collection of essential learning outcomes or competencies which every student should master in order to function effectively in Christian ministry. For example, "functions creatively with fellow staff members and other persons" pertains equally to pastors, ministers of education, ministers of music, social workers, directors of church recreation, and so forth. A core curriculum should include this outcome for *all* students.

> *A core curriculum* is not *a collection of survey courses designed to ensure that all students get a smattering of everything and to give each department equal representation in the curriculum plan.*

The program's educational goals include (a) those particular goals which relate in a special way to the program, and (b) those common learnings goals which all students in all programs should achieve. The common learnings give clues as to which cross discipline courses the program should require. A program of leadership training in religious education may require courses in ministry of music, systematic theology, and missions. The greatest requirement weight in a curriculum plan would come from those goals particularly relevant to the program. Depending upon how designers define the program name, a program would focus heavily upon an *elaboration* of the appropriately related goals. A program of leadership training in religious or Christian education would suggest learning outcomes related to foundations of education, church and denomination administration, education administration, and age-group education and administration.

If designers have given to one conceptual family (program) the name "church music," they ask, "What does *church music* mean?" They ask, "What does religious education mean? What does communication arts mean? What does 'theology' mean when we say 'School of Theology'?"

> *In the learning outcomes focus in curriculum design, a curriculum core consists of a collection of competencies which every student should master in order to function effectively as a Christian minister.*

The institution makes a decision as to which specific goals to include in a program. Other programs respect that assignment and avoid duplication of assignments among programs except for identified common learning outcomes.

If duplication occurs, it signals the need to consider the duplications as essential common learnings. The institution may have to make an arbitrary decision as to which program will implement the goal.

> *When duplication of goals in more than one program occurs, the institution will need to make an arbitrary decision as to which program will focus on that goal. Then the other programs will require their students to cross program lines to do the study.*

The following list of program educational goals includes both specialized learning goals appropriate for the program and the common learning goals appropriate for the program but assigned for implementation to another program.

To accomplish the purpose of the School of Religious Education the School provides a curriculum plan which includes the following goals.[2] Most represent goals related

---

2. These statements are translated into competency statements and appear in *Course Descriptions for the Masters Degree Programs,* School of Religious Educational, Southwestern Baptist Theological Seminary. The syllabus, which is published biannually, included these statements as early as 1974. The syllabus is the first learning-outcomes focused syllabus to be published in theological education, in which all course descriptions follow the learning outcomes (competency) format.

especially to religious education; others represent common learning goals.

The School expects learners to demonstrate the understandings involved in the specialized goals:[3]

1. guidelines for developing creative interpersonal relationships;
2. theory and design of the church curriculum;
3. principles of teaching and learning;
4. principles of administration, management, and leadership in the church and denomination;
5. principles and approaches to leadership training;
6. the nature and functions of a church;
7. principles and approaches to developing special ministries in the church (recreation, family, social work, and so forth);
8. principles and approaches in caring for and counseling persons with special needs;
9. communication theory, methods, and practice;
10. principles and approaches to education evangelism;
11. principles and methods of age-group education;
12. principles and approaches to lifelong learning; and
13. others.

The School expects learners to demonstrate the understandings involved in the following common learning goals in other programs of the seminary:

- history and tenets of the Christian faith,
- philosophical foundations of religion,
- approaches to evangelism in the church and denomination,
- theological method,
- the message of the Bible,
- the biblical basis of missions,
- music theory, and
- the ethical dimensions of life's relationships.

Theoretically, all of these, along with many others, should have appeared previously in the institution's statement of educational goals and objectives for learners. The designers select those which pertain in a special way to persons who will practice Christian ministry in religious education. Designers elaborate these goals into multiple more specific ones at the point where

---

3. The same goals are expressed as objectives or outcomes on page 164.

they need to write course descriptions. Several course descriptions may be derived from a single goal. A single program goal may become the basis for an entire department of instruction.

The wording in the introduction to the list of program goals leaves open the option to include in the program's curriculum plan those institutional goal statements which represent common learnings. Each program makes deliberate decisions as to which cross-discipline is common learning to a degree plan and what should be required.

Not all learners must achieve all the program's goals. Designers may discover that they need to develop majors or concentrations within the program. If so, they develop such plans. Then they may discover that learners involved in concentrations have need for certain *program-related* common learnings. In that case, each concentration or major includes them in curriculum plans for the concentration.

State the Program Educational Objectives: Cognitive

The structure of the learning outcomes approach to curriculum design calls for objectives to use verbs which have visualization value and a degree of observability. Verbs such as manages, counsels, trains, models, communicates, preaches, teaches, witnesses, and disciples provide strong visual imagery.

At the program level, the objectives reflect the same level of generalization chosen by designers to express the statements at the institutional level. Designers lift them from the institution's educational objective statements and transplant them into the program's statements.

> *Program objectives reflect the same level of generalization the designers chose to reflect in the institutional objectives.*

Designers find it easier to identify family-related statements if the institutional statements include specific objectives. As indicated in chapter 6, the decision as to whether to use generalized or specific statements of objectives at the institutional level is an arbitrary one.

If the institutional statements consist only of generalized statements, at some point, either at the program level or the department level, designers have to identify the specific ones. Broad statements are broad enough to house the more specific ones. At the program level, a broad objective could simply say "communicates effectively." The broad statement houses many specific means of communication such as writes news releases, lectures on assigned subjects, writes the aim of a sermon, prepares learning aids, and so forth.

Generalized educational objectives, like generalized goals, are broad enough to house all the competencies or learning outcomes which departments of instruction and individual courses may want to include. A program educational objective may say "counsels individuals and groups." That statement houses such specific counseling responsibilities as "counsels persons who have drug dependence" and "counsels persons preparing for marriage." Departments of instruction may choose to carry over the broad statement "counsels individuals and groups" and reserve the specific statements for the course descriptions. Departments make a deliberate decision as to whether to elaborate the program objectives at the department level or leave that responsibility to those who prepare course descriptions. The specific statements, regardless of whether they appear at the department level or the course description level will describe "content."[4]

The program educational goals and objectives provide the rationale for the existence of departments of instruction and courses within the departments. (See chapter 12 in part 3 for guidelines for stating the rationale for a course.) These specific objectives form the "stuff" from which teachers design course descriptions and lesson plans.

> *Specific objectives provide the "stuff" from which teachers develop course descriptions and lesson plans.*

The objectives in the following example build on the corresponding cognitive *goals* shown earlier in this chapter. In this case, both the goals and objectives represent a relatively high level of generalization.

---

4. Technically the term *content* in curriculum design includes *both* meanings and processes. Some content can only be gained through individual and group learning "processes."

The School expects learners to prove achievement of the School's educational goals by performing effectively the competencies necessary in Christian ministry in religious education.[5] The student:
- functions creatively with other professional staff and church members;
- develops, evaluates, and administers church curriculum plans;
- models the role of an effective teacher;
- organizes and manages church and education programs;
- develops and supervises leadership training programs;
- trains church members to perform the functions of a church (worship, proclaim, witness, nurture, educate, and minister);
- develops and supervises specialized ministries to meet the needs of persons (recreation, social work, and so forth);
- counsels individuals and groups;
- communicates effectively;
- plans and guides educational evangelism and outreach activities;
- organizes and supervises age-group education in the church;
- develops and follows a personal plan for lifelong learning; and
- others.

Compare and "pair" these objectives with the parent goals shown on page 161. For example, one of the goals indicates "the learner understands theory and design of the church curriculum." The corresponding objective states "develops, evaluates, and administers church curriculum plans."

A helpful way to pair the goal and objective statements is to combine them into one statement such as the following: The student demonstrates understanding of the theory and design of the church curriculum by developing a curriculum plan to meet the needs of a given church.

Few institutions have published their program educational objectives for learners. In theological education, the fields of so-

---

5. Adapted from *Course Descriptions for the Masters Degree Programs,* School of Religious Education, Southwestern Baptist Theological Seminary.

cial work, church music, and occasionally religious education
have led the way in developing and publishing such statements.

> *The fields of social work, church music, and occasionally*
> *religious education have led the way in identifying and*
> *publishing program educational goals*
> *and objectives for learners.*

Some institutions have researched the learning outcomes or
competencies needed for effective performance in Christian
ministry and expressed them in order of priority of need.

Analyze the list of cognitive objectives from the viewpoint of
their importance for church musicians, pastors, and social workers. Which objectives would, if achieved, help pastors do their
work effectively? church musicians? social workers? church recreation directors? Which items would you consider common
learnings which pastors and others should master?

The preceding list does not as yet include objectives for the
common learning goals in other programs. The list shows objectives for religious education. The parent program has the responsibility to develop those objectives and the tests which
prove achievement in its own program. A given program does
not have the prerogative to write objectives and develop evaluation instruments for programs outside its own jurisdiction.

> *A given program does not have the prerogative to write*
> *objectives and develop evaluation instruments for*
> *programs outside its own jurisdiction.*

State the Program Educational Goals: Affective

Like program cognitive goals, a program's affective educational goals for learners grow out of the institution's affective
goals. Here are some guidelines for determining affective program goals.

1. *Lift from the institution's statements (a) those goals which*
represent common affective learnings across program lines, and
(b) those goals which seem to have special relevance to the

program.—Designers experience considerable difficulty in identifying affective goals which relate especially to a given program. The pervasiveness and universality of the affective dimensions of learning cause given affective goals to apply across program lines. A given program might conceivably adopt all of the institution's affective goals with little or no change.

> *Designers experience difficulty in identifying affective goals which relate especially to a given program. The pervasiveness and universality of the affective dimensions of learning causes given affective goals to have greater application across program lines.*

2. *Discover the affective dimensions of given cognitive goals.*— As a helpful exercise, designers may analyze each cognitive program goal and attempt to specify the affective dimension of each. In course design they may analyze individually the course as described in school catalogs and ask, "What affective or attitudinal dimension does this course reflect?" In this way, they derive some affective goals which relate to specific programs. A course in Church Family Financial Planning may have a cognitive goal which states "the student demonstrates understanding of approaches to family financial planning." The designer asks, "What affective or attitudinal dimension does the statement suggest?" The affective goal could read: "The student demonstrates commitment to efficient management of personal and family finances," or "The student will demonstrate honesty and promptness in handling financial obligations."

The discovery of the affective dimension of cognitive goals comes easily when considering some courses; for other courses it requires much thought and consultation with subject matter experts to discover that important dimension. A course in elementary Greek may have as a cognitive goal the statement: "The student demonstrates understanding of the designated forms (accidence) and basic grammatical uses (syntax) of Koine Greek." Designers find it more difficult to think of an affective goal which describes affective reasons for the study of elementary Greek. The affective goals may relate to the student's *confi-*

dence that he or she can in fact learn Greek. It may relate to a *conviction* that effective communication of the gospel calls for accurate interpretation of a text. The affective goals may state: "The student demonstrates confidence in his ability to learn Greek." It may state: "The student values accurate translation of New Testament Greek as an aid to accurate interpretation of a text."

Affective goals may simply (a) reflect the affective dimensions of the cognitive goals, or (b) reflect affective outcomes which independently have value in their own right.

> *Experience shows that affective educational goals tend more toward universal application across program lines than do cognitive goals. More of them constitute common learnings than do cognitive goals.*

A course may have an affective goal as the primary goal. If so, it requires special attention in course descriptions and especially in lesson plans. Learning activities appropriate for affective learning differ considerably from those used in encouraging cognitive learning.

The following sample list of program affective goals relates primarily to a program of religious education. However, most items apply across program lines.

Analyze the goals. Which could constitute common affective learnings appropriate across programs? Which seem to relate more specifically to a program of religious education than to a program of church music?

Many of these statements suggest the affective dimension of the cognitive goals shown on page 164.

The School (program) expects learners to demonstrate achievement of such affective educational goals as these:	Possible corresponding *cognitive goals* (page 164).
1. reliance on the Bible as God's infallible guide to living,	
2. confidence and patience in the democratic process,	4

3. commitment to ministry to the total person,	7
4. compassion for the unsaved,	10
5. commitment to the teaching ministry of the total church,	2, 3, 5
6. commitment to lifelong learning,	12
7. a sense of urgency in "equipping the saints,"	5, 3
8. commitment to "decency and order" in conducting personal affairs and the affairs of the church and denomination,	4
9. faithfulness in the exercise of gifts,	12
10. loyalty to the church and denomination,	4
11. cleanliness of person and surroundings,	
12. dependability in performance of tasks,	
13. trustworthiness in counseling and interpersonal relationships,	1, 8
14. diligence in practicing communication skills,	9
15. respect for the priesthood of the believer, and	1, 6
16. others.	

State the Program Educational Objectives: Affective

Designers express affective objectives in terms of typical or representative observable actions. A given action may serve as an indicator of *both* affective and cognitive goal achievement. Designers look at the affective goals and ask, "What are some *typical* or representative responses which would indicate achievement of the affective goals?" Since few, if any institutions have specified such objectives, the example which follows serves only as a suggested approach. They will have been selected and lifted from the list of affective institutional objectives. Each derives from a corresponding affective goal. Each objective is an indicator of achievement of one or more of the program's affective educational goals.

The School of Religious Education's educational objectives (affective) for learners include such indicators of achievement of affective goals as these. The learner voluntarily and consistently . . .	Related to *affective goals* from pages 167-68.
1. reads the Bible devotionally,	1
2. witnesses consistently to the unsaved,	4
3. disciples fellow Christians,	7
4. gives of time and money to meet human needs,	9
5. schedules time for study and personal enrichment,	5
6. honors financial commitments promptly,	
7. teaches, preaches, ministers, and so forth,	5, 9
8. prays for the Spirit's guidance in changing locale of ministry,	
9. keeps confidences in counseling,	13
10. leads democratically,	10
11. plans personal study programs, and	6
12. involves church members in leadership roles.	7

Again, in stating affective objectives, designers think in terms of "representative" responses. A list of all possible responses would fill volumes. Teachers and leaders find it necessary to be alert for approach responses—indicators of goal achievement which have not been specified.

As much as possible, designers specify observable actions for objectives. Some affective goals lend themselves more easily to the specification of indicators or objectives than others. For example, designers can easily specify indicators of the goal "demonstrates compassion for the lost and for others in need." They immediately picture such precise actions as "witnesses to unsaved adults." "Pays bills on time" indicates achievement of the goal "honesty in all of life's relationships." But, designers find it more difficult to specify indicators of the goal "demonstrates pride in the denominational heritage." Subject matter experts in Christian history could doubtless help develop such a list.

As part of the validation process for this manual, I conducted feedback conferences with professors in five universities in Mexico. I posed the question, "How do you approach the implementation of affective goals and objectives in higher education?" I left the question open-ended so as not to prejudice their response. They explained that their approach did not meet needs. In undergraduate education, the universities require nine semesters of study, one semester of which the student spends in *trabajo social*. All students spend 400 hours in some acceptable form of social work, regardless of major. Thus, the doctor, architect, and chemical engineer spend 400 hours doing literacy training, caring for persons in homes for the aging, and so forth.

"Do not use this approach," they said. "The students find many diverse ways to obtain a certified indication that they have completed the work when in fact they have not."

I then asked, "What would you suggest as the best way to deal with the affective learnings a student should acquire?"

"By making the affective learning a part of *every* course," they replied. I personally see a great many values in the requirement of 400 hours of social work, but in their context many of them felt the "pervasive" approach held more promise.

One value derived from listing objectives or indicators of affective change is that action specified in the indicator may also give clues as to teaching methods.

One value derived from listing objectives or indicators of affective change is that action specified in the indicator may also give clues as to the teaching methods. For example an affective goal-objective in a course in discipling others may say, "The student demonstrates acceptance of personal responsibility for discipling new Christians by developing and following a plan for discipling a new Christian in the local church."

The objective suggests also a *method* for training the discipler—practice in discipling another person. Practice represents a learning activity at a high level of learning. The learner practices the indicator, and practice becomes a method of teaching. To a large extent, lesson plans and course descriptions consist of a sequence of appropriate contrived experiences because they consume less time than real life experiences. They can fit into the artificial time limitations imposed by the semester plan. The case study method proves helpful at this point.

> *Attitudes tend to change when learners take positive action in relation to the attitude, when they practice the attitude in situations which call for it.*

The comprehensive list of affective goals and indicators at the program level serves as the storehouse from which programs and departments choose in developing their part of the affective dimensions of the institution's curriculum plan. Some indicators relate more specifically than others to given programs and departments—and courses. For example, *all* persons engaged in Christian ministry should "witness to the unsaved." However, "witnesses to the unsaved" has special application to a department of evangelism or course in evangelism. "Reads the Bible devotionally" would have special application in a course in "Developing the Spiritual Life."

Designers of course descriptions rely upon the statement of institutional and program affective objectives for appropriate indicators of affective change to include in the course description.

State the Program Educational Goals: Psychomotor

The program educational goals (psychomotor) identify areas of skill appropriate for a given program. Psychomotor skills play a significant role in such areas of theological education as church music, church recreation, church camping, and even in ushering and performing the ordinance of baptism. The following examples show first several skills goals stated at a relatively high level of generalization in the field of church music. Then several lists of specific goals and objectives follow.

The educational goals (psychomotor) for learners in the program of leadership training in church music is that they develop such performance skills as:
- sight reading,
- choral conducting,

- instrumental conducting,
- conducting bell choirs,
- vocal performance,
- instrumental performance, and
- others.

Designers will have selected and lifted these statements from the institutional educational goals for learners. At a later stage of the design, departments of instruction find in this list the rationale for their existence. For example, a department of voice would focus on "skill in vocal performance."

State the Program Educational Objectives: Psychomotor

Statements of psychomotor objectives for a program would include all the psychomotor indicators related to the goals in the program. They would reflect the institution's specializations. For example, if the principal psychomotor skills in an institution relate to music, the institution's psychomotor objectives would relate primarily to music. In many cases designers find it easier to specify indicators of psychomotor change than to specify indicators of affective and cognitive change. For example a goal may state: "The student demonstrates skill in choral conducting (goal)." The indicator may consist simply of a rewording of the goal. For example, "The student demonstrates skill in choral conducting (goal) *by conducting choral groups* (objective)." Designers may break down "conducting choral groups" into specific groups such as "conducting children's choirs."

Since few, if any, statements of program educational objectives (psychomotor) exist, the following example suggests a form for the statements.

The School of Music's educational objectives (psychomotor) for learners are that the student demonstrates achievement of psychomotor goals as he:
- conducts children's choirs,
- plays given musical instruments,
- conducts church choirs,
- sight reads musical scores,
- others.

Resident in these rather general objectives are such very specific statements as the following which are more at home in a department description or course description. (These will receive further attention in chapter 8.)

To demonstrate skill in sight reading, the student sight reads a Bach chorale, sight reads an anthem accompaniment, sight reads an open score in four staves, and transposes at sight at the piano a single voice part up or down a whole step.

8
State Department Purposes, Educational Goals, and Objectives

Goal: A study of this chapter should help the designer understand the process of elaborating department purposes, goals, and objectives.

Objectives: The curriculum designer . . .

1. elaborates *department* purposes which are in harmony with program and institutional purpose statements.
2. elaborates *department* educational goals and objectives which are in harmony with institutional and program goals and objectives for learners.
3. identifies "conceptual families" within the program educational goals and objectives for learners.

State the Department Purpose

Department purposes grow out of the program and institutional purpose statements. For administrative purposes, institutions divide programs into divisions and/or departments. In education, designers sometimes use the phrase *department of instruction*. Like other purpose statements the department purpose tells who does what, and for whom, but it provides a sharper focus than antecedent purpose statements. Combining the several department purposes in a program equals the program purpose. Curriculum designs should specify department purposes. A purpose statement for a department of instruction would look like this:

The purpose of the Foundations of Education Department of the School of Religious Education (program) is to provide theological education for men and women preparing for the *ministry of teaching and training* in religious education.

Hierarchy of Purposes, Goals, and Objectives (Outcomes)

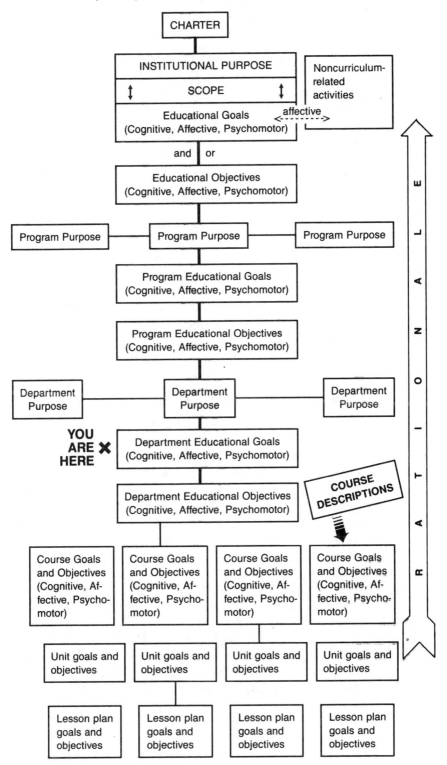

Since all purpose statements carry with them by implication all the elements of the preceding purpose statements, designers could shorten this statement to read: The purpose of the Foundations of Education Department is to prepare learners for the ministry of teaching and training.

A purpose for a Department of Psychology and Counseling might read like this: The purpose of the Department of Psychology and Counseling is to provide training in marriage and family counseling for men and women preparing for the counseling ministry.

When any doubt exists as to the purpose statement's location in the hierarchy of purpose statements, designers should use the amplified statement.

Designers may want to ask a work group to develop a "content" paper to delineate and describe content areas in a department's assignment. For example, they would in this case answer the questions: What subject areas does "foundations of education" include? Which program goals and objectives pertain especially to foundations of education?

State Department Educational Goals: Cognitive

Department educational goals (cognitive) identify the program educational goals for which a department will assume responsibility. The statement of department educational goals provides the rationale for the existence of the department. The department has a right to exist because it implements certain goals which appear in the program statements.

Designers use one of the two basic approaches to developing department educational goals.

1. *They may prefer to select from the program goals those statements which form a secondary conceptual family just as they did when establishing programs out of the institution's educational goals for learners.*—Program statements may include a sufficient number of goals to merit establishment of several departments of instruction. Designers simply lift from the program goals those which form a logical conceptual subfamily within the program. Designers who choose this approach will find it necessary to divide the department goals into more specific ones when they create and describe individual courses.

2. *The preferred approach calls for the designers to state the multiple, more specific goals at the department level.*—The designers consider one by one the *program* goals which they se-

A Flow Chart of Educational Goals and Objectives

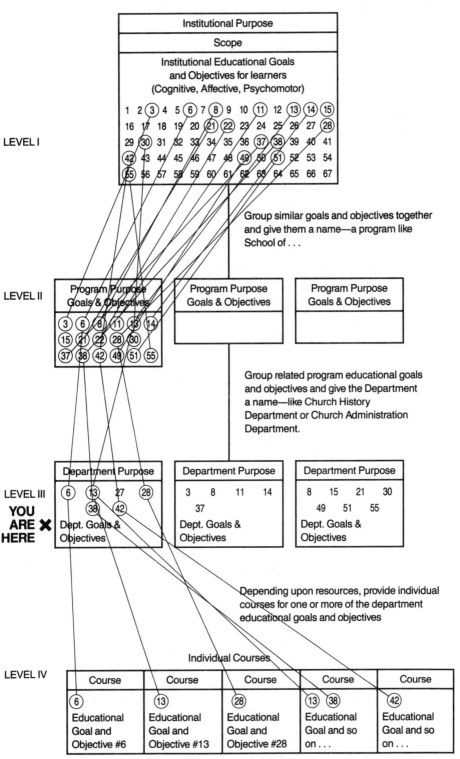

lected as department goals. They analyze the goal and determine its logical components. They ask, "What learnings would the student need to acquire in order to achieve this goal?" Designers have found it helpful to establish work groups at the department level to do this sort of study. When the multiple goal statements exist at the department level, *course* designers may pull appropriate ones from the list and develop them into course descriptions. In this way they avoid duplication of goals in courses in the department.

The list of cognitive educational goals at the program level on page 164 includes the goal "the student understands principles and approaches in caring for and counseling persons who have special needs" (8). Assuming that a department of instruction accepts responsibility for implementing that goal, designers proceed to break down the goal into its component parts and express each as a goal. Thus, the department statement would include such "subgoals" as "the student understands personality theories" and "the student will understand the methods of effective counseling in courtship and marriage." These specific expressions of the more general goal usually serve as the basis for individual courses.

An example of department educational goals for a Department of Church Administration might look like this:

> The educational goal (cognitive) for the Department of Church Administration is that learners achieve the goals of the School of Religious Education with special emphasis on these goals:
>
> The student understands principles of administration, management, and leadership in the church and denomination.
>
> The student understands . . .
>
> (a) the process of developing purpose and objective statements for the church.
> (b) the process of developing plans for providing physical resources for the church.
> (c) guidelines for preparing personal and church budgets.
> (d) process for developing church procedures manuals.
> (e) rules for conducting church business meetings.
> (f) approaches to organizing and staffing church education programs.

(g) guidelines for conducting church staff meetings.
(h) procedures for keeping church records.
(i) others.

These goals are "housed" in program and institutional statements but are specified at the department level. These goals were elaborated because of their special relevance to the work of a department of church administration as expressed in the more general department goal "demonstrates understanding of the principles of administration, management, and leadership in the church and denomination."

The list could go on and on, limited only by resources of personnel, finances, and facilities. The statements serve as the rationale for the development of courses of instruction. A task force or some other group should study the scope of the department's assignment and develop a comprehensive list of department goals and objectives.

State Department Educational Objectives: Cognitive

The department's educational objectives answer the question, "What will the learner *do* to prove achievement of the department goals?" Designers consider each goal separately. Building on the goal "demonstrates understanding of the principles of administration, management, and leadership in the church and denomination," the following *objectives* seem relevant.

Each statement assumes that the leader either *leads* in the doing of the work or when appropriate does it himself.

The Department of Church Administration's educational *objectives* for learners is that they (do such things as) . . .
1. write purpose and objective statements for a given church.
2. develop plans and recommendations for providing adequate physical resources for a given church.
3. prepare an annual church budget.
4. write a church procedures manual.
5. conduct a church business meeting according to *Robert's Rules of Order*.
6. organize and staff church education programs.
7. conduct church staff meetings.
8. develop and implement a church records system.
9. perform dozens of others.

Which of these objectives seem appropriate for a unit within a course? Which would you consider broad enough to merit development of an entire course?

Notice the parallel structure between the department *goal* examples and objective examples shown above. Designers find it helpful to combine the statements so that they appear together. Consider the first goal and the first objective in each of the sample lists shown above: The student demonstrates understanding of the process of developing purpose and objective statements for a church *by* writing purpose and objective statements for a given church.

This statement could serve as a unit goal and objective statement within a given course. The *unit* objectives sharpen and limit the statement even further. The unit objectives include such statements as "discriminates between properly stated and improperly stated purpose and objective statements for a church." The unit objective constitute the stuff out which lesson plans are made.

State Department Educational Goals: Affective

Affective goals and objectives have wide cross-department and cross-program application. Even so, a comprehensive list of affective program goals will generally include statements which relate rather clearly to a given department. Thus, a department of psychology and counseling might include in its affective goals "demonstrates fairness and impartiality in relationships with self and others by doing such things as . . ." The word *demonstrates* and the phrase *by doing such things as* serve as the "holders" for many representatives objectives which may appear later.

The use of the phrase "by doing such things as" *in statements of affective objectives becomes the "holder" for many affective indicators in addition to those specified.*

Continuing with the example of goal and objective statements for a church administration department, the department's affective goals might include such statements as these:

The educational goals for learners (affective) for the Department of Church Administration in the School of Religious Education (program) is that learners achieve such goals as these. The student demonstrates . . .

1. loyalty to the church and denomination.
2. confidence and patience in the democratic process.
3. commitment to careful planning and management.
4. fairness and impartiality in relationships with self and others.
5. others.

Notice that number 4 lends itself to cross-department and cross-program application. It could serve equally well in a Church Administration Department, Psychology and Counseling Department, or Pastoral Ministry Department. This indicates that the goal could appear in a common learnings course or core course in the core curriculum.

State the Department Educational Objectives: Affective

As in the other levels of the curriculum design, planners ask at the department level, "What are some typical or representative indicators which would prove that the learner had achieved the goals?" Designers consider each affective goal and list representative objectives or indicators of goal achievement. They are aware all the while that teachers will need to remain constantly alert to identify other unspecified indicators which may prove just as valid.

A statement of department educational objectives (affective) might appear like this:

The student demonstrates achievement of the affective educational goals of the Church Administration Department as he voluntarily *does such things as* . . .

1. attends and participates regularly in the worship services and meetings of the educational programs of his own church.
2. participates in church and associational business meetings.
3. respects congregational decisions.
4. respects church policies and procedures relating to staff relationships.

ALL NOT IN FAVOR, SAY, "I QUIT!"

A leader who conducts church business meetings according to *Robert's Rules of Order* (objective) demonstrates confidence in the democratic process (affective goal).

5. supports financially the programs of the church and denomination.
6. serves in positions of responsibility in the church and denomination.
7. involves church members in the planning process.
8. and many others.

As with cognitive goals and objectives, affective goals and objectives may appear together. Consider the first *goal* statement in the list on page 181.

The student *demonstrates loyalty to the church and denomination* (affective department goal) as he voluntarily[1] *does such things as* . . .
1. attends and participates regularly in the worship services and meetings of the educational organizations of his own church.
2. participates actively in the church's program organizations.
3. participates in church business meetings.
4. supports financially the programs of the church and denomination.
5. and others.

Note that in these examples the *same* objectives could indicate achievement of both cognitive and affective goals.

Each of these affective objectives (indicators) gives evidence that the learner has achieved or is in the process of achieving the affective goals of the department. Some institutions require students to attend regularly the services of their own church as a stopgap measure to show response to outside criticism. They may do so without ever having stated the goal "loyalty to church and denomination."[1]

State the Department Educational Goals: Psychomotor (Skills)

Some institutional programs call for greater use of psychomotor skills than others. The department selects from the list of

---

1. Controversy exists as to whether *required* affective response actually indicates affective learning. Some institutions require the student to attend regularly the services of his own church for other than educational reasons. They may require it simply because constituents complained about lack of participation in local church programs on the part of students. The requirement thus fulfills a political requirement, not an educational one.

psychomotor objectives for a program those which relate in a special way to the department. A school of church music deals with many different kinds of skills: conducting, singing, playing instruments, and so forth. A voice department in a school of church music (program of leadership training in church music) would select from the program list those which relate to skills in singing as opposed to those which call for skill in orchestral conducting. The *program* goals and objectives would include both. The following example shows the type of department objectives which might appear in a skill-oriented department in a school of church music:

> The educational goals for learners (psychomotor) for the Voice Department of the School of Church Music is that learners demonstrate . . .
> 1. skill in sight reading musical scores,
> 2. skill in pitch reproduction,
> 3. skill in music interpretation, and
> 4. others.

The list of goals would be as long as deemed necessary by the department faculty. Designers should reserve those more specific lead-up skills of which the more complex skills consist for unit descriptions within course descriptions.

State the Department Educational Objectives (Psychomotor)

In the psychomotor domain, designers find it fairly easy to express indicators of goal achievement. In most cases, the verb form of the object of the preposition in the goal expresses what the learner will *do* to prove goal achievement.

Compare the following example with the examples of psychomotor *goals* in the preceding section. In the list of goal statements, notice the objects of the preposition *in:* "sight reading," "pitch reproduction," and "music interpretation." When planners change the noun form into verb form they arrive at observable (in this case, audible) actions or competencies: "sight reads," "reproduces pitches," and "interprets music."

> The educational objectives (psychomotor) in the Voice Department of the School of Church Music are that learners:
> 1. sight read musical scores.
> 2. reproduce musical pitches accurately.

3. interpret given musical scores.
4. others.

When a psychomotor goal and objective appear together they may look like this: The learner demonstrates skill in sight reading (goal) by sight reading given musical scores (objective).

Designers run the risk of enumerating so many lead-up objectives that learners may "drown" in them!

Guidelines for developing course and unit goals and objectives appear in part 3 of this manual. Several sample course descriptions show the course and unit goals and objectives in the context of a complete description. Appendix 1 includes a great many sample course descriptions.

9
Describe the Contexts

Goals: A study of this unit should help the designer understand . . .
1. the meaning of "multiple contexts."
2. the process for describing the multiple contexts which influence and shape a curriculum design.

Objectives: The designer . . .
1. describes the hostile and the supportive aspects in each of the multiple contexts in which a curriculum design operates.
2. enumerates and defines the multiple contexts which influence and shape the curriculum design.

Context descriptions identify and elaborate those aspects of a setting (or culture) which influence and shape the curriculum in a significant way. The contexts (the "somewhere" of the organizing principle) within which the curriculum functions and lives do more than any other thing to determine the form and shape of instructional and administrative models which implement the curriculum design. The contexts influence and often dictate even the physical shape of curriculum materials. The context descriptions describe the particular target group and pinpoint cultural distinctives.

Contexts play a particularly significant role in theological education in missions. Traditionally in church curriculum design (which in a broader sense is included in theological education) designers have said the curriculum operates in the home and in the church. Because it operates in the home, the curriculum plan and its materials take on certain characteristics which fit it uniquely for use in the home. Because it operates also in the church, that context influences its viewpoint, form, and methods. Since the learner functions both in the home and in the church, a church curriculum plan reflects the influences of both contexts.

The curriculum functions within and is influenced by a number of other contextual influences. The descriptions of these contexts parallels closely a description of learners. Curriculum design in theological education *per se* calls for an expansion of the concept of contexts where the learner resides. Cross-cultural situations in missions and situations in the United States call for an expansion of the concept. When we ask, "Which contexts shape the curriculum design?" designers identify at least these:

political context	economic context
geographic context	denominational context
familial context	educational context
religious context	developmental
cultural context	

The settings in which a curriculum operates determine the relative importance of each context. For example, the political context exerts greater influence in China and Cuba than in the United States. The educational context in the United States differs from that in which illiterate tribes in Brazil live.

In most cases multiple contexts converge to influence the curriculum's design, especially its instructional and administrative models.

I once visited a K'ekchi church near Coban, Guatemala. K'ekchi adults in Guatemala cannot read (educational context). Their low incomes make purchases of cassette players difficult (economic context). (Some, however, save over a long period of time to provide funds.) The long distances which K'ekchi must walk to attend church services and the lack of transportation make it necessary for them to do much of their learning at home (geographic and economic contexts).

A K'ekchi leader responded "yes" when an unbeliever asked if he were a Christian; whereupon, the unbeliever struck him with a machete, cutting off the index finger of his right hand (religious and cultural contexts). Many of these contexts converged and resulted in the development and use of an ingenious record player consisting of a folded piece of cardboard and a low cost flexible recording. Persons could manipulate the "machine" by turning the recording with a

Diagram of Elements of Curriculum Design

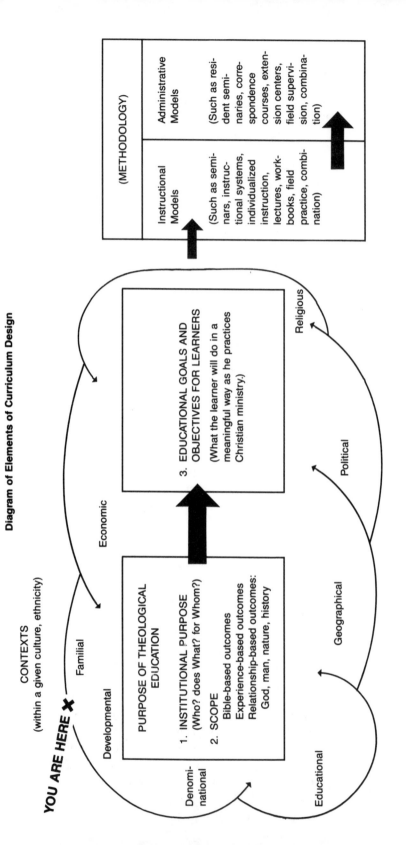

CONTEXTS
(within a given culture, ethnicity)

YOU ARE HERE ✖

Developmental

Denominational

Familial

Economic

Religious

Political

Geographical

Educational

PURPOSE OF THEOLOGICAL EDUCATION

1. INSTITUTIONAL PURPOSE
(Who? does What? for Whom?)

2. SCOPE
Bible-based outcomes
Experience-based outcomes
Relationship-based outcomes:
God, man, nature, history

3. EDUCATIONAL GOALS AND OBJECTIVES FOR LEARNERS
(What the learner will do in a meaningful way as he practices Christian ministry.)

(METHODOLOGY)

Instructional Models
(Such as seminars, instructional systems, individualized instruction, lectures, workbooks, field practice, combination)

Administrative Models
(Such as resident seminaries, correspondence courses, extension centers, field supervision, combination)

Organizing principle: Somebody—learns—Something—in Some Way—for Some Purpose

A Model for Curriculum Design Within a Given Cultural Setting

stick. Each "machine" cost about ten cents. Since the learner's educational background did not include discrimination and problem-solving exercises, the recording consisted of a recorded lecture to which the learner listened over and over and over again (educational and cultural contexts). Those who could afford a cassette player hung it on a cornstalk and listened as they tilled the soil and tended the crop.

Because of the great distances and the dangers of walking by night, the church met once on Sundays from nine o'clock in the morning until three o'clock in the afternoon (geographic context).

At noon the members walked to a nearby house where they ate, sang, and listened again to preaching. Wednesday nights they met in multiple locations to reduce walking time to attend services. Each "substation" had a pastor. On Sundays cell groups convened at the centrally located building. Because adults could not read, they spent part of the service memorizing hymns which they later sang all the way home so as not to forget the words.

A teacher used a flannelgraph to teach Bible stories. The use of slides and filmstrips required electricity, and none was available.

Multiple contexts converged to produce unique administrative and instructional models.

Geographic, economic, familial, and educational contexts also converge to suggest a new administrative model for theological education in the United States. Many ministers have an undergraduate degree and in all respects meet requirements for admission to the traditional resident seminary (educational context). However, they have families and would find it difficult and expensive to leave home and church. (familial, economic, and geographic contexts). Many are established ministers of churches which provide a salary and sometimes a residence for the family (denominational and economic contexts).

Due to the large numbers of students in the resident seminaries, most church staff positions in the surrounding area are already filled (economic and denominational contexts). But within driving distance of many prospective students, a university has an accredited library and excellent physical facilities (geographic, economic, denominational, and educational contexts).

Many professors in the centrally located resident seminary do not have classes on Mondays and are available as teachers for that time (denominational and educational contexts).

These contexts converged upon the other elements of curriculum design and suggested a new administrative model—a main, centrally located seminary *plus* several "extension centers" in locations more accessible to the target group. Thus, Southwestern Baptist Theological Seminary in Fort Worth, Texas, established extension centers in Houston; San Antonio; and Shawnee, Oklahoma. Many state universities have affiliated universities at several locations in a state, all operating on the same administrative model.

Context descriptions identify those forces within the contexts which in a significant way determine and shape the implementation processes of the design. Designers find it helpful to use these questions in describing the contexts:

1. *What within a particular setting or context is nonsupportive or even hostile to the operation of the curriculum?*— Nonsupportive factors hinder the functioning of the curriculum.

2. *What within the context is supportive of the operation of the curriculum?*—Supportive characteristics of the context facilitate the achievement of purposes, goals, and objectives. The following examples of context descriptions illustrate nonsupportive (hostile) factors and supportive factors in shaping curriculum designs. The examples focus on theological education in missions because the contextual lines are more precisely drawn and provide clearer illustrations.

(a) *The political context.*—The political context exerts more influence in some countries than in others. Designers ask, "What within the political context of Country "A" is *hostile* to the operation of the curriculum? What elements in the political context must the curriculum accommodate in order to function?"

Example 1: In Country "A," the context description included this item: The government requires that students in all schools meet to salute the flag at nine o'clock each Monday morning. Theoretically, failure to do so can result in loss of property rights. They property reverts to the government.

This item influences the shape of the curriculum by influencing the administrative model. In Country "A," students in training at a resident seminary need Mondays to travel back to school from their churches. Students travel up to 200 miles over poor roads to get to and from their churches on weekends (geographical context). They cannot afford cars (economic context). They must rely on bus transportation. The political context converges with the geographic context (200 miles away) and the economic context (cannot afford cars) to create a non-supportive influence on the curriculum. The administrative model must somehow accommodate the federal law (political context). The administrative model may have to limit enrollment to those persons who work in nearby churches or do not pastor churches. It may call for instructional models and administrative models which allow the pastors of the "far away" churches to study at home. Further study may reveal that the government in no way enforces the law!

Example 2: In Country "B," the state religion is non-Christian. A state official declared, "We have three primary enemies—first, Christianity; second, communism; third, materialism." In one state in the country the secretary of state had ordered all missionaries to leave. This hostile "political" event shaped the curriculum in at least two ways. It shaped the administrative pattern by eliminating the physical presence of teachers and administrators in the state involved. It shaped the instructional models in that learners needed self-instructional materials to take the place of the physical presence of teachers.

The curriculum designer describes and considers political, religious, and geographical contexts. The contexts even influence methods of teaching. In this case, designers considered which methods could be accommodated in written self-instructional materials or in audio instruction via radio. This model eliminated group processes for the most part, but it opened the door to the use of distance learning correspondence courses as an administrative model and to instructional systems and other forms of self-instructional materials as the instructional models.

Example 3: A radio station on the island of Bon Aire in South America broadcast religious programs throughout Latin America. Consequently, persons in a nearby communist country could hear the programs. The program encouraged *oyentes* (hearers) to request study materials. The hostile political context in that country resulted in censorship or inspection of much of the mail received by citizens. A package larger than a personal letter was especially suspect. The hostile elements of the situation prevented field workers from entering the country to work personally with the listeners. Mail censorship prevented the sending of study books.

The design group developed an eight lesson, loose-leaf format for a course entitled *Sabeis Tu?* (Did You Know?). When folded in the center, the self-instructional materials fit into a personal correspondence envelope. Instead of sending all lessons at once, the designers sent one lesson at a time in a personal correspondence envelope and omitted a return address on the outside of the envelope. The receiver already knew the return address. The political context dictated the instructional model (a self-instructional system) and the administrative model (a modified form of the correspondence course).

The curriculum planner also asks, "What within the *political context* may *support* the operation of the curriculum? What data actually encourages the operation of the curriculum or in practice tolerates the curriculum by failing to enforce statutes?"

Example 1: Country "T" through its state department held a garden party to which it invited national and nonnational church leaders. In a speech the secretary of state assured all present that a proposed national law regarding restrictions on certain religious practices would in no way limit them in their work. The law by design related to another religion. This supportive aspect of a political context opened the door to practically all administrative and instructional models.

Example 2: Country "D" does not censor the mail. Learning materials in many forms reach the learners promptly and without inspection. This supportive factor in the political context opened the door to practically all administrative and instructional models.

(b) *The economic context.*—Designers ask, "What within the economic context is *hostile* to the operation of a curriculum?"

Example 1: In Country "G" the people earn only fifty cents per day during the coffee-picking season. They find it difficult to purchase tape players. (Only 4 percent of adults read; those who do read can read only at the fourth grade level.) They cannot afford automobiles. No electricity is available. (Note how the educational context converges with the economic context to provide greater "hostility" to the operation of the curriculum.) In Country "G" the economic context shaped the format of the educational and administrative models. The economic and educational contexts called for self-instructional materials using audio channels only.

Example 2: In Country "I" pastors work full-time to support themselves and their families. Moving to a faraway city to attend a resident seminary results in disruption of the family's economic base. It leaves the "house churches" without leadership. This aspect of the economic context called for self-instructional teaching models and a "circuit-rider" administrative model. Teachers visit learners periodically on a one-to-one basis in the learner's home.

What within the *economic context supports* the operation of the curriculum?

Example 1: In Country "T" the workers earn approximately twenty-five dollars per day. In spite of a high cost of living, the people have funds for purchase of learning materials. In the cities they travel economically by taxi and bus. Many own their own cars. Several members of most families have incomes, but they share the same flat, which they own. The country has just lost its "most-favored nation" status with the United States because of its economic progress. The supportive aspects of the economic context give curriculum planners wide latitude in developing instructional and administrative models.

Example 2: In Country "M" in the state of "C" many workers find employment in the newly developed oil industry. Though they still live in small villages in substandard houses, their incomes have increased to the point that they could pay bus fare and purchase some study materials for leadership training. Most have completed elementary school. Some of the more fortunate completed one or more years in high school. Most speak Spanish in addition to the local dialect. These factors permit group seminars as well as self-instructional approaches. Such circumstances could conceivably accommodate a resident seminary model, providing evening classes only. Of course, the hostility of the geographic context could present problems.

(c) *The educational context.*—Designers ask, "What within the *educational context* would be nonsupportive or *hostile* to the operation of a curriculum?"

Example 1: In Country "G" Wycliffe translators first reduced the language to writing twenty-five years ago. As a result, only the children and youth read well. Most families have battery operated radios, but many do not speak the language used on the radio. They speak only the local dialect. Curriculum planners ask, "Shall we include reading and writing in the scope of the curriculum of theological education? Which instructional models can accommodate nonreaders?" In this case, educational and cultural contexts influence significantly the scope.

Example 2: In Country "L" 60 percent of adults read at sixth grade level. Tradition has created an educational system which does not emphasize problem solving. The system uses rote memorization and book copying as principal methods. Learners in this context may find it difficult to think abstractly in a systematic way. Curriculum planners must answer these questions: Shall we deliberately introduce instructional models which require responses at higher levels of learning? What shall we do to reach the 40 percent who do not read?

What within the *educational context* would *support* the operation of the curriculum?

Example 1: In Country "T" 99 percent of the population reads well. School is compulsory through the eighth grade (or its equivalent). Many adults take part in excellent on-the-job training opportunities where they work. Grade schools pride themselves on modern teaching methods. Many people attend night school, especially in the cities. Such supportive aspects of the educational context make possible the use of many instructional and administrative models.

(d) *The geographic context.*—What within the geographic context is *hostile* to the operation of the curriculum? What geographic influences tend to shape the instructional and administrative models?

Example 1: Country "M" consists of seven states. Some are on the mainland, some on a peninsula, and one is part of an island located six hundred miles from the mainland.

Designers ask, "Which models or combinations of administrative and instructional models would such a context accommodate?"

Example 2: In Country "B" the only north-south highway extends over a distance of two thousand miles. The country includes tropics and some arid land which experiences the four seasons. One main highway connects north with south; one connects east with west. The unpaved roads have opened up settlements in new areas at an incredible rate. People reach the remainder of the vast land by waterways and overland trails. Distance becomes a hostile element in the geographic context which curriculum planners must consider. In this case problems related to the geographic context converge with other contexts (such as economic) to limit the variety of possible instructional and administrative models.

Example 3: In Country "G" communication travels by word of mouth as persons travel over narrow trails which lead principally around fields at the base of low mountains. Many of the people have never been to the "town" several miles away. Climate is principally cool tropics, and the elevation is about five thousand feet. During the three-month rainy season, even foot travel over the trails becomes difficult. Some church attenders walk ten or more miles to church on Sunday. Distance calls for some form of self-instruction and an administrative model which reduces walking distances between home and church. The church conducts satellite meetings at four locations at midweek. Then all gather at a central location on Sundays.

(e) *The cultural context.*—As in the other contexts, the cultural context presents both hostile and supportive influences in development of the curriculum. Often, however, what appears to be negative may simply call for the designer to understand how a particular culture handles given situations.

As an example, the Indonesian TEE Association (theological education by extension) had to change its name because of government regulations. The government would not permit the use of the word for "association"—*perhimpunan.* Only certain groups can be a *perhimpunan* and TEE is not one of them. Leaders announced a *musyawarah umum.* (*Umum* means "public.")

Indonesians do not necessarily apply the scientific method in problem solving. Cultural influences affect even methodology. The Indonesians use an approach to problem solving called *musyawarah,* a unique approach in which anyone brings up anything he wants about the subject under consideration. They do not want to get to the point immediately. After all have had their say, someone whom the group recognizes as a leader restates the consensus called *mufakat.* Usually the consensus doesn't represent what either party might have proposed but a middle ground on which all can agree. Often they do not arrive at the final solution but the best one they can achieve at the time. Later on they may come back and repeat the process. They do not vote. Missionaries who understand the cultural context do not try to force the Western concept of problem solving on Indonesians.[1]

Other contexts, such as the religious, familial, cultural, and denominational contexts also have hostile and supportive elements. The curriculum planner considers all of them in planning for theological education.

Seldom do curriculum planners make instructional and ad-

---

1. This information is based on discussions with Norma Hasse, Conservative Baptist missionary in Indonesia, and Avery Willis, former Southern Baptist missionary to Indonesia.

ministrative decisions based on their analysis of only one context. Answers to design problems tend to come at the point of convergence of contexts.

In the following cases, elements in the contexts worked together to influence the shape and form of the curriculum. In the chart which follows the first case notice how multiple contexts converge to determine administrative and instructional models.

(a) Raul Trevino sits in his thatch-roofed house near Coban, Guatemala. He unfolds an ingenious double-folded cardboard device. He places a seven-inch plastic record in its proper position on one of the nine-inch folds. Then he folds the device so that a needle embedded in one fold rests on the record. He places a sharpened stick in a hole near the center of the record and turns it in a clockwise direction. He hears in the K'ekchi language an exposition of what the Bible says about the work of a pastor.

Raul cannot read. He makes fifty cents a day four months out of the year picking coffee on the *finca* where he has worked and farmed for many years. He has no electricity in his house. On Sunday, after walking eight miles to his church, he attends services from 9:00 a.m. until 3:00 p.m. Then he walks back to his candle-lit home. He carries with him the simple cardboard device which will help teach him the work of a pastor. The contexts within which Raul lives converged to determine the format of his training materials and the format of the administrative model.

(b) Jaime Ramirez sits at a table beneath a brush arbor at an orphanage in San Mateo on the south coast of Mexico. He "one-fingers" a dilapidated typewriter as he works on a lesson on the Gospel of Matthew. He reads and speaks both Spanish and Huave, his native tongue. He cannot leave the orphanage to attend the seminary in Oaxaca, 150 miles away. He slowly types out his responses to the exercises in a self-study book. Later he walks to a post office and mails the new lesson to Oaxaca. By coincidence when he calls for his mail, he receives a letter containing comments on a previous lesson. The contexts within which Jaime lives determined both the instructional and administrative models which made it possible for him to study.

(c) Hang Choo walks into a classroom in a modern building in Singapore. He carries a sophisticated self-study guide on church administration. His university background helps him appreciate the broad range of leadership and administration techniques it presents. After studying two units at home, he anticipates the opportunity he now has to discuss some of the

CULTURE	CONTEXTS	MODELS
	Geographic: Communication by word of mouth over foot trails. Must walk many miles to attend church.	**Administrative Models:** Multiple weekday meeting places within three miles of homes. Meet on Sunday in central location for training and worship. Substations meet on Wednesdays or midweek closer to homes. All come together on Sunday mornings, then go on to a home for afternoon service before returning home. Preachers in substations share Sunday program.
	Economic: Earn fifty cents per day, four months each year. Grow own food. Have no electricity.	
	Educational: Only 4 percent of adults read—at fourth grade level. Most children and youth read. Adults speak only native language; children and youth speak national language plus dialect.	Tapes loaned to pastors for home study or study in cornfields as they work. Occasional "circuit rider" visits to learner in their homes. Week-long retreats during offseasons.
The K'ekchi (Guatemala)	**Religious:** Majority have animistic background. Some practice syncretism—mixture of animism and Christian religion. Frequent persecution when one becomes a Christian. Doctrines of earlier denominational groups tend to permeate other denominational groups. Grandparents usually practice animism. Some holidays Christianized because of pagan festivals.	**Instructional Models:** Small inexpensive recordings played on cardboard players. Formal instruction for all in central location on Sundays. Some tape players with self-instructional techniques for learning music, doctrine, and leadership techniques. Oral instruction and flannelgraph.
	Familial: Large families of four to eight live in two room grass huts with dirt floors. Frequently parents of one or both spouses live with the family. Children have no "childhood" as we usually think of it. Girls take care of younger children while boys work with fathers in fields. Family is strongly patriarchal.	

materials with a teacher and colleagues at a weekly seminar. The sophisticated self-study guide provides in an educationally sound way the concepts which Choo needs as a pastor.

The contexts within which Hang Choo lives help determine the context and format of the self-study guide. The geographical context made it possible for him to attend regularly the weekly sharing sessions.

(d) Sumardi waved welcome as he saw his bicycle-riding missionary friend approaching his village. He had just finished lesson six in a self-study course on doctrine. His sixth-grade reading level made it possible for him to read the basic study guide he had received at the beginning of the course. As pastor of a "house church" and father of five youngsters, he could not afford to uproot his family to go to a resident seminary. Besides, if he did, his fellow villagers would find it difficult to accept him after he had completed his training. They would expect him to "go ahead" to bigger things. He welcomed this chance to talk to his missionary friend on a one-to-one basis about another question: Should a pastor always work full time as pastor, or could a pastor work at another occupation part time? He had heard discussion of both sides of the question.

The contexts within which Sumardi lived determined both the learning approaches and the administrative plan under which he learned. The cultural context even prompted the question he would discuss with the "circuit-rider" missionary.

(e) Franco Bernal eagerly opened the "no return address" letter he received that morning. Inside he found two letter-size worksheets on the subject "What Sin Means." Three weeks before he had returned by mail two other worksheets on "God Loves You," and he asked for the next lesson. He felt a sense of pride when he saw "well done" written in the comments about the previous lesson. Franco had heard of the course by way of radio, which penetrated political barriers. He appreciated the fact that the lessons came one at a time resembling a short personal letter. Censors would have intercepted a booklet in a larger package.

The contexts within which Franco lived determined both the approach to learning (instructional model) and the administrative model (a correspondence course) which made it possible for him to learn.

In theological education in missions all of these widely diverse approaches to training fall under the umbrella commonly called "theological education by extension" or some other similar term.[2]

The instructional devices varied from a hand-operated cardboard "turntable" and recording to a sophisticated self-instructional text. The administrative approaches (delivery systems) included correspondence courses, an extension center, and a "circuit-riding" teacher. The contexts within which the learners lived determined the particular shape and form of the learning approaches.

2. Some countries prefer not to use the phrase *theological education by extension*. Baptists in Thailand for example use TNT (Thai National Training).

10
Design Instructional and Administrative Models

Goals: A study of this unit should help curriculum designers understand . . .
1. the meaning of instructional model and administrative model.
2. the approaches to implementing the models.

Objectives: The curriculum designer . . .
1. selects delivery systems (instructional and administrative models) for theological education appropriate for a given contextual setting.
2. discriminates between instructional model and administrative model.
3. explains the rationale that "form follows function" as it relates to selection of instructional and administrative models.

Design the Instructional Model

Development of instructional models precedes the development of administrative models. Administration serves instruction, not vice versa. Form follows function. The instructional and administrative models make up the "in some way" aspect of the design.

An instructional model is an approach to instruction which implements given theories or combinations of theories of learning within the contexts which influence the design. Instructional models relate to *how* instruction and learning occur as opposed to how designers manage or administer the curriculum design.

The program purpose, educational goals and objectives for learners, scope, and multiple contexts of the curriculum determine and shape the instructional models. By allowing the unique purpose, objective, scope, and multiple contexts to reflect the cultural environment, the curriculum design becomes uniquely the possession of a given culture.

Instructional models which have resulted from such studies include the following:

1. *Instructional systems.*—An instructional system is a collection of validated learning materials designed to lead a specific target group to achieve predetermined objectives through interactive instruction. Systems include such approaches as autoinstructional devices and their variations. Study is underway to determine the feasibility of the use of computer enhanced instruction in theological education, especially in the area of languages.

Instructional systems serve well in contexts in which learners can read but cannot leave home to attend a resident school because of various hindrances. Family and church responsibilities and geographic and economic problems may call for the learner to remain "at home" or near home for training. It serves well in situations in which teachers find it difficult to go where the learner lives. Many correspondence courses use instructional systems as the instructional model.

2. *Seminars.*—Seminars consist of group meetings in which learners in a more or less structured way share insights they have gained through study and research on assigned subjects.

This model serves well in situations where learners live in a small geographic area and find it easy to get together in groups. As a rule a teacher-leader guides the group on a regular basis.

3. *Combination of instructional systems and seminars.*— Theological education uses this approach in contexts in which learners can assemble in groups only periodically. They study instructional systems at home then assemble for followup and discussion of their "at home" study. In some situations, learners do home study most of the year then get together once a year for one or more weeks for classroom instruction and fellowship. The seminars provide an added dimension to learning by providing affective association with a leader model and peers.

4. *Field experience.*—Field experience is an approach to learning in which learners, under guidance, engage in on-the-job training at the place where they serve. The needs and problems of the particular church determine what his training includes. Field experience serves well in contexts in which learners cannot leave their home and church environment without disruption of programs. It allows the learner to stay on the field and

learn at the same time. Under occasional guidance by a visiting teacher or trainer, the learner identifies the problems he faces as he leads a church. Then the curriculum planners design a curriculum plan tailored to the learner's particular needs. It involves work with guidance in a real-life situation.

5. *The case study.*—Some situations lend themselves to the use of the case study as used by the Harvard School of Business. Students "practice" in realistic but contrived settings. The approach calls for high level analysis and problem solving. Student synthesize original solutions to complex problems. The case study does not put students in the game exactly, but they get all the benefits of scrimmage.

6. *The teaching lecture.*—The most prevalent instructional model is the teaching lecture. As opposed to the "set" lecture, the teaching lecture tolerates, even encourages, student interaction. Used especially with large groups, the teaching lecture allows the teacher to present a great deal of information in a short time. Teachers can improve the lecture by combining it with other simple methods such as making listening assignments to groups within the group. Some folks do not like the lecture method. A lecturer talks in somebody else's sleep, they say. Some call it the cognitive dump! Jesus, Isaiah, and Jeremiah used it effectively! But they knew *how* to use it.

The list of methods shown on pages 261 and 264 in chapter 16, "Describe Methods and Learning Activities" introduces many additional instructional models.

Design Administrative Models

The last step in developing a curriculum design calls for development of administrative models to implement the instructional models. They serve as delivery systems. An administrative model brings the design and the target group together in such a way as to achieve the purpose and objectives of the design and to implement an instructional model.

1. *The resident school or seminary.*—A resident school is an administrative model which provides a teaching faculty and facilities at a permanent central location. Students reside at the location or commute.

The analysis of elements of design, especially the multiple contexts, may indicate that a resident seminary can best serve as a vehicle for making the curriculum of theological education happen. In missions the resident seminary serves well in contexts where travel distances are not too great and students can

Teachers and leaders use the case study to lend reality to experience.
The case study doesn't put the learner in the game exactly . . .

... BUT HE GETS ALL THE BENEFITS OF SCRIMMAGE!

In the case study, the learner does more than read.

He does more than look at a picture. (Good as that may be!)

He sort of "climbs into the picture" himself . . .
and takes a spin!

Some folks are down on the lecture!

"A lecturer is one who talks in somebody else's sleep!" they say.
Some even call it the "cognitive dump!"

But JESUS and JEREMIAH used it!
They knew <u>how</u> to use it!

finance the experience away from home. It serves well when the learner's leaving does not disrupt family and church life. In missions the resident seminary usually reaches a comparatively small number of better educated students.

In the United States the resident seminary attracts large numbers of students because the contexts include few nonsupportive elements.

2. *The extension center.*—The extension center approach is an administrative model which provides multiple locations for instruction on a more or less regular basis under guidance of a teacher or teachers. The centers may or may not operate under the umbrella of a resident institution. Accessibility to learners influences the location of centers.

The contexts of theological education may require taking the experience *to the student* where he lives and serves. Extension centers work well in situations where the learner cannot afford to leave home. If he must work to support his family or his church would go without leadership in his absence, the extension center seems appropriate. In such a model, teachers may conduct courses in theological education at multiple "centers" or locations. One teacher may reside at the location and teach all courses on a regular schedule. Teachers in a resident institution sometimes commute periodically to dispersed centers to provide instruction.

3. *The correspondence school.*—Vast distances (geographic context), government regulations (political context), and school background (educational context) may call for correspondence courses handled entirely by mail. An administrative model for correspondence work or "distance learning" calls for processing of enrollment procedures, keeping of records, handling and grading of papers, and dealing with the mail services.

The *instructional* model used in correspondence approaches usually includes some form of self-paced, interactive instruction.[1]

4. *The television model (the "electronic classroom").*—Growing in popularity and convenience is the television administrative model. Television is the "great collector" of instructional media and methods. It provides great flexibility in methodology, including teacher-pupil dialogue. Television makes possible the sharing of faculty resources among institutions.

---

1. See appendix 2 for examples of ways to provide for interactive instruction in correspondence school materials.

5. *Field supervision.*—Field supervision is the administrative side of the instructional model we call field experience. A curriculum plan whose focus calls for learning on the job calls for certain administrative processes which other approaches do not require. It may make it necessary for one teacher-leader to work intensively with only a few learners. In many cases supervision occurs on a one-to-one basis.

6. *Combinations of models.*—The contexts of the curriculum may call for such combinations as resident seminary and multiple extension centers. Widely differing target groups within the contexts may call for a combination approach. Some contexts call for a correspondence course model supplemented by a resident model in which learners assemble periodically for short periods of time for intensive follow up. Few context combinations will call for the same administrative model.

A curriculum design elaborates in relationship the institutional purpose, objectives, scope, contexts, and methodology of theological education. An effective curriculum involves . . .

Somebody in learning . . .
Something . . .
Somewhere in . . .
Some way for . . .
Some purpose . . .

Part 3
Writing the Course Descriptions[1]

---

1. Teachers who want primarily to find guidance in writing course descriptions in the learning outcomes format, may use part 3 independently from parts 1 and 2. For that reason part 3 repeats some concepts and guidelines mentioned in parts 1 and 2.

11
Review the Hierarchy of Goals and Objectives

Goals: A study of this chapter should help curriculum designers understand the relationships among the levels of educational goals and objectives for learners in curriculum design.

Objective: The designer summarizes the relationships among the institutional, program, department, individual course, and lesson plan goals and objectives for learners.

Like the proverbial hierarchy of fleas, purpose and learning intent statements for an institution's curriculum design and plan form a hierarchy.

> Big fleas have little fleas
> Upon their backs to bite 'em.
> Little fleas have lesser fleas,
> And so on *ad infinitum.*

Developers of curriculum designs see a similar picture, except the "fleas" become statements of purpose and educational goals and objectives for learners.

> Big goals have little goals
> All clustered up inside 'em.
> Little goals have lesser goals,
> And so on *ad infinitum.*

Our course descriptions ought to serve as a ready resource for personnel committees as they write job descriptions.

Purposes, goals, and objectives are like
the proverbial flea!

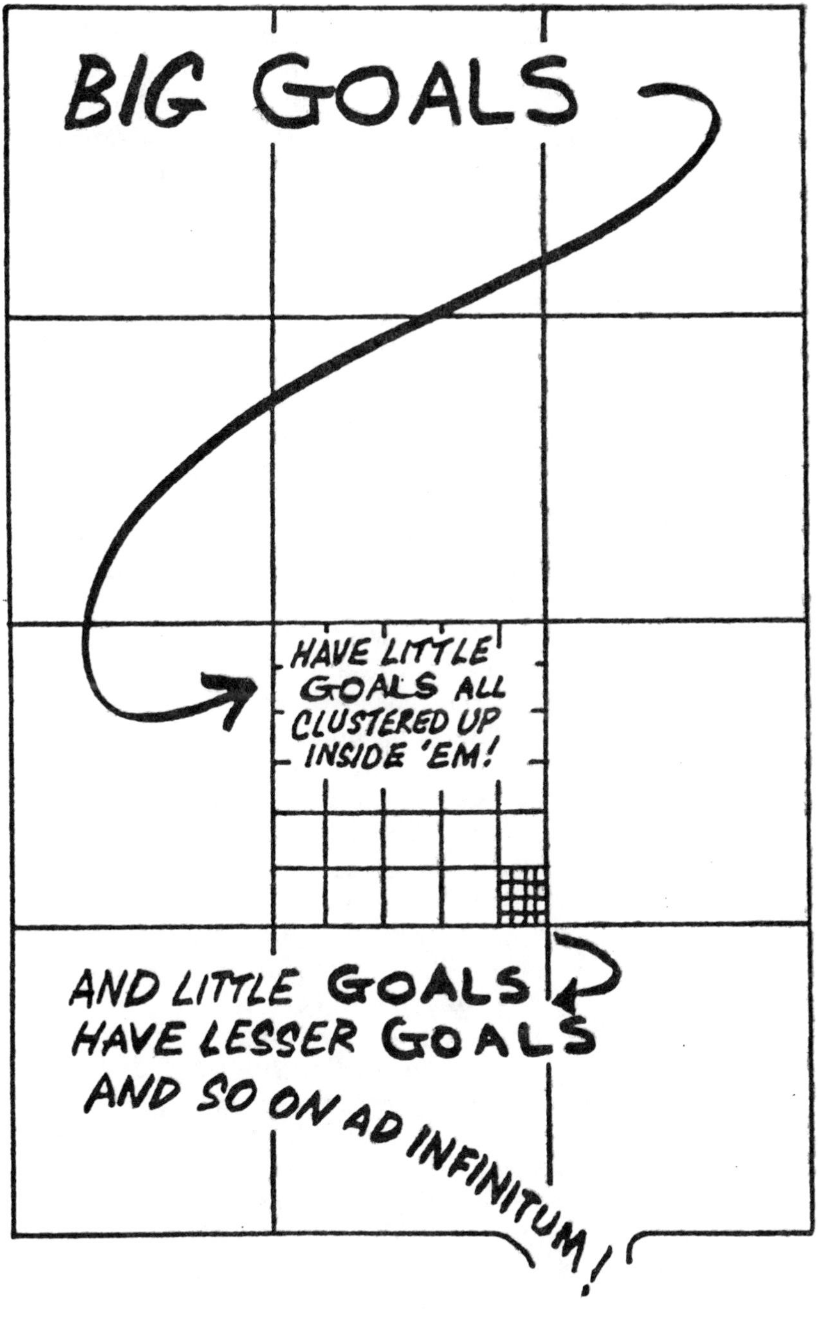
BIG GOALS
HAVE LITTLE GOALS ALL CLUSTERED UP INSIDE 'EM!
AND LITTLE GOALS HAVE LESSER GOALS AND SO ON AD INFINITUM!

The chart on page 217 shows how educational goals and objectives for course descriptions fit into the contextual framework of statements of learning intent. Educational goals and objectives at the institutional level filter down through programs, departments, and then into individual courses for implementation. Even the lesson plans which give life to the course descriptions fit into the hierarchy.

These statements of intent take several forms. Designers call them by different names depending upon their function and their position in the hierarchy. The names include institutional charter; institutional purpose; and program, division, and department purposes. Each level has its appropriate statements of educational goals and objectives for learners related to the several domains of learning. At the implementation level, the course descriptions reflect given goals and objectives. The charter and institutional purpose express learning intent at the highest levels of generalization; the course descriptions and lesson plans express the intent at the lowest level of generalization.

Level I on the chart represents the institutional level. It includes the institutional purpose and the institutional educational goals and objectives for learners.

Level II represents the program level. It includes the program purposes and the program goals and objectives for learners. Larger institutions may desire to divide the programs into divisions before reaching the department level.

Level III represents department purposes and educational goals and objectives for learners.

Level IV focuses on individual course goals and objectives. This level may even include individual lesson plans, each of which has its own set of goals and objectives.

Part 3 of this manual should help answer questions such as: What is the contextual framework within which designers write course descriptions? What should course descriptions include? How can course designers deal with some of the problems related to the affective dimensions of course planning? What forms may course descriptions take in a learning outcomes curriculum plan? What pitfalls do writers face in developing course goals and objectives? How do designers avoid them?

A Flow Chart of Educational Goals and Objectives

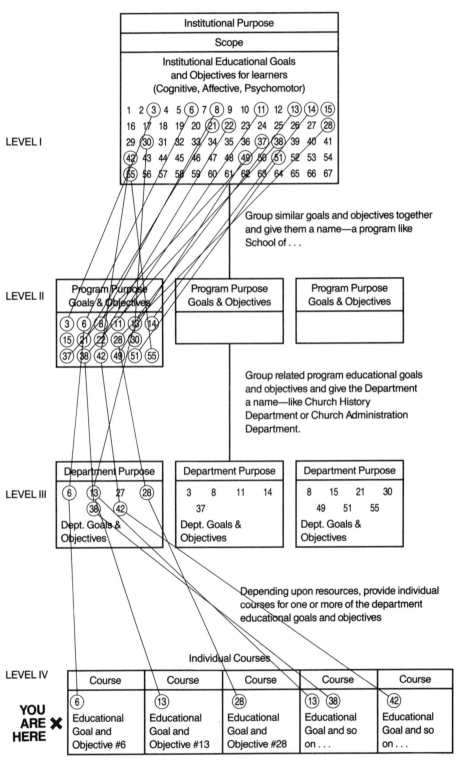

12
State the Course Title and Rationale
for the Course

Goals: A study of this chapter should help curriculum designers understand . . .
1. the forms of course titles.
2. the process for describing the rationale for a course.

Objectives: The designer . . .
1. writes course titles in the subject and process forms.
2. writes a rationale for including a given course in a curriculum plan.
3. discriminates between subject and process forms.
4. explains the reasons for including a rationale statement in a course description.

A helpful course description generally contains these elements or some variation of them:

Course title
Statement of rationale for the course
Course goal(s)
Statement of the indicators of goal achievement (objectives) for the course
Series of unit titles
Unit goal for each unit
List of lead-up objectives for each unit
Description of methods and activities used in the course
Mediography
Description of testing and evaluation approaches
Set of lesson plans if designer wants to expand the course description into a course syllabus

The Course Title

A course title should communicate readily the scope of the course. Titles generally fall into two categories.

1. *The process title.*—A process title focuses on an action. For example: Teaching Children in the Church School; Developing a Church Curriculum Plan; Preaching the Exegetical Sermon; or Exploring Schools of Philosophical Thought.

2. *The subject title.*—The subject title identifies a field of study. For example: Principles of Teaching, Introduction to Systematic Theology, The Church's Curriculum, Pastoral Ministry, or The Ministry of Music.

Generally, the process title gives students a better picture of what the course will help them do. Often the statement of course goal and objectives provides clues as to how to state the title as a process.

Certain courses like "A History of the Reformation" seem to defy the use of process titles. As a helpful exercise in such cases, designers ask, "What does one do *to* or *with* a history of the Reformation? Interpret it? Analyze it?" If designers can identify the verb, they can restate a subject title as a process title.

Catalog descriptions fall into these same categories. The subject description elaborates the subject and sets subject boundaries. The process description states the course goal and objective in performance terms. The latter communicates more readily to the student, who uses the catalog as part of his "contract" when deciding to attend or not to attend a given school.

Which of the following communicates more readily the meaningful activity required of the student?

Course Title: Developing a Church Curriculum Plan

_____1. A study of the elements of church curriculum design. Includes the steps in developing a church curriculum plan.

_____2. The student demonstrates understanding of the process of developing a church curriculum plan by developing a curriculum plan to meet the needs of a given church.

> *In a curriculum design with a learning outcomes focus,*
> *the catalog description should consist of a restatement of*
> *the course goals and objectives. The process format*
> *describes performance at the level of meaningful activity.*

Both forms find their way into institutional catalogs and bulletins. However, why develop a course goal and set of course objectives and not use them at the point where students first confront them? The catalog statement should consist of a restatement of the course goals and objectives.

Rationale for the Course

A rationale statement legitimizes the course within the institution, program, and department of instruction. It explains how the course fits into the scheme of things. For example one school (program) within an institution identified through research a series of high-level outcomes (competencies) needed by all its graduates. These competencies (school objective) included such statements as these:

- Models the role of an effective teacher.
- Communicates effectively.
- Functions creatively with staff members.
- Develops curriculum plans.
- . . . and so forth.

The school's curriculum included a course entitled "Teaching with Instructional Media." The designer chose from the school's list of high-level competencies those which the particular course supported. The course title and rationale looked like this:

Title: Teaching with Instructional Media
Rationale: This course supports the following objectives
(competencies) of the School of Religious Education:
- models the role of an effective teacher.
- communicates effectively.

In doing these two things, the course supported the purpose and objectives of the instructional department, the institutional program related to teaching, and even the institutional purpose. Finally, it was resident even in the institutional charter. The rationale statement forms the connecting link between institutional charter and purpose and the activities and units of study within the course.

The rationale for the course may consist of goal statements or objective statements—or both. When appropriate, the rationale should include statements of affective goals and objectives. For example, the rationale for a course in "Building a Church Curriculum Plan" could include an affective statement such as: "The student demonstrates conviction that the church is accountable for what it teaches."

The rationale statement may take other forms. For example, it could use as a stem the statement of institutional or program purpose. In that case, it might read like this:

> This course supports the school purpose of providing theological education for men and women preparing for the teaching ministry in religious education by helping the student . . .
> - communicate effectively.
> - model the role of an effective teacher.

Developing statements of rationale comes more easily when the institution or a program has determined the essential high-level general competencies which the student should possess. Some call these "common learnings" or "common competencies." Tragically, few institutions have identified them.

"Personal interest" does not provide adequate grounds for including a course on that subject in a curriculum plan.

Institutions use the rationale statement to legitimize courses in a curriculum plan. Often teachers decide that they should offer a course in a given subject because of their personal interest in the field. "Personal interest" does not provide adequate grounds for including a course on that subject in a curriculum plan. Each request for new courses should have to pass the "rationale test."

13
State the Course Goals and Objectives

Goals: A study of this chapter should help curriculum designers understand . . .
1. the characteristics of a course goal and objective.
2. the models for combining statements of course goals and objectives.

Objectives: The designer . . .
1. writes cognitive, affective, and psychomotor goals and objectives at the course level.
2. writes course goals and objectives which identify the affective dimensions of given cognitive goals and objectives.
3. rewrites improperly stated course goals and objectives for learners.
4. explains how one cognitive goal statement may serve as the single stem for several objectives reflecting multiple levels of learning.
5. explains the "up-the-stairs" technique for identifying the level of meaningful performance.
6. explains the problem of the approach response versus the required response in affective objectives.
7. explains the pitfalls to avoid in writing course goals and objectives.

Course goals and objectives may consist of cognitive statements only, affective statements only, psychomotor statements only, or when possible a combination.[1] Cognitive goals and objec-

---

1. Some repetition appears in part 3 so that designers can use part 3 as a separate study, complete in itself.

tives have affective dimensions; affective goals and objectives have cognitive dimensions. The sample statements in this chapter include *both* cognitive and affective statements.

State the Course Educational Goals: Cognitive

By way of review, *goal* means the broad statement of learning intent. It identifies the kind of learning expected and states the subject in a chewable bite (in this case, "chewable" in one semester). For example, a goal may say: "The student demonstrates understanding of the elements of long-range planning," or "The student demonstrates an attitude of confidence in the democratic process," Mager says. The goal is the important thing. Objectives simply tell what the teacher will accept as valid evidence that the student has achieved the important goal. Course planners "lift" individual course goals form the "bank" of department goals.

> *Teachers should be thankful for those incidental learnings which occur but are not included in goal-oriented, planned experiences.*

A course goal reflects an appropriate level of generalization. It uses terms broad enough to include all the unit goals which follow it. Yet it makes a distinct contribution to the fulfillment of all goals and purposes above it in the hierarchy.

The number of cognitive course goals appropriate for one course varies with the nature of the course. A survey course may include several units dealing with widely differing subjects. Designers either try to express an adequate generalization, or they compile the unit goals into a composite one. Generalization is the preferred approach. A generalized goal for a survey course in good health practices might say: "The learner demonstrates understanding of practices essential to good health." In this case the generalization covers such subjects as diet, exercise, rest, and mental outlook.

In stating cognitive goals, designers find it helpful to make a list of nouns which answer the question "understands what?" For example, the goal may call for understanding of principles, forms, guidelines, processes, steps, concepts, elements, relationships, causes, effects, similarities and differences, consequences, roles, influences, techniques, theories, and so forth.

The following cognitive goal is "chewable" in one course (the affective goal shows the dual-track nature of the course):

Courses title: Operating Weekday Centers for Young Children

Course goals: The student demonstrates understanding of the process of planning and operating a weekday center for children.

The student demonstrates concern for the welfare of children of working parents.

These goals would have been lifted from the composite list of department goals which in turn would have been lifted from the program goals and institutional goals.

State Course Educational Objectives: Cognitive

In education, the term *objective* means a description of an observable action or learning outcome which the teacher will accept as valid evidence that the student has achieved the course goal. In the learning outcomes focus in curriculum design, designers think of objectives in the light of their function—to *indicate* goal achievement. Course objectives have several characteristics.

1. *Objectives appear in close proximity to the educational goal.*—They tell what the learner will *do* to prove achievement. When appropriate, they specify standards of performance and the circumstances under which the learner will perform. Problems tend to arise when designers detach the objectives from the goals. Because of the importance of seeing the goal and objective together, many designers prefer to make use of a transitional word such as *by*. They may choose to emphasize in some other way the relationship between the two items. The objective qualifies the goal. Some designers find the following format helpful: The student will demonstrate understanding of the lesson planning process *by* developing a lesson plan on an assigned subject.

> *To my astonishment I was informed on leaving college that I had studied navigation!—why if I had taken one turn down the harbor I should have known more about it.—Henry David Thoreau*

Most goals listed in chapter 6 would suffice for course goals; however, depending upon resources, some could serve as goals

[handwritten marginal notes: They will work together to develop synergy in class as a model of synergy in an MCO / class as MCO / Everyone will get a class synergy grade / average of scores from each student. All students get this same score for class synergy]

for units of study. A survey course, for example, might include several of the statements.

2. *The course objective represents the highest level of performance which the student is required to achieve in the course.*—It expresses the performance in terms as close as possible to meaningful activity. Sometimes the meaningful activity does not evolve until the last course in a vertical cluster which includes prerequisite courses. Generally the course objective consists of *one* statement, but that statement represents the highest level of performance. Occasionally designers find it expedient to include two cognitive goals. (The description of the lower levels of performance usually appear in unit descriptions.) An example of a course goal and objective in close proximity and in terms of meaningful activity appears in the following example taken from a course in a Department of Christian Communications:

Course title: Writing Resource Units for the Church Curriculum

Course goals: (a) The learner demonstrates understanding of the process of designing resource units for the church curriculum using the principles of directive writing (cognitive).

(b) The learner demonstrates conviction that a church should exercise its responsibility to tailor a curriculum plan to meet its own particular needs (affective).

Course Objective: To demonstrate achievement of these goals the learner designs and writes a resource unit of at least four sessions to meet a specific need in his own church.

In this example, note that the course objective serves as an indicator of achievement of both the cognitive and affective goals.

Some designers express course goals and objectives in a form similar to the following:

The learner demonstrates understanding of the process of designing resource units by designing and writing a resource unit of at least four sessions to meet a specific need in his own church (cognitive). The learner demonstrates his conviction that an individual church should fulfill its responsibility to tailor a curriculum plan to meet its own particular needs *by* writing a resource unit of at least four sessions to meet a specific need in his own church (affective).

The following example taken from a curriculum plan for a department of psychology and counseling places the goal and objective in close proximity and expresses the objective at the level of meaningful performance: The student demonstrates understanding of the integrity therapy approach to group counseling by conducting a group counseling session using the integrity therapy model.

In this case, the learner performs primarily at the synthesis level in Bloom's taxonomy. Accomplishment at the synthesis level generally implies previous achievement of the lower, "lead-up" objectives. One function of any objective is to express which level of learning the student should reach.

> *In the final analysis, achievement of a course objective is the only "test" the learner needs to take. That achievement automatically implies achievement of the lower level objectives.*

3. *One course goal statement may serve as the single stem for several different objectives.*—The difference appears in the way the designer expresses the objectives. He states the objectives in such a way as to require performance at predetermined levels of learning. A sample goal with three separate objectives follows. Notice in the three statements that the same goal (stem) appears in each, but the objectives (indicators) reflect different levels of learning.

> *One course goal statement may serve as the single stem for several different objectives.*

(a) The learner demonstrates understanding of the steps in sermon preparation *by* writing a sermon which reflects the ten steps in preparation presented in this course.

(b) The learner demonstrates understanding of the steps in sermon preparation *by* reconstructing the parts (aim, central truth, and so forth) of a given sermon.

(c) The learner demonstrates understanding of the steps in sermon preparation *by* determining which of several given sermons best represents implementation of the steps in sermon preparation.

The designer asks, "Which of these three statements comes closest to what the learner will do the rest of his life in Christian ministry?" Although the third statement represents a higher level of learning (evaluation in the Bloom taxonomy) than the first one, the first one states the meaningful performance and would appear as the course objective. The first statement should appear as stated in the institution's catalog or bulletin.

In the following example, note that any one or all of the educational objective statements could serve as course objectives at the level of meaningful activity.

Course title: Planning Family Finances

Course goals: (a) The learner demonstrates understanding of the guidelines for family financial planning.

(b) The learner demonstrates faithfulness in stewardship of his own family finances.

Course Objectives: To demonstrate achievement of these goals, the learner . . .

(a) develops a family financial plan for his own family.

(b) assists a family in developing a family financial plan.

(c) diagnoses a family financial situation and recommends necessary actions.

The teacher makes an arbitrary decision as to which of the meaningful performances would serve as the objective in the course goal-objective statement. The teacher would probably choose the first one; however, the other two also reflect the level of meaningful activity. In a learning outcomes curriculum the course goal-objective statement and course description in the institution's catalog or bulletin should be identical.

> *In a learning outcomes curriculum the course goal-objective statement and the course description in the institution's catalog or bulletin should be identical.*

Any of the following forms serve adequately as a course description in an institution's catalog or bulletin:

(a) The student demonstrates understanding of the guidelines for family financial planning. To demonstrate achievement of this goal, the student develops a family financial plan for his own family.

(b) The student demonstrates understanding of the guidelines for family financial planning by developing a family financial plan for his own family.

(c) To demonstrate understanding of the guidelines for family financial planning, the student develops a family financial plan for his own family.

Each of the statements describes a meaningful activity in terms of the student. The student can perceive clearly the expected learning outcome. For further examples of course educational goals and objectives, see the sample course descriptions in appendix 1.

The following chart shows a technique for arriving at a course objective at the level of meaningful activity. Begin reading at the bottom. Notice how each progressive level gets closer and closer to the level of meaningful activity.

State Course Educational Goals: Affective

Affective course goals describe the affective dimension of the course. At this point, the designer searches the program and department affective goals and selects the goal most appropriate for the course. Those who want to include the affective goals may profit from studying the following format:

Course title: Practicing Education Evangelism
Course goals: (a) The student demonstrates understanding of approaches to educational evangelism in the church. (b) The student demonstrates concern for the salvation of those who already have direct or indirect relationship to the Sunday School.

The course designer decides whether the cognitive goal or affective goal should receive primary emphasis.

The inclusion of an affective goal for the course represents commitment on the part of the instructor to use learning activities geared to producing or encouraging affective outcomes. The designer considers the question *which goal* (cognitive or affective) is the *primary* goal. Course descriptions and lesson plans in the separate realms would be vastly different.

Designers state affective goals under two circumstances.

The "Up-the-Stairs" Technique
for arriving at an objective at the level of meaningful activity
(For a course in lesson planning)

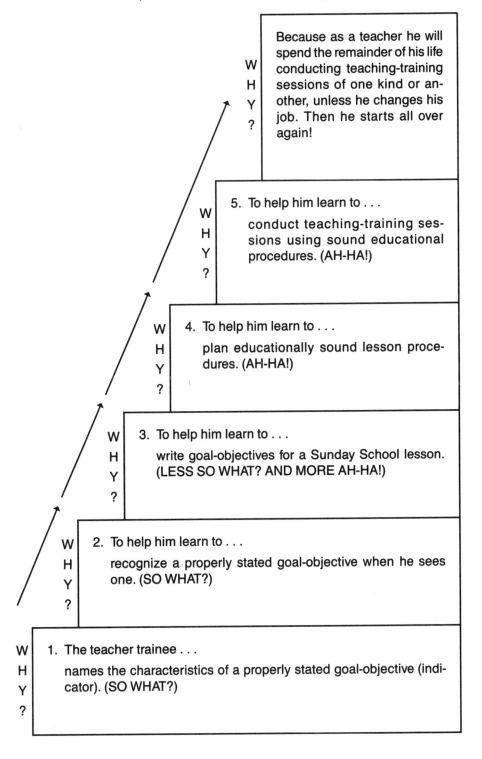

W
H
Y
? Because as a teacher he will spend the remainder of his life conducting teaching-training sessions of one kind or another, unless he changes his job. Then he starts all over again!

W
H
Y
? 5. To help him learn to . . .
conduct teaching-training sessions using sound educational procedures. (AH-HA!)

W
H
Y
? 4. To help him learn to . . .
plan educationally sound lesson procedures. (AH-HA!)

W
H
Y
? 3. To help him learn to . . .
write goal-objectives for a Sunday School lesson. (LESS SO WHAT? AND MORE AH-HA!)

W
H
Y
? 2. To help him learn to . . .
recognize a properly stated goal-objective when he sees one. (SO WHAT?)

W
H
Y
? 1. The teacher trainee . . .
names the characteristics of a properly stated goal-objective (indicator). (SO WHAT?)

Development of Course and Unit Goals and Objectives

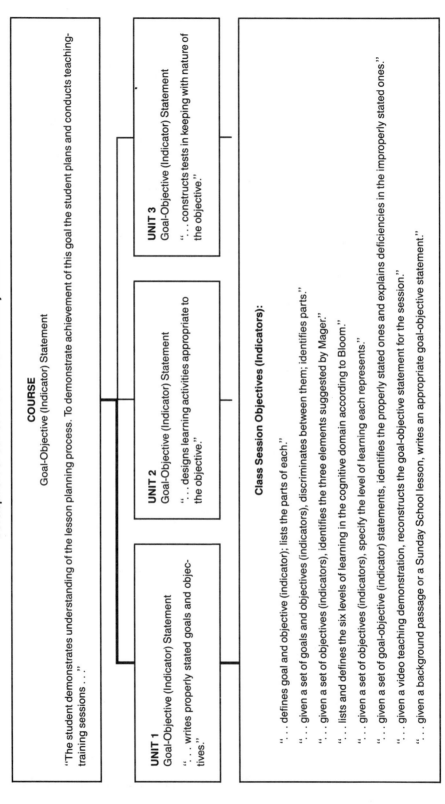

COURSE

Goal-Objective (Indicator) Statement

"The student demonstrates understanding of the lesson planning process. To demonstrate achievement of this goal the student plans and conducts teaching-training sessions . . ."

UNIT 1

Goal-Objective (Indicator) Statement

" . . . writes properly stated goals and objectives."

UNIT 2

Goal-Objective (Indicator) Statement

" . . . designs learning activities appropriate to the objective."

UNIT 3

Goal-Objective (Indicator) Statement

" . . . constructs tests in keeping with nature of the objective."

Class Session Objectives (Indicators):

" . . . defines goal and objective (indicator); lists the parts of each."

" . . . given a set of goals and objectives (indicators), discriminates between them; identifies parts."

" . . . given a set of objectives (indicators), identifies the three elements suggested by Mager."

" . . . lists and defines the six levels of learning in the cognitive domain according to Bloom."

" . . . given a set of objectives (indicators), specify the level of learning each represents."

" . . . given a set of goal-objective (indicator) statements, identifies the properly stated ones and explains deficiencies in the improperly stated ones."

" . . . given a video teaching demonstration, reconstructs the goal-objective statement for the session."

" . . . given a background passage or a Sunday School lesson, writes an appropriate goal-objective statement."

1. *Some courses need emphasis on both cognitive and affective outcomes.*—Designers describe the affective dimension of a course which is primarily cognitive (or psychomotor) in nature. They "pair" an affective goal with a cognitive (or psychomotor) one, then they state both at the beginning of a course description. The following example shows "pairing of goals."

Cognitive	*Affective*
(a) The learner demonstrates understanding of church and denominational polity.	The learner demonstrates loyalty to the church and denomination.
	or
	The learner demonstrates patience and confidence in the democratic process.
(b) The learner demonstrates understanding of approaches to witnessing and evangelism.	The learner demonstrates compassion for the unsaved.
(c) The learner demonstrates understanding of principles and approaches to counseling persons who have special needs.	The learner demonstrates sensitivity to needs for ego support in others.
	or
	The learner demonstrates commitment to confidentiality in counseling persons with special needs.
(d) The learner demonstrates understanding of the nature of the church.	The learner demonstrates commitment to the church as God's plan for reaching the world.
(e) The learner demonstrates understanding of approaches to family financial planning.	The learner demonstrates faithfulness in fulfilling family financial stewardship obligations.
(f) The student demonstrates understanding of the process of planning and operating a Christian weekday center for children.	The learner demonstrates concern for the physical, spiritual, and educational welfare of children of working parents.
(g) Others . . .	

Course planners will discover that they can pair easily the cognitive and affective goals in some courses. Other courses require more thought, but usually an affective dimension exists if planners will persist in looking for it.

2. *Some courses in and of themselves focus primarily on affective outcomes.*—If so, the course planner states that goal first, then if necessary or appropriate, adds a cognitive goal as a secondary one. For example, a course on "Confidence in Prayer" suggests an affective outcome as its primary focus. The course goal might read: "The student demonstrates confidence in prayer." *If* the course planner feels he should add a cognitive dimension, the second goal could read: "The student demonstrates understanding of what prayer means." The course planner decides which outcome should receive primary focus. Making "confidence in prayer" the primary focus means devoting a preponderance of time, energy, resources, and activity to helping students develop confidence in prayer. However, the lesson plans will of necessity include some activities directed at the cognitive dimension. (Refer to the chart "Developing Affective Goals" in chapter 6 for help in phrasing affective goal statements.)

State Course Educational Objectives: Affective

With certain changes, designers use the same process in forming affective objectives as they follow in stating cognitive objectives. Both describe performances or actions which the learner will do to prove achievement of educational goals.

Some designers prefer to use only *goals* in the course description when working in the affective domain. They use the word *demonstrates* in the goal and leave it at that because of the difficulty in leading students to achieve specific affective indicators.

Several unique considerations govern the formation of affective educational objectives, whether at the institutional, program, department, or individual course level.

1. *As is the case with goals, most courses in departments of instruction have both cognitive and affective dimensions.*—This suggests that most course descriptions include course goals in both the cognitive and affective domains. (See sample course descriptions in appendix 1 and the examples shown in this chapter.) Lesson plans for the course include learning activities oriented toward achievement of the affective as well as the cog-

nitive goals. It follows that most courses will also describe affective objectives.

2. *Teachers need a high tolerance for ambiguity when dealing with affective objectives.*—Within the bounds of time limitations such as a semester, teachers may find that all they can do is to *invite* the learner to act. The response which proves achievement of an affective goal may not come for one, ten, or twenty years. Teachers need to remember the biblical principle "one sows, another waters, and another reaps."

Notice the representative objectives in this example: "The student demonstrates concern for the physical needs of political refugees *by doing such things as* providing transportation to health clinics, teaching a course in nutrition, and delivering food to a newly arrived family." The student may *not* do any of these things, but if the teacher sees the learner interpreting for the refugee at an employment office, he recognizes that action as valid also. How much "tolerance for ambiguity" can a teacher tolerate?

Often the learner's response to an affective goal is an indicator of the instructor's performance in using appropriate learning activities. The teacher may need to identify what some call "short-range indicators." The teacher may ask students to summarize things they have done during a semester, of their own accord, which seem to indicate desirable changes in attitude. The difficulty in identifying indicators of affective change does not excuse teachers from careful planning and teaching for affective change through appropriate learning activities.

3. *Designers specify possible or representative indicators (objectives) of affective change.*—Those who prefer to specify affective course objectives (indicators) find it helpful to incorporate in the statement the phrase "by doing *such things as* . . ." That opens the door to acceptance of those valid but unspecified indicators which the learner may perform. The following example combines the affective goal and several typical or representative indicators:

Course title: Deepening the Spiritual Life
Goal-Objective (Affective): The student demonstrates commitment to the development of the spiritual life by voluntarily *doing such things as* scheduling time for daily private devotions, compiling an intercessory prayer list, joining a Bible study group, . . .

Some responses which teachers *do not* specify may prove to be the actual actions or responses which prove achievement.

4. *Two schools of thought prevail concerning whether an observed affective response is valid.*—The first says the response must come as a *voluntary* action. That is, the teacher does not assign or require such an activity. The same school says the teacher should think twice before informing the learner about the kinds of affective responses expected. Teachers reason that if the learner knows in advance, he can *fake it* just to please the teacher. In this case the attitude does not in fact change—it just appears to change.

The second school says, "Yes, let the learner know the kinds of affective responses expected." In medical school, for example, an affective goal-objective might read like this: The trainee will demonstrate represent for the dignity of patients by refraining from saying "ugh" aloud when dressing a wound. The teacher can observe in short-range response situations whether the trainee did or did not say "ugh!"

In theological education, designers might consider the fact that God gave Moses the Ten Commandments. The Commandments specify affective indicators of proper relationships between persons and God and among persons themselves. Numerous Scripture passages specify affective responses. Consider the specificity of "do good to them that, . . . despitefully use you" (Matt. 5:44). Jesus commended persons who made affective responses, "I was thirsty, and ye gave me drink" (Matt. 25:35). He instructed followers to pray without ceasing and bear one another's burdens.

Experience has shown that learners are more apt to respond affectively when invited than when not invited.

Learners are more apt to respond affectively when invited than when not invited. True or False?

Teachers may have to leave assessments of the sincerity of a response to God's judgment.

A helpful exercise in stating affective objectives for courses is to determine first the affective dimension of a cognitive course goal, then state it as a goal followed by an objective.

The following examples express the affective dimension of related cognitive goals.

(a) The learner demonstrates faithfulness in stewardship of family finances by developing and following a family financial plan. (He *understands* the family financial planning process.)

(b) The learner demonstrates concern for the welfare of children of working parents by doing such things as working voluntarily in a children's day care center. (He understands guidelines for working with children.)

After determining the affective dimension of a cognitive goal and objective, designers describe both the cognitive and the affective outcomes at the beginning of a course description. (See sample course descriptions in appendix 1.)

State Course Educational Goals: Psychomotor

Course planners select and lift from department goal statements those psychomotor goals which pertain to a given course. Psychomotor course goals describe motor actions—like riding a bicycle, singing, playing a piano, and skiing. At times teachers use the term *skills* to describe cognitive processes. But these represent "perceptual skills"—like "skills in leadership." They belong in the perceptual skills category and designers classify them as *cognitive* processes.

In the psychomotor domain, designers find it helpful to answer the question: Skill in doing what? A chart similar to the following serves as a thought stimulator:

	The skill verb	*The object*
Skill in . . .	playing	the piano, folk games, basketball
	conducting	choral music, a woodwind ensemble, congregational singing
	assembling	an outrigger canoe, playground equipment, camping equipment
	sight reading	musical scores
	operating	video cameras and recorders

> *"As oft as the song delighteth me more than that is songen, so oft I acknowledge I trespass greviously."*—*St. Augustine.*
>
> *Skills goals may also have affective dimensions.*

Statements of skills goals suitable for a single course of instruction might appear as follows. Analyze each statement and determine its appropriateness for a one-semester course.

- The student demonstrates skill in leading congregational singing.
- The student demonstrates skill in directing choral ensembles.
- The student demonstrates skill in sight reading (piano).
- The student demonstrates skill in operating video and audio recording and playback equipment.
- The student demonstrates skill in designing and operating stage lighting equipment.
- The student demonstrates skill in public speaking.
- The student demonstrates skill in swimming.
- The student demonstrates skill in assembling camping equipment.

Note that each example reflects a degree of generalization which leaves room for units of study dealing with specifics.

State Educational Objectives: Psychomotor

As in the other types of objectives or indicators, psychomotor objectives tell what the student will do to prove achievement of a goal. In the skills domain, standards of performance play a significant role. When appropriate, the statements specify how well and under what circumstances the student will perform. As in other types of objectives, designers find it helpful to express the objective in conjunction with the goal which it modifies. The following example shows a skills goal and objective in close proximity.

Course title: Sight Reading for Beginners (Vocal)
Course goal: The student demonstrates skill in sight reading musical scores (vocal).

Course objective: To demonstrate achievement of this goal the student sight reads (sings) a randomly selected musical score.[2]

The designer may add standards of performance (with fewer than three errors in pitch and timing) and circumstances (given a randomly selected musical score).

Pitfalls in Writing Course Goal-Objective Statements

A study of goal-objective statements used in course descriptions reveals that certain "pitfalls" occur repeatedly. They seem to result from (a) the designer's lack of understanding of the fundamentals of the process and (b) attempts by the designer to cover up this lack of understanding with cosmetic phrases and wordy construction to give the "feel" of sophistication. (Before continuing, review the definitions of goal and objective in the glossary.)

Wrapping Goals in the Trappings of Objectives

• Example: At the close of the semester, learners should be able to develop an understanding of the nature of the church.
• Comments: The writer inserted the Magerian phrase "should be able to" in front of a goal (broad statement of learning intent). That does not make it an objective (description of what the learner will *do* to indicate achievement of a goal). *Should be able to* suggests that an observable action should follow. True, the writer of the statement used the verb "develop," but that's a "fuzzy" when the word *understanding* becomes the direct object of the verb. Designers ask, "Can an instructor *observe* a learner developing an understanding?" No. The statement does have the characteristics of a goal. It specifies a kind of learning (understanding) and a subject (the nature of the church), but it does not tell what the learner will *do* to indicate that he understands the nature of the church. The statement expresses a goal, not an objective.
• Solution: First, simply phrase the statement as a goal. Do not attempt to make it an objective by inserting "will be able to." Add an indicator later. Simply say, "The student demonstrates understanding of the nature of the church." Then if an

---

2. When the objective indicates no standards, one assumes the standard as 100 percent. Here, it is with 100 percent accuracy.

objective is desired, ask, "What will an instructor accept as valid evidence that the student understands the nature of church?" The answer will describe a cognitive action at an appropriate level of learning. The designer describes that action—and presto, an objective! Make a beeline for the cognitive action when stating an objective. A combined statement could look like this:

> The student demonstrates (or will demonstrate) understanding of the nature of the church by summarizing the five functions of a New Testament church (or "by evaluating the degree to which a given church fulfills the functions of a New Testament church").

Note how the last example lends itself to the use of the case study method. The statement requires response at the evaluation level of the Bloom taxonomy.

Majoring on Minors

• Example: The student demonstrates understanding of the characteristics of a properly stated objective by (a) underlining the performance verb, (b) drawing a circle around the performance conditions, and (c) drawing a wavy line under the performance standards.

• Comments: The objective as stated does not zero in on the cognitive action. Underlining simply provides a convenient means for indicating a cognitive action which has *already taken place*. The use of the terms *underlining, drawing a circle,* and *drawing a wavy line* would be acceptable when teaching the learner to draw circles and wavy lines!

Such a statement confines the teacher unnecessarily to one format for test construction. The unnecessary details tend to create a feeling of child's play. The designer should determine the proper cognitive action and express it.

• Solution: Determine the cognitive action involved. The cognitive action which precedes the underlining and circling is probably the act of discriminating between or among items. The instructor decides what he or she will accept as valid evidence of understanding. Any of the following would suffice, depending on the level of understanding the teacher desires.

> The student demonstrates understanding of the process of writing learning objectives by . . .

(a) discriminating between properly stated and improperly stated objectives,
(b) rewriting improperly stated objectives,
(c) identifying the parts of given objectives, and
(d) writing objectives based on given resource material.

Stated together, the goal and objective would look like this:

The student demonstrates understanding of the characteristics of an educational objective by discriminating between properly stated and improperly stated objectives. (In this case, the student discriminates among givens.)

Focusing on Methods Rather than Cognitive Action

Sometimes an objective calls for the same action that a method specifies. In such cases the objective should express the desired cognitive action. This example focuses on method.

• Example: The student will demonstrate understanding of the elements of curriculum design in theological education by designing a graphic representation showing the relationships among the elements.

• Comments: The first part, the goal, is adequate. The last part of the statement is intended as an objective, but in the objective one needs to go straight for the *cognitive action* which precedes the development of the graphic. What is it? What does the student do cognitively that results in a graphic? He *analyzes the relationships among elements.* "Designing a graphic" is a method—a means for picturing the cognitive analysis which took place previously. "Designing a graphic" would serve well as an objective in a course in graphic arts, when the student must design a graphic or fail the course. However, the not-so-small matter of individual differences and individual learning styles comes into play here. As stated, the objective assumes that *all* students are equally adept at converting concepts into graphic forms.

As stated, the instructor fences himself in. If he later decides that the student can prove in better ways that he understands the relationships, what then?

The graphic indicators not so much the student's ability to analyze relationships as it does his ability to create visual displays. What about the student who has great analytical powers but cannot express them visually? What about the student who has great facility with words but who must essentially eliminate them because the objective (or test) calls for production of a graphic?

• Solution: Again go straight for the cognitive action—analyzing relationships. A simpler goal-objective statement would sound like this:

> The student demonstrates understanding of the elements of curriculum design (goal). To demonstrate achievement of this goal, the student *analyzes the relationships* among the elements.

The teacher has greater freedom in designing test items. The phrase *designing a graphic* belongs in the description of *methods* in the course description along with some other vehicles used in the study.

• Example: The student demonstrates understanding of the elements of curriculum design in theological education by writing a paper on the elements.

• Comments: This very common statement seems to serve as a catch-all used by instructors who do not know what else to say. They have written papers all their lives because their instructors did not know what else to ask them to do. By assigning a paper one can always require strict adherence to form, and form is easy to grade—much easier than the cognitive performance which resides in the form. Such an objective belongs in a course in *composition,* but even then the teacher should identify the cognitive action desired.

• Solution: Like "designing a graphic," "writing a paper" is a method—a means, a vehicle. The phrase hides the cognitive action expected. Go straight for the cognitive action which *may* or may not be clothed in the words of a "paper." State the cognitive action. Decide which cognitive action the student should use as an approach to development of the paper. Then describe that action. A "paper" may or may not be the best vehicle for dealing with ideas. Include "writing a paper" in the description of methods in the course description, but a teacher who understands individual differences in learning will probably avoid limiting the vehicle to writing a paper. Great injustice may be done to the student when form precedes substance in writing papers. Form should be a minor consideration in writing a paper—unless the course deals with how to write papers.

Consider this revision:

> The student demonstrates understanding of the elements of curriculum design in theological education by comparing

the elements of curriculum design in theological education with the elements of design in public education.

Such a statement allows for flexibility in determining the vehicle for making the comparison. It is the *comparison of elements,* not the vehicle, that is the critical factor in the learning.

Of course, if one teaches a course in English composition, then writing a paper would seem essential as an indicator.

If writing a paper does in fact turn out to be the best vehicle, then the student knows what to do cognitively in the paper (compare the elements). The instructor then knows what to look for in evaluating the paper. He grades on the basis of the cognitive action the paper carries, not totally on the student's ability to conform to a style manual.

Measuring Distance with a Pair of Scales

• Example: The student will demonstrate confidence in the democratic process in church administration by comparing the characteristics of the democratic process with the hierarchial concept.

• Comments: The word *confidence* casts the goal as an *affective* one, dealing with attitudes and values. The objective says that the act of comparing the democratic approach with the hierarchial approach is an indicator that the learner possesses *confidence* possibly, but not necessarily. Generally, "comparing" requires a cognitive process. There are affective values in comparing one with the other, and diffusion of learning among the domains says that comparing could produce *some* attitudinal change. However, comparing primarily requires cognitive action. In writing goals and objectives, designers need to make a deliberate decision as to the primary direction the lesson or unit will take. Course designers pair affective goals with affective indicators or objectives. They pair a cognitive goal with a cognitive indicator. Measure distance with an odometer, not a set of scales! You don't drive nails with a stick of butter!

• Solution: Decide first of all whether to focus on the affective outcome or the cognitive outcome. In this case the designer could take either or both directions. If he decides on both directions, he will need two goal-objective statements. Consider these examples:

(a) The student demonstrates understanding of the forms of church government by analyzing the advantages and disadvantages of the four principle forms (cognitive).

(b) The student demonstrates confidence in the democratic process by voluntarily doing such things as participating in the business meetings of the church (affective). In the realm of national politics the learner could demonstrate an attitude of confidence in the democratic process by doing such things as registering with the political party of his choice, enlisting as a volunteer at that party's campaign headquarters, . . .

(c) The student demonstrates understanding of the democratic process in church life by comparing the democratic process as used in a Baptist church with the hierarchial process used in another religious group.

Attempting the "Layered Look"

• Example: The student should be able to identify, apply, analyze, evaluate, and demonstrate an understanding of the modern philosophies of education (cognitive objective).

• Comments: The layered look has definite disadvantages in the world of writing course descriptions. As stated, the objective makes quite an order! The writer seems afraid that he might omit something, so he lists many levels of learning (layers) in one statement. If one layer doesn't give enough latitude, the others will! Then as a fool-proof catch-all, he added "demonstrates an understanding of." True, the statement includes both a goal and an objective—but in this case the layered objectives blur the focus.

• Solution: First, the description writer needs to pull forward the goal: "The pupil demonstrates understanding of modern philosophies of education." Then the objectives should follow. In stating the objective, the writer needs to decide on the highest level of learning expected (or feasible) and reflect that *one* in the course objective. As a rule of thumb, designers specify in a course objective the *highest level only,* since a high level *implies* achievement at the lower levels. The decision as to the level of learning expected depends on the scope of the course. If the situation does not provide time and resources for synthesis level performance, then the designer must decide *which level* does seem feasible under the circumstances. Then he calls for performance at that level.

Consider these revisions:
(a) The student understands the modern philosophies of education. To demonstrate achievement of this goal, the

student designs lesson plans based on each of the philosophies (synthesis level).

(b) The student demonstrates understanding of the modern philosophies of education by analyzing the philosophies employed in instructional case studies (analysis level).

Disguising or Hiding the Essential Cognitive Actions

• Example: The student completes the learning packet on *How to Make a Hospital Visit.*

• Comments: "Completing the learning packet" disguises the essential cognitive action. The phrase gives no indication as to the level of learning or performance expected. The learning packet may or may not consist totally of recall items. Or, it may involve complicated problem solving. The reader doesn't know. As stated, the required performance is "completing learning packets." That action would suffice if the designer intends to teach students how to complete learning packets. Obviously, the learning packet houses some specific goals and objectives. The goals and objectives may specify the cognitive action, but the packet hides them. The designer needs to go on a treasure hunt and discover the goodies provided in the packet. The teacher may use "completing the learning packet" as a *learning strategy*—but not as an objective. He should list the learning packet under "mediography." It serves as a *resource*, not as an objective.

• Solution: The designer should search the learning packet and study the goals and objectives it contains. He should identify the goal-objective statement which represents the highest, most meaningful performance level. That statement then becomes the cognitive action which the goal-objective should reflect. The teacher has no idea at this point what the packet contains, but one could make a good guess that the course description ought to contain a statement similar to this one:

The student demonstrates understanding of the principles of hospital visitation by (a) evaluating a given hospital visitation simulation and (b) visiting a patient in a hospital.

Then the designers would list the learning packet in the mediography or perhaps describe it in a methods section. "Analyzing a simulation" could serve both as a method (practice) and as a test.

• Example: The student demonstrates understanding of present, middle, or passive voice Greek verbs by passing the mid-term exam with a grade of 90 percent.

• Comments: The phrase *passing a test* hides the cognitive action in a test of undisclosed nature or purpose. True, the student must perform in order to "pass a test," but "passing a test" does not disclose the cognitive action involved in passing the test.

• Solution: The designer needs to analyze and classify the cognitive actions involved in the test, then state them as objectives. And the objectives will not refer to a test at all! The objectives *reflect* the test. As stated, the student has no indication of the complexity of response the test requires. In this case the properly stated goal does not have a cognitive objective as an indicator.

Consider this revision:
The student demonstrates understanding of the present, middle, or passive voice of Greek verbs by parsing and declining present tense, middle, and passive voice verbs.

The objective as revised tells the *kinds* of questions which the instructor may include in a test, but he may use whatever form of items he desires as long as they match the objective.

Focusing Unnecessarily on Process

• Example: The student demonstrates understanding of the prospect analysis approach to educational evangelism by planning and modeling a large group simulation of prospect analysis in cooperation with assigned groups of fellow learners through videotape and playback.

• Comments: The fact that the teacher will use as methods "cooperative groups of fellow students" and video playback has nothing to do with the objective. The description of the processes and methods belongs under methodology in the course description. "Simulation" as a method belongs in the description's methodology—not in the objective.

• Solution: Rephrase the objective in this way: Plans and conducts a prospect analysis meeting. This approach allows the teacher flexibility in selecting methods. He is not confined to the group process and video production unless the course deals with how to do a simulation.

Saying What One Does Not Mean

• Example: Define the meaning of the elements of curriculum design.

• Comment: One does not define *meanings*. He defines words or terms.

• Solution: The designer should say simply what he means: Define the five elements of curriculum design.

14
Develop Unit Titles and Patterns of Organization

Goals: A study of this chapter should help curriculum designers understand . . .
   1. the patterns of organization for course descriptions.
   2. the forms of unit titles.

Objectives: The designer . . .
   1. organizes units of study in a course into the linear, anchor, and wheel patterns.
   2. discriminates among unit organization patterns.
   3. writes unit titles in the subject and process forms.

Like course titles, unit titles may state a subject or express a process. Regardless of the form, designers use parallel construction in stating the titles.

If a unit title could speak, it would say, "My title, plus the other unit titles, equals the course title." A unit is a logical subdivision of the scope of a course. A unit of study identifies manageable segments or chewable bites of a subject. Depending upon the scope of the unit and number of objectives it has, completion of a unit of study may require use of several lesson plans.

Course and unit titles may take any of several forms.[1]

1. *The anchor pattern.*—In this pattern the first unit introduces a basic concept or principle. The second and succeeding unit reflect logical breakdowns of the basic concept or principle. They may show the application of the basic concept to specific concerns. The anchor pattern diagram looks like this:

---

1. The patterns for unit arrangement used here were originally developed by Raymond Rigdon, director of Seminary External Education Division, the Southern Baptist Convention.

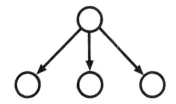

ANCHOR PATTERN

A course entitled "The Nature of the New Testament Church" might have a unit arrangement like this:

Course title: Understanding the Nature of the New Testament Church
Unit Titles: Unit 1, "The New Testament Church"
    Unit 2, "The Church as the Body of Christ"
    Unit 3, "The Church as a Fellowship of Learners"
    Unit 4, "The Church as a Functioning Organism"

Designers could change these subject titles to process titles by making changes like these: The Church Lives as the Body of Christ, The Church Learns in Fellowship, or The Church Functions as an Organism.

2. *The linear pattern.*—The linear pattern consists of several units, each following in a logical sequence. In a sense, each unit grows out of a preceding unit. The units may follow a developmental sequence. The linear pattern looks like this:

LINEAR PATTERN

A course in missions, following the linear pattern, could include unit titles such as these:

Course title: Accepting the Challenge of Missions
Unit titles: Unit 1, "Accepting the Challenge of World Missions"
    Unit 2, "Accepting the Challenge of Missions in America"
    Unit 3, "Accepting the Challenge of Missions in the State"
    Unit 4, "Accepting the Challenge of Associational Missions"

Unit 5, "The Individual Church Responding to the Challenge of Missions"

3. *The wheel pattern.*—The wheel pattern consists of several units organized around a central theme, but they have no logical sequence. We could picture this arrangement of units this way:

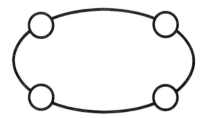

WHEEL PATTERN

A course on "Managing the Church's Business" included these units of study. The central theme is "the church's business." Notice the random sequencing order involved. Unit 1 does not serve as an "anchor."

Course title: Managing the Church's Business
Unit titles: Unit 1, "Managing the Church's Finances"
    Unit 2, "Managing the Church's Records"
    Unit 3, "Managing the Church's Properties"
    Unit 4, "Managing the Church's Insurance Program"
    Unit 5, "Managing the Church's Policies and Procedures"

As in stating the course title, the unit title may take the form of a subject title or process title. Some designers use the declarative sentence form. From an educational viewpoint, the declarative sentence title seems to have more teaching value. It makes a declaration, and the declaration itself teaches. Notice in the following example how the short statements tell something the church does. A student who reads only the unit titles learns the five functions of a church. Notice also the "wheel" pattern.

Course title: The Functions of a Dynamic Church
Unit titles: Unit 1, "The Church Worships"
    Unit 2, "The Church Witnesses"
    Unit 3, "The Church Ministers"
    Unit 4, "The Church Educates"
    Unit 5, "The Church Applies"

15

State Unit Goals and Objectives

Goals: A study of this chapter should help designers understand . . .
1. the relationship between course and unit goals and objectives.
2. the process for writing units goals and objectives which relate properly to statements at the course level.
3. the process of arranging "meaningful performance" objectives with essential "lead-up" objectives in units of study.

Objectives: The curriculum designer . . .
1. designs a unit of study which identifies a "meaningful performance" objective and essential "lead-up" objectives in the cognitive domain.
2. writes affective objectives at the unit of study level.
3. explains reasons for using in affective objectives the phrase "by doing such things as . . ."

Unit Educational Goals

Unit goals describe learning intent appropriate for a subdivision of a course. The designer asks, "Will accomplishment of this goal, along with other unit goals, result in achievement of the course goal?"

State the Unit Educational Goals: Cognitive

Unit educational goals deal with a smaller segment of the scope of the course than course educational goals. The course goal reflects a greater degree of generalization than unit goals. Notice how the unit goals in the following example, when taken together equal the course goal.

Course goal: The student demonstrates understanding of
the lesson planning process.
Unit 1: The student demonstrates understanding of the
process of writing goals and objectives.
Unit 2: The student demonstrates understanding of the
process of designing learning activities for cognitive
learning.
Unit 3: The student demonstrates understanding of
the evaluation process in learning in the cognitive domain.

Achievement of the three "unit bites" results in achievement
of the course goal "bite."

As in other goal statements at higher levels in the hierarchy,
unit goals specify the kind of learning and indicate the subject
in a chewable bite. The "chewable bite" in a unit goal is much
more limited than a course goal.

State the Unit Educational Goals: Affective

Generally affective goals for units of study are the same as
for the course, sometimes with a further limitation of the subject. For example, a course goal "the student demonstrates
concern for the unsaved" becomes "the student demonstrates
concerns for unsaved college students (or adults, migrant workers, and so forth) at the unit level.

Some courses may focus primarily on affective goals. They
lend themselves to inclusion of affective unit goals. A course
goal may state, "The student demonstrates confidence in
prayer." An affective unit goal within the course may state, "The
student demonstrates confidence in intercessory prayer." The designer has asked, "What *kinds* of prayer?" The answer constitutes the framework for logical divisions of the course into units.

A complete list of unit goals in the affective domain might
appear like this:

Course goal: The student demonstrates confidence in
prayer.
Unit 1: The student demonstrates confidence in intercessory prayer.
Unit 2: The student demonstrates confidence in prayers
of petition.
Unit 3: The student demonstrates confidence in prayers
for forgiveness.
Unit 4: The student demonstrates commitment to a consistent prayer life.

State the Unit Educational Goals: Psychomotor

Designers state unit goals in the psychomotor domain by "breaking down the job." They determine the subskills needed to achieve the course goal. Usually the breakdown reveals prerequisite skills, each of which becomes the basis for a unit. Thus, a course goal "the student demonstrates skill in conducting congregational singing" becomes a unit goal such as "the student demonstrates skill in conducting in 4/4 time."

The technical aspects of stating a unit goal are the same as for the course goal, except the unit goal appears at a lower point on the generalization scale. If a designer placed all the unit goals in a container, he could label the container "course goal."

State the Unit Educational Objectives: Cognitive

These crucial statements form the stuff out of which teachers make lesson plans. Units of study include as many "lead-up" objectives as necessary to lead the student progressively to achievement of the unit objective. The designers make judgments as to how much the student already understands about the subject. If the student already knows certain essential facts, the designer omits objectives calling for their recall.

> *Unit educational objectives are the stuff out of which teachers build lesson plans.*

As in writing the course goal, a unit goal once specified may accommodate objectives at various levels of learning. Designers may attach to *one* cognitive goal a list of indicators of goal achievement at whatever levels of learning the course calls for. Study the following goal statement. Note how it remains constant while the objectives imply various levels of learning.

> *One educational goal may accommodate many objectives at various levels of learning.*

Because of the close relationship between unit goals and their objectives at the unit level most designers choose to treat them together.

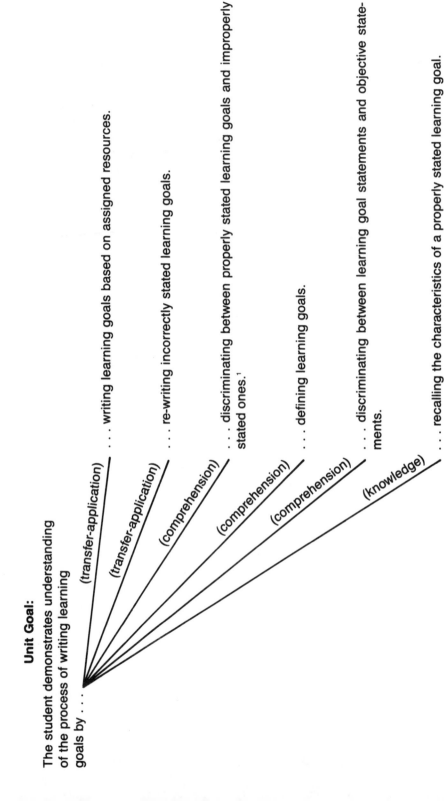

Unit Goal:

The student demonstrates understanding of the process of writing learning goals . . . .

(transfer-application) . . . writing learning goals based on assigned resources.

(transfer-application) . . . re-writing incorrectly stated learning goals.

(comprehension) . . . discriminating between properly stated learning goals and improperly stated ones.[1]

(comprehension) . . . defining learning goals.

(comprehension) . . . discriminating between learning goal statements and objective statements.

(knowledge) . . . recalling the characteristics of a properly stated learning goal.

1. Some educators classify *recognition* of a properly stated item as representing the application level.

Designers usually state the unit goal, then list as many objectives as necessary. The objective which expresses performance at the highest level becomes the unit objective. Teachers develop lesson plans and tests from unit objectives. Study this example:

Unit goal: The student demonstrates understanding of the process of writing sermon aims.
Unit objectives:
To demonstrate achievement of this goal the student . . .
- writes sermon aims on assigned subjects.
- rewrites improperly stated sermon aims.
- discriminates between properly stated sermon aims and improperly stated ones.
- discriminates between sermon aims and central truths.
- explains the difference between a sermon aim and a central truth.
- recalls the characteristics of sermon aims.

Notice the progression in complexity from "recall" of characteristics (last objective) to the actual writing of sermon aims on new subjects. The first objective becomes the "unit objective." The others serve as necessary "lead-up" objectives and guides in developing lesson plans.

In the preceding list of unit objectives, note that they appear in descending order of complexity, from higher level (transfer-application) to knowledge. The first one approximates meaningful activity, but it is not as meaningful as a *course* objective which requires the learner to develop a complete sermon. The designer must make a deliberate decision as to how high a level of learning the student should reach in the unit. The decision is relative, depending upon the nature of the course. The decision to include the lower levels of learning—knowledge and comprehension—implies that the learner has not mastered those levels before. If the designer believes that learners have already achieved those levels (that these are "entering behaviors" brought to the class), then he could omit them and include in the unit description only those objectives which the learners have not already achieved.

For the sake of clarity, study the following models of unit goals and objectives. Notice how the first objective in examples 1 and 4 represent the highest level of learning in the list. The others represent "lead-up" objectives, ending with the simplest. Study also the sample course descriptions in the appendix 1.

1. Unit Title: Using Creative Writing to Teach Children
   Unit Goal: The student demonstrates understanding of the guidelines for using creative writing in teaching children.
   Unit Objectives:
   To demonstrate achievement of this goal the student . . .
   - demonstrates the use of creative writing in a teaching situation.
   - writes choral readings, litanies, songs, stories, and poems for use in teaching children.
   - guides a group of children in a creative writing activity.
   - recognizes good examples of creative writing.
   - defines creative writing.
   - recalls five forms of creative writing.

2. Course Title: Elementary Greek
   Unit Title: Understanding Imperfect Tense Verbs
   Unit Goal:[2] The student demonstrates understanding of the parsing and conjugating of the imperfect tense indicative verb in the active, middle, and passive voice forms.
   Unit objectives: To demonstrate achievement of this goal the student . . .
   - *parses* specified imperfect, indicative verbs.
   - *conjugates* specified imperfect, indicative verbs.
   - *translates* correctly the meaning of specified English and Greek sentences and words.
   - *diagrams* specified Greek sentences.
   - *reads* specified Greek sentences.

3. Unit Title: Using Community Resources in Social Ministry
   Unit Goal:[3] The student demonstrates understanding of the role of community resources in social ministry by . . .

---

2. A related affective goal, usually the same as the affective course goal, might read: "The student demonstrates conviction that believers and unbelievers need to hear the gospel clearly and accurately," or "commitment to accuracy in interpreting the New Testament."

3. A related affective goal, usually the same as the affective course goal, might read: "The student demonstrates conviction that every person has a right to receive help in overcoming life's problems," or "demonstrates commitment to bear one another's burdens."

Unit objectives:
- referring persons to appropriate community agencies.
- analyzing social work cases to determine which community agency should serve as a referral sources.
- analyzing the consequences of failure to refer.
- explaining the special areas of concern of community referral agencies.
- recalling the referral sources available in the community.

State the Unit Educational Objectives: Affective

One approach to using affective goals in a unit of study is to use the same goal as stated for the course itself, with no further delineation of content. For example, in a course in elementary Greek, the goal stated, "The student *values* Greek as a tool for interpreting accurately the New Testament." Though it could be done, it would seem somewhat redundant in a unit of study to say, "The student *values* the parsing and conjugating of the imperfect tense indicative verb in the active, middle, and passive voice forms as tools in interpreting the New Testament."

An exception to this approach would occur when the unit itself is of such magnitude and importance that it requires a separate delineation or breakdown of the affective course goal. This would be especially true in a survey course which deals with several related but essentially separate subjects. For example, a course called "Survey of Education Administration" included such widely diverse units of study as "The Educational Functions of a Church," "Principles of Planning for Organization and Growth," and "Enlisting and Training Volunteer Leaders." Possible affective goals for these units appear below:

Unit Title	*Possible Affective Goals*
The Educational Functions of a Church	The student views the education function of a church as being Bible-based.
Principles of Planning for Organization and Growth	The student values the time conservation which careful planning tends to produce.
Enlisting and Training Volunteer Leaders	The learner demonstrates confidence in the potential of volunteer workers.

The development of attitudes and values seems to require a maturing process. Though some attitudes may change dramatically in a moment because of a traumatic experience, many attitudes require a longer gestation period than a single unit of study provides.

How do designers determine "indicators" of achievement of affective goals? The "projection of time" technique has proven helpful. In this approach, the designer assumes he has taught for achievement of an affective goal. Then, he imagines that at an appropriate time later he observes the learner in his own environment. He follows the learner around, making notes of what he sees him do. For example, assume that a goal reads, "The learner demonstrates honesty in dealing with others." The designer writes in his notes, "The learner told a cashier that she had given him too much change. He paid his bills on or before the due date. After scraping the fender of a parked car, he left a note on the car telling how to contact him." The instruction at that point says "ah-ha!" That student *did indeed* demonstrate honesty in dealing with others. He based his decision on observed indicators of affective change.

The designer would accept these indicators as *representative* ones only. The unit goal and indicators would then read like this:

The learner demonstrates honesty in dealing with others by doing *such things as . . .*
- refusing to accept too much change in a sales transaction.
- paying bills on time.
- informing the owner when he damages property.

However, the learner may *not* do any of these things. He may do something entirely different. At this point evaluation calls for a high tolerance for ambiguity on the part of the teacher. The learner may not respond until *after* he has completed the course! The teacher sows the seeds and extends an invitation to respond.

State the Unit Educational Objectives: Psychomotor

Because of the nature of complex psychomotor skills, their development often requires an entire semester or even years of practice. For this reason, given music skills objectives apply over an entire semester. Students cannot achieve the objectives in a short unit of study. For example, *when* does a student learn to sight read musical scores for the piano? During a unit of study? Over a period of semesters and even years?

Many schools of church music have identified precise objectives for proficiency in piano, voice, conducting, and other areas of music. These statements prove helpful in writing course descriptions.

The statements which follow break music skills objectives down into specific requirements (the statements serve as examples and are not intended to constitute a comprehensive list):

1. *Piano.*—Music schools have specified such objectives as the following for piano students—and sometimes for all students.

The student . . .

- sight reads a four-part open score in choral style.
- plays scales, arpeggios, and cadences of I-IV-I-V-I in all major keys and white-tonic minors and plays cadences in root position and their inversions.
- transposes a single voice part up or down a whole step at sight.
- supplies a choral accompaniment to a melody at sight.
- plays from memory two hymns, one Bach chorale, a homophonic piece, and a polyphonic piece.
- plays a simple anthem accompaniment at sight.
- plays vocal scores using G and F clefs on four staves at sight.
- plays a simple keyboard harmony passage from a figured base.

2. *Voice.*—Objectives required a voice students include the following:

The student . . .

- sings with pitch and rhythmic accuracy.
- uses clear diction in singing.
- sings with acceptable singing quality, a reasonable variety of color tone, dynamic range, and musical sensitivity.
- sings prescribed vocalises to exhibit basic vocal techniques.
- demonstrates correct principles of breathing, phonation, resonance, diction, and coordination.
- performs from memory four vocal compositions in English at an appropriate level of difficulty.
- sings at sight a hymn selected by a jury panel.

3. *Conducting.*—Conducting students often must exhibit both instrumental proficiency and conducting proficiency. Music schools have stated such objectives as these:

The student . . .

- sight reads at the piano a Bach chorale, an anthem accompaniment, and an open score in four staves.
- plays all major and minor scales and arpeggios, root positions, four voice parts, and all major and minor keys.
- transposes at the piano a single voice part.
- plays a hymn at sight while supplying three parts at the keyboard and vocalizing a specified fourth part.
- performs one polyphonic piece.
- coordinates the right hand and arm to conduct the traditional rhythmic meter designs of one through twelve beats per measure.
- gestures to conduct all subdivisions of basic meter designs.
- "melds" smoothly from one beat to another and from nondivided beats to subdivision and the reverse.
- achieves through the conducting gesture a precise release on any pulse or anacrusis of all meter designs.
- achieves through coordinated gesture of the right hand and arm any expressive element within musical thought.
- communicates effective cuing of any part on any pulse of all meter designs.

Psychomotor objectives in the field of church recreation relate primarily to teaching sports and camping skills. Theological institutions do not always teach students in church recreation actually to perform skills. Many students generally enter church recreation training possessing the skills as entering behaviors. They train others. Leaders who work with missions organizations for boys or Boy Scouts and Girl Scouts find it helpful to state psychomotor objectives such as these:

The student . . .

- sets up a two-person tent in six minutes.
- starts a fire using flint and steel.
- shoots five free throws in a row.
- mounts, pedals, brakes, and dismounts both stationary and free-wheeling bicycles.

When a unit description includes specific lead-up objectives or indicators, the instructor has a ready-made basis for preparing lesson plans and developing valid examinations.

16
Describe Methods and Learning Activities

Goals: A study of this unit should help curriculum designers understand . . .
  1. the guidelines for determining and describing methods used in a course.
  2. the formats for describing methods.

Objectives: The curriculum designer . . .
  1. writes "Descriptions of Methods" portion of course descriptions.
  2. summarizes the guidelines for describing methods for instruction.
  3. explains the relationships among goal and objective statements, learning activities, and test.
  4. discriminates between process and nominative (subject) formats in describing methods.
  5. explains what *economics of methodology* means.

The description of methods used in a course usually appear in narrative form in the course description. (See sample course descriptions in appendix 1.) These guidelines should help teachers in developing the description.

1. *Match the methods and activities to the goal-objective statements.*—Stewardship of time does not give teachers the luxury of using just any method which comes to mind. Goals and objectives provide clues to appropriate methods. For example, if an objective says the learner will *analyze* something, appropriate methods include the case study, the research report, the production of flow charts and diagrams, observation reports, excursions, and so forth. Designers could think of this guideline as the "economics of methodology" guideline.

Often teachers can use a given activity to achieve both cognitive and affective responses. The teacher controls the response by the kinds of questions he asks. A given case study consisted of a letter a runaway teenager had written to his parents. He described childhood events and feelings. The teacher used the case to elicit both cognitive and affective responses. He asked these questions: What principles of Christian family living does the case suggest? (cognitive) Which principles of Christian family living are *you* violating in your own home? (affective)

> *Teachers can control the kind of response
> (cognitive-affective) and the level of learning
> by the kinds of questions they ask.*

2. *Use activities which focus on the higher levels of learning.—* The objective implies the level of learning desired. Activities should provide practice at the same level of learning that the objective suggests.

3. *Use learning activities which support the affective goals and objectives.—*Teachers find it easier to design learning activities appropriate for affective outcomes than to measure achievement of the outcome. The key to the use of activities designed for attitudinal change lies in the parable of the sower. The teacher "sows" appropriate activities, but some fall on good ground and some on rocky ground—but he sows!

> *The key to the use of activities and methods designed
> to produce attitudinal change lies in
> the parable of the sower.*

4. *Provide for variety in methods.—*Individual differences in learners call for variety in methods and activities. Not all students learn equally well and with the same speed when listening to a lecture. Some students need to hear it twice. Another may learn better when he reads it.

I once taught a course "Developing a Church Curriculum Plan." I required each student to produce a graphic which depicted the relationships among the elements and subelements of church curriculum design. One third of the grade depended upon the performance on this assignment! Some could do it; some could not. Some had the ability to visualize a concept; some did not. I soon realized that I was violating the principle of individual differences. I changed the assignment so that students could choose from among several mediums of expression which would allow them to express in their own way their perception of the relationships among the elements.

> *Two reflective middle school students conversed on the way home from school. Said one, "I'm learning at my own rate. Whose rate are you learning at?"*

5. *Try to focus on the learner learning rather than the teacher teaching.*—Some find it helpful to use a present participle first when specifying a method in order to focus on the learner. The descriptions of methods might read: The course may involve the student in *analyzing* case histories, *writing* research reports, *writing* proposals, *designing* training programs; *diagnosing* cases, *producing* video tapes, *preaching* sermons, *interviewing* counselees, *guiding* therapy sessions, *observing* teaching sessions, and *designing* floor plans. Focus on interactive instruction.

> *Tell me and I'll forget; show me and I may remember; involve me and I'll understand.—Chinese proverb*

6. *Give attention to the "determiners" of methods and activities.*—The size of the group, the educational level of the pupil, the size of the room, the nature of the subject, the ability of the teacher, the arrangement of the room, and the nature of the goals and objectives all influence the choice of methods and activities.

7. *In listing methods and activities, follow the procedure used in listing the "contents" on a food label.*—List the most used methods first.

You Don't Drive a Nail with a Stick of Butter!

Match the methods and activities to the
goal-objective statement.

Give attention to "determiners" of methods –
like size of the group! – and time available!

8. *Remember to list methods and activities which focus on affective dimensions.*

This inventory of methods should prove helpful in preparing the methods section of the course description. Which of the methods could a teacher use to encourage affective responses? (teaching lecture, set lecture, research report, demonstration, videotape production, role play, drama, case study, observation report, creative writing, production of charts and graphics, panel, excursion, practice teaching, simulation, academic games, computer programs, supervised field work, experimentation, interviews, product development, individual and group projects, problem solving, instructional systems, question and answer, lecture-forum, group discussion, multimedia presentations, laboratory experiences, personal conferences, practicums, seminars, on-the-job training, brainstorming, and so forth).

9. *Base methods and activities on sound principles from educational psychology.*—Lesson planners ask, "Which activities will put into practice a given principle of learning?" The lists of guidelines in appendix 3 summarize some principles for teaching for knowledge, understanding, skills, attitudes and values.[1]

Designers may use various formats in presenting the description of methods:

1. *The process format*—
Course title: Evangelistic Preaching
Methods of Instruction: analyzing sermons of great evangelists, writing evangelistic sermons, practice preaching, producing videotapes, evaluating evangelistic sermons

2. *The subject format*—
Course Title: Teaching for Results
Methods of Instruction: observation, case study, videotape production, practice teaching, production of lesson plans

The target group for the course description consists of students. The process format seems to communicate more readily to that target group.

The following format has been used in many course descriptions:

---

1. For an elaboration of these principles, see *Design for Teaching and Training: a Self-study Guide to Lesson Planning* by LeRoy Ford.

Methods of Instruction:
Methods and activities used during the course grow out of the statement of goals and objectives. The nature of the goals and objectives suggests such activities as these:

> This statement commits the teacher to plan the course so as to help the student achieve precisely what the goals and objectives call for.

preparing sample sermons and sermon briefs, delivering an original sermon, analyzing and evaluating videotaped sermons

> The highest level practice activity parallels the action called for in the course goals and objectives.

(case studies), evaluating sermons presented by peers, preparing sample sermon titles, central truths, aim, outlines, and conclusions; discriminating among properly and improperly stated parts of a sermon; observing in churches and class

> The lower level practice activities serve to develop enabling learnings which equip the learner to perform the higher level requirements.

The chart on page 266 illustrates the relationship among goals and objectives, methods and learning activities, and tests and evaluation instruments. The chart suggests a rule of thumb in selecting methods and activities: The goal-objective statement, the methods and learning activities, and the test should all focus on the *same level of learning*.

Sequence of Goals, Objectives, Learning Activities, and Tests[2]

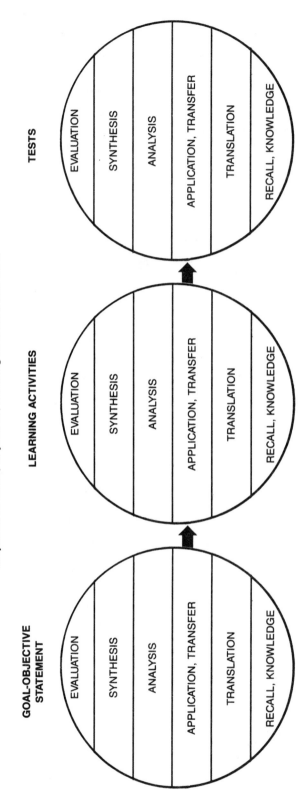

GOAL-OBJECTIVE STATEMENT

LEARNING ACTIVITIES

TESTS

EVALUATION
SYNTHESIS
ANALYSIS
APPLICATION, TRANSFER
TRANSLATION
RECALL, KNOWLEDGE

1. The teacher and/or pupils decide the highest level of learning involved.
2. Assume that they *have* or *have not* achieved the preceding levels.
3. If they *have* already achieved, write the goals and objectives at the highest level involved.
4. If they *have not* already achieved the lower levels, write goal-objective statements on all the lower levels as well as the highest levels involved.
5. Teach and test on all the levels specified in the goal-objective(s).
6. Emphasize in the learning experience the *highest level* involved and allot "grade weight" accordingly.

2. Adapted from Benjamin S. Bloom *Taxonomy of Objectives: Cognitive Domain.*

17
Describe the Testing and Evaluation Approaches

Goals: A study of this chapter should help curriculum designers understand . . .
1. the guidelines for describing evaluation procedures in a course description.
2. the meaning of test, criterion-referenced testing in learning outcomes curriculum.
3. the rationale for using criterion-referenced testing in learning outcomes curriculum.
4. principles for testing in the learning outcomes curriculum.

Objectives: The curriculum designer . . .
1. writes descriptions of testing and evaluation procedures for inclusion in course descriptions.
2. summarizes the principles for testing in the learning outcomes curriculum.
3. defines test, criterion-referenced testing, and norm-referenced testing.
4. explains the rationale for using criterion-referenced testing in the learning outcomes curriculum.

Preparing the Description

Test means any activity which indicates whether and to what degree a learner has achieved a goal. The test reflects the same subject, the same kind of performance, and the level of learning called for in an objective.

> **Test** *means any activity which indicates whether and to what degree a learner has achieved a goal.*

In the learning outcomes approach to curriculum design, teachers use criterion-referenced grading as opposed to norm-referenced grading—the curve. However, norm-referenced grading must have some merit because many institutions use that approach and have not as yet fallen apart.

What should characterize the description of testing and evaluation procedures in a course description?

1. *The description conveys clearly the relationship between the "test" and the course and unit objectives.*—The test description sends the learner back to the course goals and objectives for a description of expectations. In the learning outcomes curriculum, tests and objectives are the two sides of the same coin.

> *In the learning outcomes curriculum, tests and objectives are the two sides of the same coin.*

The absence of a learning outcomes course description keeps students guessing what the course goals and objectives are—until exam time. The missing statements are the "secrets we keep from students!"

2. *The testing description focuses on the highest level of performance called for in the course.*—The *course* objective describes the performance. In a vertical cluster of courses, the highest level in the lower courses in the cluster may not call for performance at the high level of meaningful performance. However, the last course in the sequence will include it.

3. *The description should explain the grade weight assigned to required performance.*—If the "test" calls for the same high-level performance the course objective specifies, then that portion of the semester grade should receive much of the grade weight. For example, if the course objective calls for the learner to compose an original anthem, the original anthem will constitute the primary test. Many teachers would assign two thirds or more of the grade weight to that project. "Lead-up" examinations would then count for the remaining one third of the grade weight.

In a course in preaching, a demonstration sermon as a test would receive much greater grade weight than an objective test which required the learner to do such things as list the steps in sermon preparation or identify a properly stated sermon aim—even though such a test occurred on "final examination" day. The high-level performance in this case (preaching the sermon)

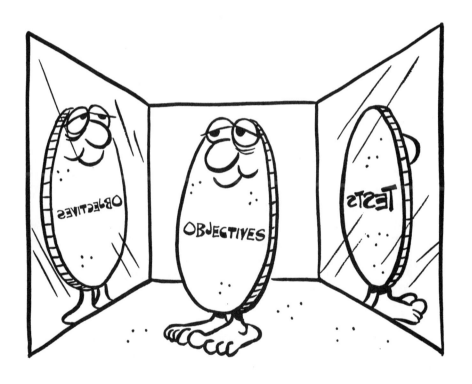

Objectives and tests are two sides of the same coin.

is in fact the "final" examination. Teachers in the learning outcomes approach have to adjust to a new concept of what "final exam" means.

> *In the learning outcomes curriculum, teachers must adjust to a new concept of what "final examination" means.*

> *In the final analysis, personnel committees in the churches write the final examinations for our courses—in the form of job descriptions.*

Learners need lead-up examinations in addition to the high level performance test to provide early and periodic assurance of satisfactory progress. They provide immediate confirmation of their accomplishments.

If an objective states "to prove achievement of this goal the learner conducts a Sunday School teaching session," the learner must conduct a teaching session which the teacher observes and evaluates. A teacher could hardly fit this test into the traditional two-hour final examination period, especially if the class consists of thirty students. Such tests require performance at the synthesis level. Many such tests require days or even weeks for adequate preparation.

> *The traditional exam week may become a relic of the past when the curriculum design focuses on learning at the level of meaningful activity.*

4. *The description informs the learners in an organized way about any evaluation criteria involved in "testing".*—If the teacher uses an "evaluation sheet" for evaluating student performance, he should provide the learner *in advance* a copy of the form. In the Magerian concept of teaching and testing, this information tells the learner not only about the required performance but the *standards* by which the teacher will evaluate the performance.

When course goals and objectives are not clear . . .

. . . students enroll
in a course . . .

. . . and wait for
results.

Then comes the
final exam!

—Cindy

The use of standards of performance benefits the teacher as well as the learner. Standards commit the teacher to keep on teaching until the learner achieves; they commit the learner to reach minimum acceptable performance. This creates a problem in view of the fact that the four-and-a-half month semester imposes an artificial standard (time limit of four-and-a-half months) on achievement. In real life, however, the learning outcomes curriculum plan must accommodate itself to certain "bounds of limitation" which lie beyond its control.

5. *The student should understand clearly on first reading the test and evaluation procedures.*—Ambiguous descriptions have little value. One description detoured to ambiguity street with this statement: "Heavy emphasis will be placed on student participation in class activities and dialogue." The statement in reality says, "In this course you will be graded on your involvement in the group process—not on whether you achieved the goals and objectives of the course." However, if the course goal-objective called for involvement, then such a requirement belongs. However, it would be more appropriate in a course in group dynamics. The artist-teacher assumes personally the responsibility for creating a climate for dialogue.

Another description included this line, "Written examinations will be utilized in connection with selected units." Such "sheet lightning" statements seldom "hit" anything. Another inadequate description indicated, "Criteria for evaluation will be class participation[1] (20 percent), regularity in attendance (10 percent), and demonstrated growth as a professional (20 percent)." None of these reflects clearly the subject related performance called for in the goals and objectives. Any of these descriptions could appear at the end of any course description on any subject.

In course descriptions in the learning outcomes curriculum some teachers correctly inform the learner, "Tests will consist of whatever activity the objectives of the course and its units of study call for. Study carefully the goal and objective statements." However, learners who do not understand design theory may need more precise information.

In a course description on "Principles of Teaching in the

---

1. Assigning a lot of grade weight to class attendance seems to represent a superficial attempt to ensure attendance. Teachers should ask, "Have I designed the course in such a way that it invites absenteeism?"

"An examination based on fuzzy objectives gets fuzzy answers!"

Church," the following description of testing and evaluation procedures appeared.

> Tests will consist of whatever activity the course and its units of study call for. The lesson plans you submit and the demonstration teaching sessions will count for two thirds of the grade weight. You will receive in advance a copy of the evaluation sheet the professor will use in grading your lesson plans and demonstration.
>
> All other tests will count for one third of the grade weight. The test items will consist of discrimination exercises, recall items, rewrite items, and composition items related to the unit objectives. Study carefully the entire course description for details.

In a learning outcomes curriculum the student who asks, "What will our tests be like?" has not carefully studied the course description. Many students expect "trick questions" on examinations and find it difficult to accept the "no tricks" testing approach used in the learning outcomes curriculum.

> *In a learning outcomes curriculum students should not have to ask, "What will the test cover? What will the test be like?" If a student does ask such questions, the teacher should ask, "Have you studied your course description carefully?"*

Considering Implications of the Testing Process

Several observations relative to testing and evaluation in the learning outcomes curriculum should help designers and teachers understand better the concept.

1. *Any teacher who "tests" learners or gives grades already uses to some extent the learning outcomes approach to curriculum design.*—Designers can look at a "test" and reconstruct the learning outcome involved, but the learner may have had to wait until the final examination to discover what the course goals and objectives were.

> *Any teacher who tests learners already uses to some extent the learning outcomes focus in curriculum design.*

2. *The learning outcomes curriculum provides a logical basis for inclusion of a "barrier examination" in degree plans.*—The common learnings identified through research may constitute a basis for a barrier examination. Since the design specifies the meaningful performances, planners can select the most meaningful ones and require the student to pass a battery of performance tests to quality for graduation. In a learning outcomes curriculum, these "tests" normally would consist of a series of demonstrations, projects, or other similar high-level performances.

For example, a school of religious education might include in a barrier examination such performances as these: a videotaped teaching session which reflects a given philosophy of education, conducting a church business meeting according to *Robert's Rules of Order,* analyzing a recorded counseling case study, and so forth.

3. *Testing is only as valid as the teaching and training methodology which precedes the testing.*—The breakdown in the instructional sequence lies not so much in the writing of goals and objectives and the preparation of appropriate testing procedures as in the methodology which bridges the space between them. Many teachers teach as if the teaching objectives and testing procedures had absolutely nothing to do with choice of teaching methods and activities.

> *Many teachers teach as if the teaching objectives and testing procedures have absolutely nothing to do with choice of teaching methods and activities.*

An institution which uses learning outcomes oriented goals and objectives and which uses tests based on the objectives does not necessarily have a learning outcomes focused curriculum. Such a curriculum plan requires not only goals, objectives, and appropriate testing procedures but appropriate methods—an absence of any one of them cripples the design.

> *A learning outcomes curriculum requires objectives, appropriate tests, and appropriate teaching methods—an absence of any of one of them invalidates the design.*

A LEARNING OUTCOMES CURRICULUM
REQUIRES OBJECTIVES, APPROPRIATE
TESTS, AND APPROPRIATE TEACHING
METHODS — THESE THREE.

THE ABSENCE OF APPROPRIATE
METHODS INVALIDATES THE PLAN.

In the learning outcomes approach, designers specify a kind of performance in the objectives; the teacher develops lesson plans which involve the learner in guided practice of that same or analogous performance; and the student takes a test which requires that same performance or an analogous one at the same level of learning specified in the objective.

4. *In the learning outcomes curriculum, tests at the lower performance levels can be made more palatable if teachers help learners see at the beginning how the low-level learning contributes to performance at the higher levels of meaningful activity.*— For "political purposes" teachers should show the learner the promised land!

5. *The multiple choice questions is a workhorse among written test items in much of the learning outcomes curriculum.*—Even though the learning outcomes curriculum focuses on performance in real-life or contrived situations, teachers can test many outcomes in written examinations. They can design the stem of the multiple choice question in such a way that the question tests at the higher levels of learning such as analysis and evaluation in the Bloom taxonomy. For example, at the analysis level a question stem could say, "Based on the following social work case description, which action should the case worker take? The student then chooses one of four possible actions. The answer calls also for evaluation.

> *Properly designed, a multiple choice question can test performance at most of the higher levels of learning.*

Some objectives which require complex synthesis of many factors or which require learners to synthesize their stance regarding a subject can best be tested with essay questions. However, the grader will need to keep in mind certain standards while grading.

6. *Teachers should validate all test items to eliminate misunderstanding.*—A classic "fuzzy" states, "Describe the universe and give two good examples!" The fact that a student's future hangs in the balance makes validation necessary. Validation "tests" the teacher's ability to construct clearly the test items. Validation would prove unusable such item stems as, "The leader of the Reformation in Germany was _____." (a monk, a Roman Catholic, born in

Eisleben.) The stem should provide a clue to the correct family of responses. The item could read, "The *name* of the leader of the Reformation in Germany was _____."

Matching test items should (a) relate to *one* family of responses—dates, persons, places, and so forth; and (b) include in one column *more items* than appear in the other.

7. *The learning outcomes curriculum calls for criterion-referenced testing.*—Norm-referenced grading evidently has worked in many instances, but the learning outcomes curriculum calls for a different approach. Testing measures the student's progress against stated objectives—not against a student's standing in the light of the performance of other students (the curve or norm-referenced grading). Norm-referenced grading tends to impose an artificial template over instructional data. It can easily bear "false witness" to a learner's performance. If an institution insists on norm-referenced grading, perhaps the teachers should submit *both* the letter grade and numerical grade for transcript purposes. Consider the implications of a grade of C-93. It means that the vast majority of the students scored 93 or above on a test, but the *C* says he or she was an "average" student. The *C* may reflect more on the teacher's inability to state meaningful objectives and goals and to evaluate the "entering behavior" of students than it reflects on the ability of the student. The teacher may need to revise the course goals and objectives. Students already knew more than he thought. If only a *C* appears on the transcript, one might say, "he's average," but if one saw *C-93,* one would (a) see the student as better than the concept of "average," (b) ask whether the instructor's grading system was valid, and (c) how long it has been since the teacher revised the course description. A grade of *C-93* or *A-65* says to the teacher, "Revise your course description now!"

A grade of A-69 raises the question, "How did the student do so well when obviously he did not do so well in reaching the course goals and objectives?" An A-69 suggests that the teacher accepted a rather low "minimum acceptable performance." The teacher may have overestimated the student's "entering behavior." The course goals and objectives may need loosening up. The goals and objectives may have been valid, but the instructional methodology may not have supported adequately the objectives. The student obviously failed to reach the course goals and objectives because the highest grade was 69 out of a possible 100. In criterion-referenced instruction, students compete against standards expressed in goals and performance objectives; not against each other. The imposed template of norm-referenced grading (the curve) can make instructional management look good, but it can easily hide deficiencies in a teacher's preparation for the ministry of teaching. Can the student for whom an institution exists become victim of instructional inefficiency?

8. *Grading in the affective domain depends largely upon the teacher's alertness in detecting "approach responses"—voluntary actions—and on his ability to recognize "representatives of responses."*—Such responses may be other than those anticipated.

18
Compile the Mediography

Goal: A study of this chapter should help curriculum designers understand the process for compiling the mediography for a course description.

Objective: The designer compiles a mediography for a given course description.

Some designers prefer to use the term *mediography* over the traditional *bibliography* because it recognizes that information sources come in numerous formats. The mediography should include all sources which have been selected because of their bearing on the course, primarily those which either the instructor or learner will use in completing the course.

The instructor uses discretion in determining the number of items to include; however, it seems that a few or several highly relevant and selective items are more likely to receive attention by the learner than a not-so-selective list.

Since learners generally use the title and the author's name in locating the books in a library, some designers list only the title and author in the mediography.

In a course "Understanding Group Dynamics," one course designer included this mediography:

Books:
Effective Small Group Communication, Bormann and Bormann
Group Development, Bradford, ed.
Group Dynamics, Cartwright and Sander
Growth Groups, Clinebell
People to People Therapy, Drakeford
Small Groups and Self Renewal, Kemp
Introduction to Group Dynamics, Knowles and Knowles
Carl Rogers on Encounter Groups, Rogers

Theory and Practice of Group Psychotherapy, Yalom

Films and Videotapes:
Computer Programs:
Periodicals:

Institutional policy may require following established forms. Institutions whose course descriptions occupy hundreds of pages in a syllabus of descriptions may opt to use the shorter form to conserve space.

19

Select an Appropriate Form for the Course Description

Goal: A study of this chapter should help the designer understand the structure of the various forms a course description in a learning outcomes curriculum plan may take.

Objectives: The designer . . .

1. writes a course description in a selected form.
2. defines long form, short form, miniform, and elaborated form of course descriptions.

Course descriptions may take any of several forms, depending upon the circumstances. The short form deals only with course and unit goals and objectives. The long form treats goals and objectives more fully and includes "lead-up" objectives in the units of study. The elaborated form includes elements of the long form but adds lesson plans based upon the lead-up objectives in the units of study. The miniform includes only the title and a list of meaningful performance objectives.

1. *The short form.*—The short form of course descriptions includes only the statement of the course goals and objectives, unit goal, and high-level performance objective. It omits the lead-up objectives in the units of study. It assumes that the instructor will furnish the lead-up objectives later. The short form has several advantages. (a) Students are not discouraged by excessive length of the description. Students may tend to experience some frustration if they receive very long course descriptions for each of six or seven different courses. (b) In a large educational institution a course syllabus containing dozens, even hundreds of long course descriptions may require a publication of three or four hundred pages. The printing and distribution costs may prohibit publication.

The short form has some disadvantages. (a) Instructors generally must supply supplementary descriptive material when introducing a unit of study. (b) Some instructors may neglect the detailed subject analysis required when specifying lead-up objectives.

A sample of a short form for a course description follows:

Course Title: Developing Teaching and Training Systems[1] (This course was designed to assist foreign missionaries in developing self-study materials for theological education by extension [TEE].)

I. Course Goal and Objectives

The student demonstrates understanding of the process of designing instructional systems for theological education in missions.

To demonstrate achievement of this goal the student:

- designs and validates an instructional system on an approved subject.
- demonstrates conviction that students should have access to leadership training regardless of the settings in which they live.

II. Unit Goals and Objectives

Unit 1: "Writing Goals and Objectives"

The student demonstrates understanding of the process of writing goals and objectives.

To demonstrate achievement of this goal, the student:

- writes goals and objectives which reflect appropriate levels of learning, based on approved resources.

Unit 2: "Analyzing a Subject"

The student demonstrates understanding of the process of analyzing a subject for an instructional system.

To demonstrate achievement of this goal, the student:

- develops a subject analysis for an approved subject, using declarative sentences.

Unit 3: "Designing Practice Cycles"

The student demonstrates understanding of the

---

1. The author used this design in numerous mission workshops, *preceded* always by a study of curriculum theory and design for theological education.

process of designing practice cycles for an instructional system.

To demonstrate achievement of this goal, the student:

- designs practice cycles for each item in a subject analysis.

Unit 4: "Constructing Tests for Instructional Systems"

The student demonstrates understanding of the principles and processes of designing tests for instructional systems.

To demonstrate achievement of this goal, the student:

- constructs multiple forms pretests and posttests for an instructional system.

Unit 5: "Validating an Instructional System"

The student understands the process of validating instructional systems.

To demonstrate achievement of this goal, the student:

- validates with the appropriate target group an instructional system of his own design.

Note: Unit descriptions may be further shortened by expressing the goal and objective in one statement. For example:

Unit 3: "Designing Practice Cycles"

To demonstrate understanding of the process of designing practice cycles, the student designs practice cycles for each item in a subject analysis.

2. *The miniform.*—The miniform includes only the course title and major course and unit objectives. An example follows:

Course title: Basic Sermon Preparation
The student . . . .

- prepares and delivers a sermon.
- selects a Bible truth to preach.
- interprets the text.
- writes a thesis or central truth.
- writes general and specific objectives.
- gathers appropriate materials and illustrations.
- prepares the parts of the sermon, including the introduction, body, and conclusion.

3. *The long form.*—The long form of course descriptions includes all parts of the short form but includes these additions: lead-up objectives for the units of study, description of methods of instruction, mediography, and description of testing and evaluation procedures. The addition of unit lead-up objectives is the major factor in making the course description longer.

The long form has some advantages. (a) The lead-up objectives for the units provide "stuff" from which the teachers design lesson plans; (b) the lead-up objectives provide the foundation for developing unit test items; and (c) the lead-up objectives call for the designer to do exhaustive analysis of the subject.

The long form has some disadvantages. (a) If the course description becomes too detailed, the student may "drown" in it; (b) if a school publishes a large number of long form course descriptions in a syllabus, the publication may be too large and costly to be feasible.

A sample of a long form course descriptions follows. For purposes of comparison the description deals with the same subject as the sample of the short form. Notice that in the list of lead-up objectives in the unit descriptions, the objective representing the highest level of learning dealt with in the unit appears first. This is the only objective which is expressed when using the short form for course descriptions. The unit lead-up objectives then reflect progressively the lower levels of learning. The list begins with the highest level treated and ends with the lowest level of learning dealt with. Assumptions about what the learner *already* knows and understands determines how low the designer will go in specifying objectives.

Course Title: Developing Teaching and Training Systems (This course was designed to assist foreign missionaries in developing self-study materials for theological education by extension [TEE].)

I. Rationale for the Course

This course focuses on the following student outcomes as expressed in the goals and objectives of the School of Religious Education:

- Develops and administers curriculum plans.
- Models the role of an effective teacher.
- Develops and supervises leadership training programs.

II. Course Goal and Objectives

The student demonstrates understanding of the process of designing instructional systems.

To demonstrate achievement of this goal, the student:

- designs and validates an instructional system on an approved subject.
- demonstrates conviction that students should have access to leadership training regardless of the contextual setting in which they live.

III. Unit Goals and Objectives

Unit 1: "Writing Goals and Objectives"

To demonstrate understanding of the process of writing goals and objectives, the student:

- writes goals in the cognitive, affective, and psychomotor domains.
- writes cognitive objectives which reflect appropriate levels of learning.
- writes affective objectives (indicators) for affective goals.
- writes psychomotor objectives which reflect appropriate levels of learning.
- restructures improperly stated goals and objectives.
- identifies the level of learning represented by given objectives.
- discriminates between goals and objectives.
- defines the levels of learning in the cognitive domain.
- defines the terms *goal* and *objective*.

Unit 2: "Analyzing a Subject"

The student demonstrates understanding of the process of analyzing a subject as he:

- writes a subject analysis using declarative sentences.
- organizes analysis items in a meaningful order.
- selects critical items in a subject analysis.
- identifies the significant components of a subject.
- reconstructs the sentence-point outline used as a basis for given instructional systems.

Unit 3: "Designing Practice Cycles"

The student demonstrates understanding of the process of designing practice cycles for an instructional system.

To demonstrate achievement of this goal, the student:

- designs practice cycles for each item in a subject analysis.
- designs feedback components for practice cycles.
- designs practice components which provide appropriate practice responses.
- designs input components based on items in a subject analysis.
- identifies components in given practice cycles.
- defines practice cycle.

Unit 4: "Constructing Tests for Instructional Systems"

To demonstrate understanding of the principles of test item construction for instructional systems, the student:

- constructs multiple forms pretests and posttests.
- constructs discrimination test items which reflect specific levels of learning (multiple choice, matching, and so forth).
- designs constructed-response test items which reflect appropriate levels of learning.
- designs motor response test items.
- reconstructs test items which do not relate properly to objectives.
- identifies test items which do not reflect proper level of learning, subject, and form.

Unit 5: "Validating an Instructional System"

The student demonstrates understanding of the validation cycle (test, evaluate, revise) used in the validation process as he:

- validates with the representative target group an instructional system of his own design.
- revises practice cycles based on analysis of pretest and posttest results.

- evaluates given instructional systems.
- explains the validation process.

IV. Mediography

Books:

Stating Behavioral Objectives for Classroom Instruction, Gronlund

Goal Analysis, Mager

Taxonomy of Objectives: Cognitive Domain, Bloom

Taxonomy of Objectives: Affective Domain, Krathwohl

Instructional Systems:

Assuring Learning with Self-Instructional Packages, Johnson and Johnson

Design for Teaching and Training, Ford

Designing Effective Instruction (a multimedia system), Cramm

Videotapes:

V. Methods of Instruction

Methods and learning activities grow out of the statements of goals and objectives. These include preparation of an original instructional system, case analysis, project method, film forum, small group discussion, lecture demonstration, and practice exercises.

VI. Testing and Evaluation

Tests consist of whatever activities the objectives call for. The course goal-objective describes the highest level of learning required in the course. It requires production of a new product—an instructional system. Because of the significance of this project, it will serve as the basis for two thirds of the course grade. The remaining one third of the grade will derive from "test your progress" exams based on the activities described in the lead-up objectives in each unit. In advance you will be furnished with an "Instructional System Evaluation Sheet" which the instructor will use in evaluating your instructional system.

4. *The elaborated form.*—The elaborated form of course descriptions includes not only the course description itself but the lesson plans for each unit, based on the goals and objectives for

the units described in the long form. It is based on the assumption that the complete list of goals and objectives for a unit constitute the "stuff" out of which teachers make lesson plans. Experience has shown that an adequate lesson plan includes (a) the unit title, (b) a statement of the unit goals and objectives, (c) a description of one or more learning readiness activities, (d) a selection of descriptions of learning activities and aids based on objectives in the unit description, and (e) a sample of test items appropriate for the unit.

The elaborated form would constitute a rather large volume. It is rather like a collection of resource units which the instructor uses as an instructional guide. A given unit may require several lesson plans, depending upon the number of lead-up objectives in the unit description.

20
Master the Techniques of Generalization

Goals:	A study of this chapter should help curriculum designers understand the role of generalization in stating educational goals and objectives in curriculum design.
Objectives:	The designer . . .
	1. writes educational goals and objectives at given levels of generalization.
	2. defines *progressive generalization*.

The concept of "progressive generalization" constitutes the framework within which designers develop statements of learning intent. The highest level of generalization occurs at the highest level of the hierarchy of statements—the institutional charter and institutional purpose. The lowest level of generalization occurs at the lesson plan level.

What does *generalization* mean? To *generalize*, means to derive or to induce a general concept or principle from particulars. In that sense, generalization in statements of learning intent progress upward from the very specific found in lesson plan goals and objectives.

Notice the progressive generalization in the chart on the next page. If each item in the chart were a course in a curriculum, the school with very limited resources would offer a survey course in "Modes of Transportation;" the school with adequate—but not unlimited—resources would offer courses in "Steam-Driven Vehicles," "Solid-Fuel Vehicles," "Animal-Powered Vehicles," "Gasoline-Powered Vehicles," and "Electricity-Powered Vehicles." The school with unlimited resources in money, endowment, personnel, and facilities could offer courses on "One-Horse Open Sleighs" and "Surreys with the Fringe on the Top!"

The chart on page 292 shows progressive generalization flowing in the opposite direction.

The chart on page 293 shows progressive generalization at work in a curriculum setting. Actually, additional higher-level

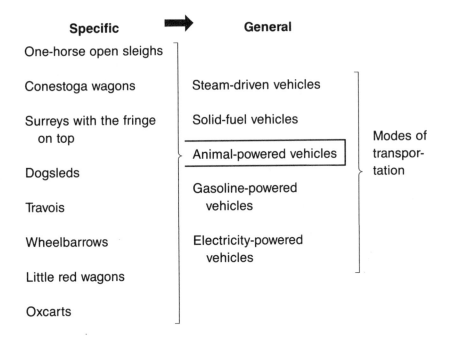

generalizations could appear "off the chart" to the left. For example, the institutional purpose, though not specifying the statement, would have resident in it the program objective "models the role of an effective teacher."

Another way of summarizing the progressive generalization flowing through a curriculum design would appear much like this:

The institutional purpose encompasses
　All program purposes, goals, and objectives.
　　The program purposes, goals, and objectives encompass
　　　All department purposes, goals, and objectives.
　　　The department purposes, goals and objectives encompass
　　　　All course goals and objectives.
　　　　The course goals and objectives encompass
　　　　　All unit goals and objectives.
　　　　　The unit goals and objectives encompass
　　　　　　All lesson plans goals and objectives.

Apples ⟶	Red delicious apples
Pears	Yellow delicious apples
Bananas	McIntosh apples
FRUIT	
Apricots	Canned apples
Peaches	Dried apples
Raspberries	Johnnies

Using the principle of generalization, designers express learning intent at any given level in such a way as to (a) encompass everything below and (b) provide residence for everything above.

Progressive generalization should be evident in (a) titles of courses and units; (b) names of departments, divisions, and programs; and (c) statements of learning intent called purposes, goals, and objectives.

Just as there is progressive generalization in the hierarchy of purposes, goals, and objectives for an institution, there is progressive generalization in titles and goal-objective statements for courses.

The degree of generalization depends upon the degree of specialization to which the institution is committed by its purpose.

Progressive Generalization

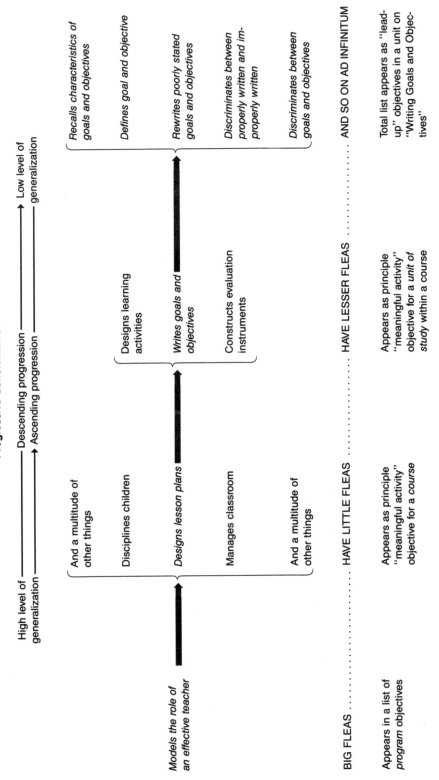

High level of generalization ← Descending progression →

Ascending progression → Low level of generalization

Models the role of an effective teacher

And a multitude of other things

Disciplines children

Designs lesson plans

Manages classroom

And a multitude of other things

Designs learning activities

Writes goals and objectives

Constructs evaluation instruments

Recalls characteristics of goals and objectives

Defines goal and objective

Rewrites poorly stated goals and objectives

Discriminates between properly written and improperly written

Discriminates between goals and objectives

AND SO ON AD INFINITUM

BIG FLEAS .... HAVE LITTLE FLEAS .... HAVE LESSER FLEAS ....

Appears in a list of *program* objectives

Appears as principle "meaningful activity" objective for a *course*

Appears as principle "meaningful activity" objective for a *unit of study* within a course

Total list appears as "lead-up" objectives in a unit on "Writing Goals and Objectives"

Glossary

Administrative model—An administrative model is a plan for bringing together a curriculum design and a target group in such a way as to achieve the purpose and objectives of the design and to implement an instructional model.

Competency—A competency is a performance deemed essential to effective handling of a task. In this manual competency represents performance at the level of meaningful activity and is usually referred to as a learning outcome.

Conceptual family—A conceptual family refers to a set of learning goals and objectives or subject items in a scope description which relate in a significant way to a given concept.

Context—Context is an element of curriculum design which describes where curriculum occurs. Context refers to the various influences which converge to help shape and form a curriculum plan. The convergence of the educational, cultural, political, geographical, familial, economic, and religious contexts influence in a significant way the elaboration of the other elements of curriculum design, especially the instructional and administrative models.

Correspondence School—A correspondence school is an approach to theological education in which students through interactive instruction participate in planned courses of study mediated by way of the postal service or some other such service. The phrase *distance learning* which implies participation by students who because of distances cannot otherwise take part is in vogue today.

Course description—A course description is a document which describes in varying degrees of specificity the learning goals and objectives for a given course. It may also include a description of methods of instruction, explanation of testing and evaluation procedures, and a mediography.

Criterion-referenced grading and testing—Criterion-referenced grading is an approach to grading in which students receive grades based on the degree to which they have achieved goals and objectives.

Curriculum—Curriculum means the sum of all learning experiences resulting from a curriculum plan and directed toward achieving educational goals and objectives. Curriculum means what happens to persons as they become involved in an institution's curriculum plan.

Curriculum design—A curriculum design is a statement and elaboration of the institutional purpose, educational goals and objectives for learners, scope, contexts, methodology, and instructional and administrative models considered by an institution in developing its approach to doing its work.

Curriculum plan—A curriculum plan is a more or less detailed blueprint for implementing a curriculum design. Ultimately, a curriculum plan resides in course descriptions, lesson plans, and study materials. The difference between a curriculum design and a curriculum plan is the difference between a curriculum planned and a curriculum "had."

Department—A department is a division of a program or a division in the departmentation scheme of an institution. Designers refer to departments as "departments of instruction."

Departmentation scheme—A departmentation scheme is a plan an institution implements in order to divide into progressively smaller parts its responsibility for achieving the institutional purpose.

Extension center—An extension center is a local training center in an administrative model which provides multiple locations for instruction on a more or less regular basis under guidance of teachers.

Field experience—Field experience is an approach to learning in which the learner, under guidance, engages in on-the-job training at the church or in the position where he serves.

Foundation discipline—A foundation discipline is a great field of thought from which designers may derive assistance in curriculum planning.

Generalization—Generalization is word or phrase used to infer from particulars and is an umbrella term or phrase in which reside many particulars. For example, resident in the phrase *institutional purpose* are all the purposes subsumed under it such as program, division, and department purposes.

Goal—In the field of education, a goal is a broad statement of learning intent which identifies the domain of learning and states the subject in a chewable bite.

Indicator—An indicator is a term which means the same as objective. It states what the learner will *do* to prove or "indicate" achievement of a goal. The term *indicator* reflects more accurately the *function* of an objective.

Instructional model—An instructional model is an approach to instruction which implements given theories or combinations of theories of learning. The teaching lecture and instructional system represent instructional models.

Norm-referenced grading—Norm-referenced grading is an approach to grading in which students receive grades based upon their standing in relation to performance of other students.

Objective—In education, an objective is a statement of learning intent which expresses what learners should be able to do well as a result of a program's fulfillment of its purpose and goals.

Process description—A process description is a catalog description which repeats verbatim the course goal and objective.

Program—A program is a primary division of responsibility in an institution. Institutions form programs when they group together into conceptual families similar goals and objectives and give each grouping a name.

Purpose—A purpose is a statement of the primary reason for being for an institution, a program, or a department in theological education. It tells who, does what, and for whom.

Rationale—The part of a course description which legitimizes a course from the viewpoint of the institution's educational goals and objectives for learners. It specifies the institutional goals and objectives which a particular course supports.

Scope—Scope is an element of curriculum design which identifies the subject areas which designers legitimately may include in the curriculum plan. Designers derive scope by analyzing the Bible, experience, and human relationships to oneself and others, God, history, and nature.

Seminar—A seminar is an instructional model which consists of group meetings during which learners share in a more or less structured way insights they have gained through study and research.

Subject description—A subject description is a catalog description which identifies the boundaries of the subject to be dealt with in a course.

Test—A test is any activity which measures the degree to which a learner has achieved learning goals and objectives.

Theological education by extension—In general, theological education by extension is an approach to theological education which implements a variety of administrative and instructional models consistent with the principle of taking the training to the learner as opposed to bringing the learner to a central institution. Thus theological education by extension can accommodate many instructional models. When learners must of necessity learn on their own generally apart from the group process, institutions often use self-instruction approaches such as the instructional system as the instructional model.

Appendix 1
Sample Course Descriptions
in Theological Education

Course Title: Building a Church Curriculum Plan[1]

I. Rationale for the Course:

This course supports the following goals and objectives as expressed in the statements of educational goals and objectives for learners in the School of Religious Education.

The student . . .

- understands the process of building a church curriculum plan.

---

1. This course description was developed by LeRoy Ford, professor emeritus of Foundations of Education, Southwestern Baptist Theological Seminary. This model places the "meaningful activity" at the *end* of the unit descriptions.

- demonstrates conviction that each church is accountable and responsible for what is taught in its education program.

To demonstrate achievement of these goals the student designs a church curriculum plan to meet the needs of his own church.

II. Course Goal and Objective:

The student demonstrates understanding of the process of developing a church curriculum plan.

To demonstrate achievement of this goal the student designs a valid church curriculum plan in keeping with particular goals and needs of a given church. In order to accomplish this, the student achieves the goals and objectives indicated in the units of study.

III. Unit Goals and Objectives:

Unit 1: "Elements of Curriculum Design"

The student demonstrates understanding of the elements of curriculum design.

To demonstrate achievement of this goal the student:

- names and defines the elements of curriculum design according to Colson and Rigdon.
- analyzes the relationships among the elements of design and among certain terms such as curriculum and curriculum plan.
- identifies in given lesson course periodicals evidences of the expression of the elements of curriculum design.
- explains the similarities between the elements of curriculum design according to Colson and Rigdon, and the concepts of Ralph Tyler in *Basic Principles of Curriculum and Instruction.*

Unit 2: "Approaches to Curriculum"

The student understands possible approaches to curriculum.

To demonstrate achievement of this goal the student:

- explains the various approaches to curriculum according to Hyman.
- interprets or predicts the effect various curriculum approaches would have on curriculum materials if each was adopted as a curriculum focus.

Unit 3: "Interpreting Denominational Curriculum Series"

The student demonstrates understanding of denominational curriculum materials by interpreting to others the distinctive characteristics of the denominational curriculum series and the periodicals within the series.

To demonstrate achievement of this goal the student:

- names and describes the curriculum series used in his own denomination.
- identifies the curriculum series involved when given a statement which describes the stance of a particular series in regard to selection and development of content, use of Scriptures, educational approach, art design, and vice versa.
- indicates the curriculum series and age group when given the names of particular curriculum periodicals.
- evaluates given age-group periodicals in the light of criteria included by Colson in *Tests of an Adequate Curriculum*.

Unit 4: "Practice in Building a Church Curriculum Plan"

The student demonstrates understanding of the process of building a church curriculum plan.

To demonstrate achievement of this goal the student:

- writes specific church goals.
- recognizes properly stated church goals.
- lists and explains the steps involved in leading a church to develop a curriculum plan to meet its own particular need.
- selects appropriate units of study for use in helping a church reach specific goals.
- develops a church curriculum plan for a given church.

IV. Methods of Instruction:

This course involves primarily the use of the project method. All methods are consistent with the performances called for in the goals and objectives. Methods include writing and analyzing case studies, developing an original curriculum plan project, and, in a few cases, preparing descrimination and recall exercises. A great deal of curriculum plan evaluation will occur in small groups.

V. Tests and Evaluation:

Since the primary goal and objective for the course call for the development of an original curriculum plan for a church, that project will account for two thirds of the grade. You will receive in advance a copy of the "Curriculum Plan Evaluation Sheet" which the professor will use in evaluating your project. Other examinations based on the unit objectives will account for one third of the semester grade. Your project is considered the "final examination."

VI. Mediography:

Books:

Beauchamp. *Curriculum Theory*. 2d ed. 1964.

Colson and Rigdon. *Understanding Your Church's Curriculum*. rev. 1985.

Hyman. *Approaches in Curriculum*. 1973.

Tyler. *Basic Principles of Curriculum and Instruction*. 1949.

Wyckoff. *Theory and Design of Christian Education Curriculum*. 1961.

Videotapes:
Colson. *Tests of Adequate Church Curriculum*. 1970
Wyckoff. *Curriculum Design*. 1976

Periodicals:
Denominational lesson course periodicals

Course title: Elementary Greek[2]

I. Rationale for the Course:

This course focuses on the following learning outcomes as expressed in the educational goals and objectives of the School of Theology:

- understands New Testament Greek.
- views accurate translation of the New Testament as a requirement for effective communication of the gospel.
- translates into English the New Testament in its original languages.
- demonstrates confidence in ability to learn Greek.

II. Course Goals and Objectives:

The student demonstrates understanding of the designated forms (accidence) and basic grammatical uses (syntax) of Koine Greek.

The student values accurate translation of the New Testament as a requirement for effective communication of the gospel.

The student views New Testament Greek as a learnable language.

To demonstrate achievement of this goal, the student translates the correct meaning of selected passages of Scripture.

The student values accurate translation of the New Testament as a requirement for effective communication of the gospel.

---

2. This course description was developed by Lorin Cranford, associate professor of New Testament, Southwestern Baptist Theological Seminary.

III. Unit (Lesson) Goals and Objectives:
   Lesson 1: "Getting Underway"

The student demonstrates understanding of the Greek alphabet, essential concepts of pronunciation and punctuation, and description of basic grammar.

To demonstrate achievement of this goal, the student:
- *writes* the Greek alphabet (capital and small letters).
- *identifies* the various types of vowels, consonants, and diphthongs of the Greek alphabet.
- *identifies* the breathing, accent, and diacritical marks.
- *identifies* the punctuation marks.
- *defines* the basic parts of speech and additional grammatical terms.
- *classifies* sentences according to their form and function.
- *diagrams* an English sentence according to the specified pattern.
- *transliterates* Greek words into the equivalent English spelling.
- *reads* with correct pronunciation Greek sentences.
   Supplementary Lesson One: "John 1:11-14"

The student demonstrates understanding of the parsing, translating, and diagramming of the forms studied thus far.

To demonstrate achievement of this goal, the student:
- *parses* specified words in John 1:11-14.
- *translates* the correct meaning of John 1:11-14.
- *diagrams* specified sentences in John 1:11-14.
- *reads* the sentences in John 1:11-14.
- *classifies* specified dependent clauses in John 1:11-14.
   Supplementary Lesson Two: "John 1:15-18"

The student demonstrates understanding of the parsing, translating, and diagramming of the forms studied thus far.

To demonstrate achievement of this goal, the student:
- *parses* specified words in John 1:15-18.
- *translates* the correct meaning of John 1:15-18.
- *diagrams* specified sentences in John 1:15-18.
- *reads* the sentences in John 1:15-18.
- *classifies* specified dependent clauses in John 1:15-18.
   Lesson 2: "Getting Acquainted with the Verb"

The student demonstrates understanding of the parsing and declining of present, active, indicative verbs and εἰμί and of the guidelines for accenting verbs.

To demonstrate achievement of this goal, the student:

- *Parses* specified present, active, indicative verb stems, and the εἰμί verb.
- *Conjugates* specified present, active, indicative verb stems and the εἰμί verb.
- *Defines* the categories of the parsing model for verbs.
- *Accents* specified verbs according to the rules of accents.
- *Translates* the correct meaning of specified Greek and English verbs.
  Lesson 3: "Getting Acquainted with the Noun and the Article"

The student demonstrates understanding of the parsing and declining of first declension nouns, guidelines for accenting nouns, and declension of the article.

To demonstrate achievement of this goal, the student:

- *defines* the categories of the parsing model for nouns.
- *parses* any of the five patterns of first declension nouns.
- *declines* any of the five patterns of first declension nouns.
- *accents* specified nouns according to the rules of accents.
- *declines* the article in the masculine and feminine genders.
- *translates* the correct meaning of specified Greek or English words and sentences.
- *diagrams* specified Greek sentences.
- *classifies* specified Greek sentences.
- *reads* specified Greek sentences.
  Lesson 4: "Understanding Second Declension Nouns"

The student demonstrates understanding of the parsing, declining, and accenting of second declension nouns and the use of negatives, conjunctions, and proper/geographical names.

To demonstrate achievement of this goal, the student:

- *parses* either pattern of second declension nouns.
- *declines* either pattern of second declension nouns.
- *accents* second declension nouns according to the rules of accents.
- *translates* the correct meaning of specified Greek or English words and sentences.
- *diagrams* specified Greek sentences.
- *reads* specified Greek sentences.
- *parses* proper/geographical names.
  Lesson 5: "Understanding Adjectives and Adverbs"

The student demonstrates understanding of the parsing, declining, accenting and use of adjectives and the translation of adverbs.

To demonstrate achievement of this goal, the student:
- *parses* any of the gender forms of adjectives.
- *declines* any of the gender forms of adjectives.
- *accents* adjectives according to the rules of accents.
- *translates* the correct meaning of specified Greek or English adjectives, adverbs, and sentences.
- *diagrams* specified Greek sentences.
- *reads* specified Greek sentences.
- *parses* specified Greek nouns and verbs.
- *declines* specified Greek nouns.
- *conjugates* specified Greek verbs.

Lesson 6: "Understanding Prepositions"

The student demonstrates understanding of the form, translation, and use of prepositions.

To demonstrate achievement of this goal, the student:
- *translates* the meaning of specified prepositions in each of their case uses.
- *translates* specified sentences containing prepositional phrases.
- *diagrams* specified Greek sentences containing prepositional phrases.

Lesson 7: "Understanding the Present, Middle, or Passive Voice Verb"

The student demonstrates understanding of the parsing and declining of the present tense middle and passive voice verbs and of deponent verbs, and the form and function of dependent clauses.

To demonstrate achievement of this goal, the student:
- *parses* specified present, middle, or passive indicative verbs.
- *conjugates* specified present, middle, or passive indicative verbs.
- *parses* specified present, deponent, indicative verbs.
- *translates* the correct meaning of specified English and Greek sentences and words.
- *diagrams* specified Greek sentences.
- *reads* specified Greek sentences.
- *classifies* the form and function of specified Greek sentences.
- *classifies* the form and function of specified Greek dependent clauses.

Lesson 8: "Understanding Pronouns (Part 1)"

The student demonstrates understanding of the parsing; de-

clining, and use of personal, intensive, demonstrative, recipro-
cal, and reflexive pronouns.

To demonstrate achievement of this goal, the student:

• *parses* specified pronouns.
• *declines* specified pronouns.
• *translates* the correct meaning of specified English and
Greek sentences and words.
• *reads* specified Greek sentences.

Lesson 9: "Understanding Imperfect Tense Verbs"

The student demonstrates understanding of the parsing and
conjugating of the imperfect tense indicative verb in the active,
middle, and passive voice forms.

To demonstrate achievement of this goal, the student:

• *parses* specified imperfect, indicative verbs.
• *conjugates* specified imperfect, indicative verbs.
• *translates* the correct meaning of specified English and
Greek sentences and words.
• *diagrams* specified Greek sentences.
• *reads* specified Greek sentences.

Lesson 10: "Understanding First Aorist Tense Verbs"

The student demonstrates understanding of the parsing and
conjugating of the aorist tense indicative verb in the active, middle, and passive voice forms.

To demonstrate achievement of the goal, the student:

• *parses* specified first aorist verbs.
• *conjugates* specified first aorist verbs.
• *translates* the correct meaning of specified English and
Greek sentences and words.
• *diagrams* specified Greek sentences.
• *reads* specified Greek sentences.
• *parses* specified Greek nouns, pronouns, and adjectives.
• *declines* specified Greek nouns, pronouns, and adjectives.

Lesson 11: "Understanding Second Aorist Tense Verbs"

The student demonstrates understanding of the parsing and
conjugating of the second aorist tense indicative verb in the active, middle, and passive voice forms.

To demonstrate achievement of this goal, the student:

• *parses* specified second aorist verbs.
• *conjugates* specified second aorist verbs.
• *translates* the correct meaning of specified English and
Greek sentences and words.
• *reads* specified Greek sentences.

Lesson 12: "Understanding the Infinitive"

The student demonstrates understanding of the parsing and the use of the infinitive.

To demonstrate achievement of this goal, the student:

- *parses* specified infinitives.
- *translates* the correct meaning of specified English and Greek sentences and words.
- *diagrams* specified Greek sentences.
- *reads* specified Greek sentences.

Lesson 13: "Understanding Future Tense"

The student demonstrates understanding of the parsing and conjugating of the future tense indicative verb in the active, middle, and passive voice forms.

To demonstrate achievement of this goal, the student:

- *parses* specified future indicative verbs.
- *conjugates* specified future indicative verbs.
- *translates* the correct meaning of specified English and Greek sentences and words.
- *diagrams* specified Greek sentences.
- *reads* specified Greek sentences.

Lesson 14: "Understanding Contract Verbs and Relative Pronouns"

The student demonstrates understanding of the parsing and conjugating of the contract verbs and the parsing, declining, and use of the definite relative pronoun.

To demonstrate achievement of this goal, the student:

- *parses* specified contract verbs.
- *conjugates* specified contract verbs.
- *parses* specified relative pronouns.
- *declines* specified relative pronouns.
- *translates* the correct meaning of specified English and Greek sentences and words.
- *diagrams* specified Greek sentences.
- *reads* specified Greek sentences.
- *classifies* specified Greek dependent clauses.

IV. Methods of Instruction:

Methods and learning activities grow out of the statements of goals and objectives for the course. Those used in this course include completion of all exercises in *Workbook for Elementary Greek,* a paper which analyzes the chosen word in each of the designated sources, practice drills on parsing, and oral reading of assigned passages.

V. Tests and Evaluation:

Tests will consist of whatever activities the objectives call for. Study carefully the course and lesson goals and objectives for descriptions of what you may expect on examinations. Three major exams shall be given during the semester. On each exam you will translate given passages, parse specified forms, classify given sentences by form and function(s), classify subordinate clauses by form and function(s), and diagram given sentences. No pop tests will be given. The three major exams will constitute _____ percent of the grade; the term paper will count for _____ percent of the grade; and completion of the workbook will count for 20 percent of the grade.

VI. Mediography:

> *An Introduction to New Testament Greek,* Drumwright
> *The Greek New Testament,* edited by Kurt Aland, et. al.
> *Workbook for Elementary Greek,* vol. 1, Cranford
> *A Reader's Greek-English Lexicon of the New Testament,* Sakae Kubo

Course Title: Basic Musicianship[3]

I. Rationale for the Course:

This course focuses on the following learning outcomes as expressed in the educational goals and objectives of the School of Church Music.

The student . . .

- understands music theory.
- understands the principles of music notation.
- demonstrates skills in sight singing, discriminatory listening, and dictation.
- views music as a means of helping persons reach their highest aspirations in worship.

II. Course Goal and Objective:

The student demonstrates skills in the basic areas of musicianship: sight singing, discriminatory listening, and dictation. To demonstrate achievement of this goal, the student:

- sings melodies at sight with the correct pitch, intonation, and rhythm using the movable do system.
- identifies intervals, rhythms, melodies, or chords heard.

---

3. This course description was developed by Janis Watkins, instructor in Music Theory, Southwestern Baptist Theological Seminary.

- uses standard musical notation to transcribe intervals, rhythms, melodies, or chords that are played.

III. Unit Goals and Objectives:

Unit 1: "Sight Singing"

The student demonstrates skill in singing melodies in modes and in major and minor keys, using movable do.

To demonstrate achievement of this goal, the student achieves such objectives as these:

- *sings* diatonic melodies in simple or compound time, using movable do.
- *sings* melodies with chromatic tones not implying modulation, using movable do.
- *sings* modal melodies.
- *sings* a given line in a multivoiced score, using movable do, with other students singing other parts.

Unit 2: "Chords"

The student demonstrates skill in identifying and writing chords by dictation.

To demonstrate achievement of this goal, the student achieves such objectives as these:

- *writes* figured bass, major and minor triads in root position, and first and second inversion.
- *identifies* figured bass, major-minor seventh chords, diminished seventh chords, and diminished triads in root position and first inversion.
- *identifies* chord progression in a key by writing figured bass and Roman numerals.
- *notates* chords (all four parts) of chorale-type examples by dictation.

Unit 3: "Rhythm"

The student demonstrates skill in identifying and writing rhythms by dictation.

To demonstrate achievement of this goal, the student achieves such objectives as these:

- *identifies* rhythms played on tape or the piano.
- *writes* rhythms that are played in simple or compound time with neutral pitch.
- *identifies* errors in rhythms played from a given score.
- *notates* rhythms of melodies written by dictation.

Unit 4: "Melodies"

The student demonstrates skill in notating melodies by dictation.

To demonstrate achievement of this goal, the student achieves such objectives as these:

- *writes* melodic intervals, ascending or descending, given the first pitch.
- *writes* soprano and/or bass line of a chorale-style example by dictation.
- *writes* alto and/or tenor line of a chorale-style example by dictation.

IV. Methods of Instruction:

The nature of the goals and objectives suggests methods such as the following: individualized instruction, using taped exercise; group study (practice as a class or by division into smaller groups to work on specific weaknesses); singing individually before the class; or singing individually one part of multipart music with others singing respective parts.

V. Tests and Evaluation:

Tests will involve sight-singing examples before the class every two weeks. Written exams in dictation will be given after completion of each unit. Test items will involve performance in keeping with the objectives included in each unit. Sight-singing tests will count for 50 percent of the grade. Unit tests will count for 50 percent of the grade.

VI. Mediography:

Workbook in Ear Training, Bruce Bonward

Selected recordings of chords and so forth.

Course title: The Epistle to the Galatians (Greek Text)[4]

I. Rationale for the Course:

This course focuses on the following learning outcomes as expressed in the educational goals and objectives of the School of Theology.

The student . . .

- understands New Testament Greek.
- analyzes, translates, and exegetes the meaning of the books of the New Testament.
- demonstrates conviction that effective communication of the gospel requires accurate interpretation of the New Testament.

---

4. This course description was developed by Lorin Cranford, associate professor of New Testament, Southwestern Baptist Theological Seminary.

II. Course Goals and Objectives:

The student demonstrates understanding of the historical and literary meaning of Galatians.

The student values accurate translation as a requirement for effective communication of the teachings of the Book of Galatians.

To demonstrate achievement of these goals, the student translates the correct meaning of the Book of Galatians.

III. Unit Goals and Objectives:

Lesson 1: "Praescriptio, Galatians 1:1-5"

The student demonstrates understanding of the historical and literary setting of Galatians 1:1-5.

To demonstrate achievement of this goal, the student:

- *identifies* the basic elements of the ancient epistolary form as evidenced in Galatians 1:1-5 (according to appendix 5 in the *Student Workbook*).
- *recognizes* the literary relationship of this epistle to the ancient epistolary form as evidenced in the Book of Galatians.
- *parses* all substantives and verb forms in Galatians 1:1-5.
- *determines* the most likely reading of Galatians 1:1-5 where variants are listed.
- *assesses* the literary structure of Galatians 1:1-5. (*Analyzes* how Paul follows or deviates from ancient epistolary form.)
- *evaluates* the exegetical issues in Galatians 1:1-5. (*Analyzes* the differing interpretative viewpoints of the North-South theories, for example.)
- *recognizes* the basic design of the literary structure of the epistle, according to the structural outline in appendix 5.

Lesson 2: "Propositio, Galatians 1:6-10"

The student demonstrates understanding of the historical and literary setting of Galatians 1:6-10.

To demonstrate achievement of this goal, the student:

- *parses* all substantives and verb forms in Galatians 1:6-10.
- *translates* by dynamic-equivalent method all sentences in Galatians 1:6-10.
- *classifies* all sentences in Galatians 1:6-10.
- *classifies* all subordinate clauses in Galatians 1:6-10.
- *determines* the most likely reading of Galatians 1:6-10 where textual variants are listed.
- *assesses* the literary structure of Galatians 1:6-10.
- *evaluates* the exegetical issues in Galatians 1:6-10.
- *completes* the exegetical outline of Galatians 2:6-10 (or *outlines* exegetically Galatians 1:6-10).

Lesson 3: (All of the lessons which follow use essentially the same format as shown for lesson 2; only sections of the Book of Galatians change.)

IV. Methods of Instruction:

Methods of instruction grow out of the statements of goals and objectives for the course and its lesson. Those used in this course include completion of the *Study Manual* exercises, practice drills on parsing, translation of assigned sentences, classification exercises, oral reading, and so forth. The first work in each lesson objective (a verb) suggests the type of learning activity involved.

Class procedures for each lesson begin with an oral reading of each text. This is then followed by a translation of the text into English. Drill work over parsing of individual words and classification of sentences and clauses follows. Exegetical analysis of the textual meaning follows and is usually done by lecture in combination with question and answer.

V. Tests and Evaluation:

Three major exams will be given during the semester, including the final exam. The semester grade will be determined from an average of the following sources: major exam 1, major exam 2, final exam, weekly recitation grades, and the workbook. Each source counts for 20 percent of the grade.

VI. Mediography:

A Study Manual of the Epistle to the Galatians: Greek Text, Lorin Cranford

Galatians, Hans Dieter Betz

The Epistle to the Galatians, F. F. Bruce

The Epistle to the Galatians, Ernest De Witt Burton

The course designer may want to substitute some or all of the following objectives for the objectives show for lesson 1 and 2.[5]

- *Compares* the epistolary structure of Galatians with the ancient epistolary form as modified by Paul (using the Semantic Diagram in appendix 4 and appendix 5 for division of text pericopes).
- *Compares* the content of the Galatians praescriptio to the others in Paul.
- *Analyzes* similarities and differences between the Galatians praescriptio and the others in Paul.

---

5. These objectives also apply to a course in "The Epistle to the Galatians (English Text)."

- *Identifies* in the superscriptio the elements which constitute the tutelary aspects.
- *Explains* the interpretative alternatives for the phrase "not from man neither through man."
- *Identifies* the two expressions of the traditional material in the praescriptio and explains their role in this passage.
- *Identifies* geographically the adescriptio and *explains* the significance of the North Galatians Theory and the South Galatians Theory in regard to identity, time of writing, place of writing, and supportive scholars.
- *Explains* how the salutatio differs from the pure Hellenistic form.
- *Explains* the Jewish chronological presupposition behind the "so what" clause statement in verse 4.
- *Describes* the structural pattern of thought development in Galatians, using the Structural Outline in appendix 5 as the basis for assessment.

Course title: The Epistle to the Galatians (English Text)

Note: The course structure for the course which uses the English text is quite similar to the structure used for the course based on the Greek text. The number and nature of the unit objectives differ in appropriate ways.

The two units shown below illustrate the differences between the objectives for the two courses. The designer may also choose the alternate objectives shown on page 311.

I. Rationale for the Course:

This course focuses on the following learning outcomes as expressed in the educational goals and objectives for the School of Theology:

The student . . .

- analyzes and exegetes the meaning of Paul's Epistle to the Galatians.
- demonstrates conviction that effective communication of the gospel requires accurate interpretation of the New Testament.

II. Course Goals and Objectives:

The student demonstrates understanding of the historical and literary meaning of Galatians.

The student values accurate translation as a requirement for effective communication of the teachings of Galatians.

To demonstrate achievement of these goals, the student exegetes the meaning of the text of Galatians in keeping with what it most likely meant to those who read it or heard it read.

III. Unit Goals and Objectives:

Lesson 1: "Praescriptio, Galatians 1:1-5"

The student demonstrates understanding of the historical and literary setting of Galatians 1:1-5 (English text).

To demonstrate achievement of this goal, the student:

- *identifies* the basic elements of the ancient epistolary form.
- *recognizes* the literary relationship of this epistle to the ancient epistolary form.
- *assesses* the literary structure of Galatians 1:1-5.
- *evaluates* the exegetical issues in Galatians 1:1-5.
- *recognizes* the basic design of the literary structure of the epistle.

Lesson 2: "Propositio, Galatians 1:6-10"

The student demonstrates understanding of the historical and literary meaning of Galatians 1:6-10 (English text).

To demonstrate achievement of this goal, the student:

- *assesses* the literary structure of Galatians 1:6-10.
- *recognizes* the literary context of Galatians 1:6-10.
- *evaluates* the exegetical issues in Galatians 1:6-10.
- *outlines* exegetically Galatians 1:6-10.
- *produces* a semantic diagram of Galatians 1:6-10.

Lesson 3: (All of the lessons which follow use essentially the same format as shown for lesson 2; only the text under consideration changes.)

IV. Methods of Instruction:

(With appropriate changes, course follows the format established for the course based on the Greek text)

V. Tests and Evaluation:

(With appropriate changes, course follows the format established for the course based on the Greek text)

VI. Mediography:

(With appropriate changes, course follows the format established for the course based on the Greek text)

Course title: The Biblical and Philosophical Worlds: A Twentieth-Century Dialogue[6]

I. Rationale for the Course:

This course supports these educational goals and objectives of the School of Theology:

The student . . .

- understands the biblical and philosophical world views of the meaning of life.
- understands theological methods.
- demonstrates conviction that the biblical world view has the answers to universal religious questions.

II. Course Goals and Objectives:

The student demonstrates understanding of the biblical and philosophical world views related to the meaning of life's ultimate questions.

The student demonstrates conviction that the biblical world view has the answers to universal religious questions.

To demonstrate achievement of these goals the student:

- explains in a comparative and apologetic manner the relevance and superiority of the biblical world view over philosophical world views.
- preaches, teaches, and witnesses convincingly that the biblical world view is superior to the philosophical and religious world views and has the answers to universal religious questions.

III. Unit Goals and Objectives:

The student demonstrates understanding of the differences among the biblical and the philosophical views of the meaning of history.

To demonstrate achievement of this goal, the student:

- *analyzes* the Old Testament and New Testament views of the meaning of history and representative views influenced by biblical emphases (or *identifies* the central concepts in the biblical and philosophical views of the meaning of history).
- *analyzes* the pessimistic-cyclical views of world history, the optimistic-inevitable progress philosophical views, and the sense of uniqueness as a chosen people view of the meaning of history. *Identifies* the central concepts in each.

---

6. This course description was developed in consultation with John Newport, vice president for Academic Affairs and Provost and professor of Philosophy of Religion, Southwestern Baptist Theological Seminary.

- *outlines* the basic differences between the biblical and philosophical views of the meaning of history.
Unit 2: "Views of Revelation, Authority and Religious Language"

The student demonstrates understanding of the biblical and philosophical views of revelation, authority, and religious language.

To demonstrate achievement of this goal, the student:
- *analyzes* the biblical view of revelation, authority, and religious language so as to include:
  (a) the meaning of special revelation;
  (b) the approach to stories of the beginning and the end;
  (c) the unique function of biblical language;
  (d) objections to the biblical view; and
  (e) the view of authority, canon, and interpretation.
- *analyzes* the philosophical view of revelation, authority, and religious language so as to include:
  (a) the emphasis on exemplary rather than emissary approach,
  (b) the emphasis on abstract rather than particularistic,
  (c) the emphasis on inner confirmation,
  (d) the emphasis of major groups and movements, and
  (e) the emphasis on allergorical rather than grammatical-historical-literary approach.
- *outlines* the basic differences between the biblical and philosophical views of revelation, authority and religious language.
Unit 3: "Views of the Origin of Nature and Humans, Providence and Prayer, Miracles and Science

The student demonstrates understanding of the differences between the biblical and philosophical views of the origin of nature and humans, providence and prayer, and miracles and science.

To demonstrate achievement of this goal, the student:
- *analyzes* the biblical view so as to include:
  (a) Old Testament and New Testament views and alternative interpretations of the biblical view of the origin of nature,
  (b) Old Testament and New Testament views and alternative interpretations of the origin and nature of man (Adam),
  (c) the biblical viewpoint toward providence and prayer, and

(d) the biblical viewpoint toward miracles and science.
- *analyzes* the philosophical views so as to include:
  (a) the philosophical views of the origin of nature;
  (b) the philosophical views of the origin and nature of humans;
  (c) the philosophical views of alchemy, ceremonial magic, witchcraft, prayer, and worship;
  (d) the views of astrology and human relationships to the universe;
  (e) the philosophical views of miracles and miracle workers;
  (f) the views of occultism and modern science; and
  (g) the views which adapt to natural law.
- *summarizes* (or *outlines*) the differences between the biblical and philosophical views of the origin of nature and humans, providence and prayer, and miracles and science.

Unit 4: "Views of Evil, Suffering, and Satanic Forces"

The student demonstrates understanding of the differences between the biblical view and the philosophical views of evil, suffering, and satanic forces.

To demonstrate achievement of this goal, the student:
- *analyzes* the biblical view toward evil, suffering, and satanic forces so as to include:
  (a) a statement of the problem,
  (b) review of basic principles,
  (c) a systematic explanation of natural and moral evil,
  (d) the view toward satanic and demonic forces and,
  (e) the view toward spiritual healing.
- *analyzes* the philosophical views toward evil, suffering, and satanic forces so as to include:
  (a) the view of evil as ignorance and involvement in matter,
  (b) the view of evil as related to the law of Karma,
  (c) the view of evil as due to personal supernatural forces, and
  (d) the viewpoints related to spiritual healing.
- *outlines* the differences between the biblical and objective views of evil, suffering, and satanic forces.

Unit 5: "Views of the Life to Come and Immortality"

The student demonstrates understanding of the biblical and philosophical views of the life to come and immortality.

To demonstrate achievement of this goal, the student:
- *analyzes* the biblical view so as to include:
  (a) the early and later Old Testament views, and

    (b) the views of Jesus and the apostolic community in the
       New Testament.
- *analyzes* the philosophical views so as to include:
    (a) the Western version;
    (b) the Eastern roots;
    (c) the view of spiritualism;
    (d) the views of Theosophy and other related groups;
    (e) viewpoints toward ghosts, hauntings, poltergeists, and
       astral body;
    (f) viewpoints toward reincarnation; and
    (g) views toward U.F.O. contacts.
- *summarizes* the differences between the biblical and philosophical views of the life to come and immortality.

Unit 6: "Views of Religious Experience and Mysticism"

The student understands the biblical and philosophical views of religious experience and mysticism.

To demonstrate achievement of this goal, the student:
- *analyzes* the biblical view so as to include:
    (a) the Old Testament and New Testament views,
    (b) contemporary interpretations of the biblical view,
    (c) the view of reacting mysticism,
    (d) the view of religious experience and charismatic emphases (glossolalia/tongues),
    (e) the view of religious experience in Judaism, and
    (f) the view of religious experience in Christianity (conversion, sanctification, Catholic way, Protestant way).
- *analyzes* the philosophical views so as to include:
    (a) views rooted in animistic or primitive thought, and
    (b) views rooted in Hinduism and Buddhism (central beliefs and representative groups).
- *summarizes* the differences between the biblical and philosophical views of religious experience and mysticism.

Unit 7: "Views of the Place of Reason and the Knowledge of the Nature of God and Reality"

The student demonstrates understanding of the differences between the biblical and philosophical views of the place of reason and the knowledge of the nature of God and reality.

To demonstrate achievement of this goal, the student:
- *analyzes* the biblical view so as to include (or *identifies* the central concepts in):
    (a) the place of God's particularistic self-disclosure in the biblical view,
    (b) the place of obedience in the biblical view,

(c) the relation of sin and general revelation,

(d) the subordinate place of the rational arguments, and

(e) the view of ultimate proof-fulfillment of biblical promises.

- *analyzes* the philosophical views so as to include the:

(a) views of groups rooted in Hinduism,

(b) views of Buddhism,

(c) views rooted in Islam,

(d) views developed in the West, and

(e) views rooted in Judaism.

- *outlines* the differences between the biblical and the philosophical views of the place of reason and the knowledge of the nature of God and reality.

Unit 8: "Views of Moral Responsibility, Freedom, and Ethics"

The student demonstrates understanding of the biblical and philosophical views of moral responsibility, freedom, and ethics. To demonstrate achievement of this goal, the student:

- *analyzes* the biblical view of moral responsibility, freedom, and ethics so as to include (or *identifies* the central concepts in):

(a) the Old Testament covenant concept,

(b) the New Testament gratitude and kingship concept,

(c) the centrality of idolatry and *agape* love,

(d) the centrality of the ethical prophet,

(e) the group consciousness concept,

(f) the view of the ethical and conscientious humans,

(g) the views of communes, and

(h) the fulfillment in history emphasis.

- *analyzes* the philosophical views of moral responsibility, freedom, and ethics so as to include the philosophical views of Kant, Sartre, and Marcel.

- *analyzes* the occult views of moral responsibility, freedom and ethics so as to include:

(a) the life-style and enlightenment of Hinduism, Buddhism, Theosophy, and Church of Satan;

(b) the individual consciousness view of the Church of Satan, Hare Krishna, Baha'i, Church of All Worlds; and

(c) the problem of freedom and determinism in the Church of Light, astrology, and law of Karma.

- *outlines* the differences between the biblical and the philosophical views of moral responsibility, freedom, and ethics.

Unit 9: "Views of Beauty, Aesthetics, and Culture in the Knowledge of God (Reality), Worship, and Life-style"

The student demonstrates understanding of the biblical and the philosophical views of beauty, aesthetic, and culture in the knowledge of God, worship, and life-style.

To demonstrate achievement of this goal, the student:

- *analyzes* the biblical view so as to include (or *identifies* the central concepts in the biblical view):
  (a) the view of nature as sister rather than mother or semi-illusory;
  (b) the Brahamic view and the Romantic view compared to the biblical view;
  (c) the concept of balance between the transcendence and immanence of God;
  (d) the view of worship as rooted in God's historical acts of creation and redemption;
  (e) the positive and evaluative approach to culture;
  (f) the false theories and positive values of the arts in a useful way but secondary role; and
  (g) the view toward literature, drama, and painting.
- *analyzes* the philosophical views of beauty, aesthetics and culture in the knowledge of God, worship, and life-style so as to include:
  (a) the view of nature as mother (in religious Greeks, Romantic movement, new-pagan groups, Feraferia, Church of All Worlds, witchcraft, the Church of Eternal Source, and Sabaianism);
  (b) the views of extremes of transcendence and immanence;
  (c) the view of the symbolic and ecstatic (in polytheism, new-paganism, Romanticism, Builders of the Adytum, Hare Krishna, and Zen);
  (d) the tendency toward idolatrous use of symbols; and
  (e) the tendency toward the magical.
- *summarizes* the differences between the biblical view and the philosophical views of beauty, aesthetics, and culture in the knowledge of God, worship, and life-style.

IV. Methods of Instruction:

The methods of instruction include those appropriate for analytical study. These include the research report, the case study, the teaching lecture, and other related methods. Each student will prepare four five-to-six page analysis reports on selected topics dealt with in the units of study. The reports will focus on the central concepts in the particular viewpoint and the differences and similarities among the viewpoints. The reports will explain in a comparative and apologetic manner the relevance of the superiority of the biblical world view over philosophical world views. (See the course objective.) The student may make the report in the form of graphics, a formal paper, an illustrated videotaped presentation, or some other format approved by the professor.

V. Tests and Evaluation:

Three major tests will be given during the semester, one each at the end of three units of study. As indicated in the objectives, the tests will focus on the central concepts of the viewpoints and the differences between the biblical and philosophical views. Many of the test items will involve matching and multiple-choice responses. Each of the four analysis reports will be evaluated in accordance with the "Report Evaluation Sheet" provided at the beginning of the semester. The three examinations will count for 50 percent of the grade; the four analysis reports will count for the remaining 50 percent of the grade.

VI. Mediography:

Philosophy and the Christian Faith, Colin Brown

Religious and Spiritual Groups in Modern American, Robert W. Ellwood

Judaism and Modern Man, Will Herberg

God and Reason, Ed L. Miller

Christ and the New Consciousness, John Newport

What Is Christian Doctrine?, John Newport

Course title: Basic Sermon Preparation[7]

I. Rationale for the Course:

This course focuses on the following learning outcomes as expressed in the educational goals and objectives of the School of Theology:

The student . . .

• understands the process of sermon preparation.

• plans and delivers sermons.

• communicates effectively.

---

7. This course description was written by LeRoy Ford, professor emeritus of Foundations of Education, Southwestern Baptist Theological Seminary. It is based primarily on Brown, Clinard, and Northcutt, *Steps to the Sermon.*

- demonstrates commitment to disciplined sermon preparation.
II. Course Goals and Objectives:
The student demonstrates understanding of the steps in sermon preparation.

The student demonstrates commitment to careful planning for preaching.

To demonstrate achievement of this goals, the student:
- plans and delivers sermons on approved subjects or passages of Scripture.
- analyzes given sermons to determine whether they reflect the steps presented in this course.
- evaluates sermons according to criteria presented in the course.
III. Unit Goals and Objectives:
Unit 1: "Understands What Preaching Means"

The student demonstrates understanding of what preaching means.

To demonstrate achievement of this goal, the student defines preaching so as to indicate what preaching proclaims, what contains the truth proclaimed, who does the proclaiming, and the purpose and content of proclamation.

Unit 2: "Find a Bible Truth to Preach"

The student demonstrates understanding of the approaches to finding a Bible truth to preach.

To demonstrate achievement of this goal, the student:
- defines "Bible truth."
- explains four idea sources for Bible truths to preach.
- locates Scripture passages which relate to given truths.
Unit 3: "Interpret the Bible Text"

The student demonstrates understanding of the principles for interpreting the Bible text.

To demonstrate achievement of this goal, the student:
- recalls and explains the six principles of interpretation.
- interprets a given Scripture passage using the six principles.
- exegetes a given passage in preparation for preparing the sermon.
Unit 4: "Decide on the Central Thesis of the Sermon"

The student demonstrates understanding of what central truth means and the characteristics of a central truth.

To demonstrate achievement of this goal, the student:
- defines central truth.

- discriminates among examples those which properly express a central truth.
- rewrites improperly stated central truths.
- states a central truth or thesis for a sermon so as to reflect given characteristics.
  Unit 5: "Determine the General Objective (Aim) and Specific Objectives"
The student demonstrates understanding of what "aim" (general objective) means and characteristics of an aim.
To demonstrate achievement of this goal, the student:
- defines sermon aim.
- discriminates among examples those which express properly a sermon aim.
- rewrites improperly stated sermon aims.
- states original sermon aims which reflect properly the characteristics of an aim.
  Unit 6: "Gather the Material"
The student demonstrates understanding of the sources from which to gather sermon material and the purposes of illustrations.
To demonstrate achievement of this goal, the student:
- recalls the sources of sermon material.
- locates materials for given subjects.
- explains the purposes of illustrations.
- finds illustrations for given ideas.
- gathers materials, including illustrations, for a sermon on an approved subject.
  Unit 7: "Allow Time for Preparation to Mature"
The student demonstrates understanding of the conditions which foster the maturing process in sermon preparation.
To demonstrate achievement of this goal, the student explains the role of time, input, divine leadership, and the subconscious mind in the maturation process.
  Unit 8: "Complete the Sermon as You Will Preach It"
The student demonstrates understanding of the process of developing the structure of a sermon (title, introduction, outline, body, conclusion).
  The Title:
The student demonstrates understanding of the process for stating an appropriate title for the sermon.
To demonstrate achievement of this goal, the student:
- recalls and explains the four kinds of sermon titles (em-

phatic word, question, imperative sentence, and declarative sentence).

- discriminates among titles those which represent each form.
- writes original examples of the four kinds of sermon titles.

The Introduction:

The student demonstrates understanding of the eight forms of an introduction and process for developing an introduction.

To demonstrate achievement of this goal, the student:

- recalls and explains the eight kinds of introductions.
- classifies given examples of sermon introductions according to form.
- writes original examples of each form of sermon introductions.

The Body:

The student demonstrates understanding of the steps in preparing the body of a sermon and the four ways to develop sermon points (explanation, illustration, application, argumentation).

To demonstrate achievement of this goal, the student:

- explains the guidelines for developing a sermon outline.
- explains the three ways to develop sermon points.
- develops a sermon outline following the three guidelines.
- develops given sermon points, using appropriately the three development approaches.
- develops the body of a sermon, following the guidelines presented in the course.

The Conclusion:

The student demonstrates understanding of the types of sermon conclusions and the process for writing them.

To demonstrate achievement of this goal, the student:

- explains the functions and characteristics of a conclusion.
- recalls and explains five types of conclusions (application, illustration, poetic, summary, and direct appeal).
- classifies given examples of the kinds of conclusions according to the type each represents.
- writes original examples of the five types of conclusions.

The Invitation:

The student demonstrates understanding of the guidelines for giving an invitation.

To demonstrate achievement of this goal, the student:

- explains the nine guidelines for giving an invitation.

- evaluates given invitations according to the nine guidelines.
- prepares invitations appropriate for a given kind of sermon (such as an evangelistic sermon).

Unit 10: "Putting It All Together"

The student demonstrates understanding of the process of combining the sermon elements into a complete sermon.

To demonstrate achievement of this goal, the student:

- evaluates given sermons.
- writes sermon briefs.
- prepares and delivers original sermons.

IV. Methods of Instruction:

Methods and learning activities grow out of the statements of goals and objectives for the course and its units. Those used in this course include discrimination exercises, case analysis, evaluation of recorded sermons, preparation and evaluation of sermon briefs, practice preaching, preparation and evaluation of original sermons, and evaluation of peers.

V. Tests and Evaluation:

Tests will consist of whatever activities the objectives call for. The *course* goal and objective statements describe the highest level of learning expected in the course. The course goal and objective calls for the student to prepare and preach an original sermon. This performance, evaluated according to criteria presented in the course, will constitute two thirds of the grade weight for the course. The other third will be derived from grades given on sermon briefs and from periodic "test your progress" examinations based on the lead-up objectives in each unit. In advance, the professor will furnish you a copy of a "Sermon Evaluation Sheet" which he will use in evaluating your sermon.

VI. Mediography:

Books:

Fire in Thy Mouth, the Way to Biblical Preaching, Donald Miller

How to Give an Invitation, Roy Fish

Preparation and Delivery of Sermons, John A. Broadus

Steps to the Sermon, Brown, Clinard, and Northcutt

Recordings:

Selected audio and video recordings of sermons.

Course title: Educational Programming for Family Life Ministry[8]

I. Rationale for the Course:

This course focuses on the following learning outcomes as expressed in the educational goals and objectives of the School of Religious Education.

The student . . .

- understands the process for developing a plan for family life ministry.
- views the family as God's instrument for fulfilling His purpose for humankind.

To demonstrate achievement of these goals, the student develops a plan for a family life ministry in a church.

II. Course Goal and Objective:

The student demonstrates understanding of educational programming in meeting family-related needs.

To demonstrate achievement of this goal the student designs family enrichment learning activities to meet needs of a specified group in the church, such as family life conferences, marriage enrichment retreats, parenting or communication workshops, and sex education seminars.

III. Unit Goals and Objectives:

Unit 1: "Rationale for a Church's Family Ministry"

The student demonstrates understanding of the basis of the church's concerns for family ministry.

To demonstrate achievement of this goal, the student achieves such objectives as these:

- recalls biblical passages indicating the importance of the family.
- explains the fundamental needs of humankind that are family related.
- identifies influences in modern society which are of concern to families and churches.

Unit 2: "Family-Related Needs of Developing Individuals"

The student demonstrates understanding of the scope of family-related needs of children, youth, and single and married adults at successive stages of life.

To demonstrate achievement of this goal, the student achieves such objectives as these:

---

8. This course description was written by Pat Clendinning, professor of Psychology of Religion and Counseling, Southwestern Baptist Theological Seminary.

- differentiates between general developmental needs and those that are family related.
- recognizes those needs that will be met solely by family members and those which can also be met by the church.
- identifies the personal needs of individuals as they develop and the skills needed in guiding the growth of other family members.
- predicts the changing expression of a need at various stages of life.

Unit 3: "Planning to Meet Family Needs"

The student demonstrates understanding of the process of determining and planning to meet family-related needs.

To demonstrate achievement of this goal, the student achieves such objectives as these:

- explains the procedure for surveying the community and the church to determine family needs.
- develops methods of establishing priorities for age groups and the whole church within specified planning periods.
- produces an annual calendar of family ministry events that is balanced and comprehensive.

Unit 4: "Meeting Crisis Needs of Families"

The student demonstrates understanding of how the church is organized to meet crisis needs.

To demonstrate achievement of this goal, the student achieves such objectives as these:

- differentiates between the developmental needs of individuals and the crisis possibilities affecting families.
- identifies existing organizations that have ministry potential in crises.
- proposes a training plan for church leaders to equip them for meeting crisis needs.

Unit 5: "Developing Family Enrichment Activities to Meet Family Needs"

The student demonstrates understanding of the principles of designing learning activities on the basis of specified family-related needs.

To demonstrate achievement of this goal, the student achieves such objectives as these:

- designs learning activities meeting family-related needs of a specified nature and in a given setting.
- demonstrates experiential learning activities for communicating certain content.

- chooses visual aids, resource materials, and illustrations to recommend to class members.

IV. Methods of Instruction:

Methods of instruction grow out of the performances indicated in the course and unit goals and objectives. Each student would design one of the following projects: a family life conference, marriage enrichment retreat, parenting-communication workshop, or sex education seminar. Methods used in the classroom will include demonstrations of project planning meeting, the teaching lecture, and group research projects.

V. Tests and Evaluation:

The course goals and objectives call for the student to design a family life project (conference, worship, retreat, seminar). These projects will be graded using the "Project Evaluation Form" as a guide. Each student will receive a copy of the form at the beginning of the course. This project will count for two thirds of the semester grade. Other tests based on the unit goals and objectives will count for one third of the semester grade.

VI. Mediography:

The Intimate Marriage, Clinebell
Growing Parents, Growing Children, Grant
Christian Marriage: Growing in Oneness, Howell
Marriage Enrichment in the Church, Mace
Ministering to Families, Money
Marriage and Family Enrichment: New Perspectives and Programs, Otto
Family Ministry, Sell

Course Title: The Church and Community Intervention (Social Work)[9]

I. Rationale for the Course:

This course supports these educational goals and objectives of the School of Church Social Ministries:

The student . . .

- understands the concepts of social work intervention.
- demonstrates concern for persons facing personal problems.

To demonstrate achievement of this goal, the student plans intervention strategies appropriate for given situations.

II. Course Goal and Objective:

9. This course description was written by Bob Brackney, associate professor of Social Work, Southwestern Baptist Theological Seminary.

The student demonstrates understanding of the concepts of social work intervention with communities by analyzing a community's needs and resources and planning intervention strategies appropriate to the situation (a strategy-planning project).

III. Unit Goals and Objectives:

Unit 1: "Historical Development and Context of Community Intervention"

The student demonstrates understanding of community intervention, history, and context of its practice by achieving objectives such as these:

- lists six significant movements in the history of community intervention in the nineteenth and twentieth centuries.
- describes the three major types of community intervention practice.
- explains the sociological concepts of community and organization.
- explains the interplay of demographic, ecological, and cultural themes.

Unit 2: "The Practice of Community Intervention"

The student will demonstrate understanding of the community intervention process by achieving objectives such as these:

- lists and describes the major components of the community intervention process.
- describes the technical tasks involved in the community intervention process.
- explains the development of a support constituency.
- explains the role of the social worker as a change agent.

Unit 3: "Community Intervention Strategies"

The student will demonstrate understanding of methods and strategies used in community intervention by achieving objectives such as these:

- lists the elements of a community analysis.
- describes the organizational process used in the implementation and completion of a community analysis.
- explains the planning and implementation process of various intervention strategies.

Unit 4: "The Church and Community Intervention"

The student will demonstrate understanding of the church as a community change agent by achieving objectives such as these:

- describes the elements of conflict management.

- develops an analysis of the needs and resources of a given church community.
- explains the role of the minister as a change agent.

IV. Methods of Instruction:

The methods of instruction include those appropriate for achieving the course goals and objectives. The course goals and objectives call for planning intervention strategies based on an analysis of community needs and resources. Students may choose from the following approaches to development of such a project: research report, graphic presentation, videotaped simulation of the strategy-planning process, or another approach approved by the professor. Other methods include the teaching lecture, the case study, simulations, and on-site experiences.

V. Tests and Evaluation:

The strategy-planning project will count for two thirds of the semester grade and will be considered the "final exam" for the course. Other tests based on other unit goals and objectives will count for one third of the grade. The student would analyze carefully the unit goals and objectives for guidance in preparation for tests.

VI. Mediography:

Strategies of Community Organization, Cox, et. al.
Community Organization, Ross.
Community Organizing and Development, Rubin and Rubin.
The Change Agent, Schaller.

Course Title: Systematic Theology[10]

I. Rationale for the Course:

This course focuses on the following learning outcomes as expressed in the educational goals and objectives of the School of Theology:

The student . . .
- understands theological method.
- synthesizes theology and theological perspective within the context of the believing community.
- views systematic theology as a dynamic process.

II. Course Goals and Objectives:

---

10. This course description was developed in this format by LeRoy Ford after consultation with David Kirkpatrick, associate professor of Theology, Southwestern Baptist Theological Seminary.

The student demonstrates understanding of the primary theological questions which the Christian theologian confronts.

To demonstrate achievement of this goal, the student:

- writes a personal theology and theological perspective within the parameters of this course.[11]
- interprets and evaluates critically the nature, sources, scope, the doctrines of theology.

The student views systematic theology as a dynamic process rather than a static discipline.

The student views systematic theology as a discipline which one cannot separate from the other disciplines of theological education.

To demonstrate achievement of the preceding two goals, the student evaluates and synthesizes continually his own theology and theological perspective

III. Unit Goals and Objectives:

Unit 1: "God and Revelation"

The student demonstrates understanding of the Christian doctrine of God and revelation.

To demonstrate achievement of this goal, the student:

- writes a Christian doctrine of God and revelation using exegesis, the Bible, Christian history, and content as sources. Student writes within the context of the work of a pastor, youth worker, and so forth and in the broader context of the church where he or she serves. (Note: The designer may specify a time frame if desired.)
- summarizes what revelation means as related to the doctrine of God.

Unit 2: "God and Creation; Providence and Man"

The student demonstrates understanding of the doctrines of creation, providence, and anthropology.

To demonstrate achievement of this goal, the student:

- reconstructs from specified sources the Christian doctrine of creation.
- reconstructs from specified sources the Christian doctrine of providence.

---

11. This objective assumes that the student uses in a meaningful way what has been learned by doing such things as preparing and delivering sermons on basic doctrines and planning and leading group studies on doctrines. In this sense, systematic theology is a prerequisite to other courses in a vertical cluster which require understanding of theological method.

- reconstructs from specified sources Christian doctrine of humans (anthropology).
- explains his own theology and theological perspective of the doctrines of God and creation, providence, and anthropology.

Unit 3: "Christology; Soteriology"

The student demonstrates understanding of the relationship of Christology to the doctrines of creation, providence, and anthropology.

To demonstrate achievement of this goal, the student:

- analyzes the relationship of Christology to these doctrines.
- explains the significance of this relationship for the doctrine of God.
- explains a personal theological perspective of this relationship.

Unit 4: "Pneumatology"

The student demonstrates understanding of the place of the Holy Spirit in the Trinity and Christian life.

To demonstrate achievement of this goal, the student:

- analyzes the place of the Holy Spirit in the Trinity and in the Christian life.
- explains a personal theological perspective of the place of the Holy Spirit in the Trinity and Christian life.

IV. Methods of Instruction:

Dialogical-inductive analysis is the primary instructional approach. Students do critical evaluation of sources of theology. The vehicle for the dialogical-inductive approach is the teaching lecture (lecture-dialogue). Each student prepares periodically a three-page research brief on topics dealt with in the class sessions and assigned reading materials.

V. Tests and Evaluation:

Tests will consist of whatever activity the course goals and objectives call for. For example, if the objective says, "The student explains a personal theology and theological perspective of the doctrine of God," the examination item will call for such an explanation. Four major examinations will be given—one for each major unit of study. These examinations will count for one fourth of the final grade. Daily examinations over assigned material will consist generally of objective questions related directly to the subject. These examinations will count for one fourth of the grade. The research briefs will be evaluated primarily on the basis of evidence of thorough research, organization, and clarity. These briefs will count for one fourth of the grade. In keeping with the principal goal and objective for the course, each student will prepare a paper or some other approved project which reflects a synthesis of a personal theology and theological perspective. This paper or project will count for one fourth of the final grade and will constitute the "final examination."

VI. Mediography:

> *Essentials of Evangelical Theology,* vol. 1, Donald G. Bloesch
>
> *Early Christian Doctrines,* J. N. D. Kelly
>
> *Foundations of Dogmatics,* vol. 1, Otto Weber, translated by Darrell L. Guder

Course Title: The Teaching Ministry of the Church[12]

I. Rationale for the Course:

This course supports these educational goals and objectives of the School of Religious Education:

The student . . .

- understands the principles and dynamics of teaching in the church.
- understands the process of developing a church curriculum plan.
- demonstrates commitment to the teaching task as a biblical function of the church.

To demonstrate achievement of these goals, the student designs and conducts a teacher-training event.

II. Course Goal and Objective:

The student demonstrates an understanding of the role of the Christian educator in the teaching-learning process within the local church.

To demonstrate achievement of this goal, the student . . .

- formulates a biblical basis for the teaching ministry in the church.
- designs lesson plans for given denominational curricula.
- completes a literature order form based on a church case description.
- designs and conducts a teaching-training event.

---

12. This course description was developed as a joint project by professors Daryl Eldridge, William A. (Budd) Smith, and Charles Ashby, Foundations of Education Department, Southwestern Baptist Theological Seminary.

III. Unit Goals and Objectives:
   Unit 1: "Dynamics in the Teaching Situation"
   The student demonstrates understanding of the roles that God, the teacher, the learner, the curriculum, and methodology have in the educative experience.
   To demonstrate achievement of this goal, the student achieves such things as these:
   - explains the relationship of God, learner, and teacher in the teaching ministry of the church.
   - explains the role of the teacher.
   - describes the content of Christian teaching.
   - formulates a biblical basis for the teaching ministry in the church.
   Unit 2: "Lesson Preparation"
   The student demonstrates an understanding of the steps involved in lesson preparation.
   To demonstrate achievement of this goal, the student achieves such objectives as these:
   - lists and explains the steps in lesson preparation.
   - identifies aids utilized in lesson preparation.
   - outlines a unit of study for given curriculum.
   - writes a background study for a given passage of Scripture using principles of biblical interpretation outlined in class.
   - evaluates teaching procedures based on criteria given in class.
   - develops a lesson plan using denominational curriculum materials.
   Unit 3: "Practical Curriculum Problems"
   The learner will demonstrate an understanding of the role of curriculum in the educational practice of the church.
   To demonstrate achievement of this goal, the student achieves such objectives as these:
   - solves practical curriculum problems in given case studies.
   - explains the advantages of using denominational literature.
   - explains the "tests of an adequate curriculum as proposed by Colson and Rigdon.
   - completes a literature order form based on a church case description.
   Unit 4: "Equipping Others in the Teaching Ministry"
   The student demonstrates an understanding of the educator's role in the weekly workers' meeting and other teaching-training events.

To demonstrate achievement of this goal, the student achieves such objectives as these:
- leads a simulated weekly lesson planning meeting.
- designs and conducts a teaching training workshop.

IV. Methods of Instruction:

Methodology for the course grows out of the statements of goals and objectives. The nature of the goals and objectives suggests methods such as the following: case studies, simulations, lectures, and group work.

V. Tests and Evaluation:

"Tests" will consist of whatever activity is called for by the objectives. For example, the course and unit goals and objectives call for designing and conducting a teacher training workshop, writing a biblical basis for the teaching ministry of the church, leading a weekly workers' meeting, designing lesson plans for given lesson course material, and completing literature order forms. These "products" constitute the major "tests" for the course. Objective tests will cover the en route objectives listed for each unit of study. The workshop and the weekly workers' meeting will each count for two thirds of the semester grade. Other tests and assignments will count for one third.

VI. Mediography:

Why the Church Must Teach, Coleman
Preparing to Teach the Bible, Colson
Helping the Teacher Teach, Edge
The Teaching Ministry of the Church, Smart
Twelve Dynamic Bible Study Methods, Warren

Course Title: Using Computers in Christian Education[13]

I. Rationale for the Course:

This course focuses on the following learning outcomes as expressed in the educational goals and objectives of the School of Religious Education.

The student . . .
- understands the principles of teaching.
- understands the role of computer systems in Christian education.
- demonstrates conviction that the church is responsible for

---

13. This course description was developed by Rick Yount, assistant professor in Foundations of Education, Southwestern Baptist Theological Seminary.

providing high quality teaching and training in the community of learners.

To demonstrate achievement of these goals, the student develops teaching and training approaches which result in effective learning.

II. Course Goal and Objective:

The student demonstrates understanding of the process of designing computerized instructional materials in Christian education.

To demonstrate achievement of this goal, the student designs a computerized tutorial on a selected Bible passage or church-related training topic.

III. Unit Goals and Objectives:

Unit 1: "Using Computers in the Local Church"

The student demonstrates understanding of the use of computers in the local church.

To demonstrate achievement of this goal, the student achieves such objectives as these:

- defines major components of computer systems.
- explains the characteristics of operating systems and languages.
- describes functions of the church which can be assisted by computers.

Unit 2: "Educational Foundations of Computer Enhanced Learning (CEL)"

The student demonstrates understanding of the educational foundations of computerized instruction.

To demonstrate achievement of this goal, the student achieves such objectives as these:

- explains the philosophical foundations of computer enhanced learning.
- describes the relationship of the theories of learning to CEL.
- analyzes CEL by way of selected principles of teaching.
- explains the systems approach to instructional development.

Unit 3: "The Language of Basic"

The student demonstrates understanding of the Basic programming language.

To demonstrate achievement of this goal, the student achieves such objectives as these:

- defines each of the Basic commands and statements.
- analyzes program segments written in Basic.

- writes selected Basic program segments as assigned.

Unit 4: "Developing CEL Programs with Basic"

The student demonstrates understanding of computerized instructional design using the Basic language.

To demonstrate achievement of this goal, the student achieves such objectives as these:

- produces an interactive tutorial program on a selected Bible passage or study topic.
- produces pre and posttesting programs to measure student understanding of tutorial content.
- produces a drill and practice computer program over the commands of PILOT.

IV. Methods of Instruction:

This course focuses on the project method. Each student produces an interactive tutorial program on a selected Bible passage or a church leadership training topic. Other methods include individualized instruction, demonstration, teaching lecture, small-group work sessions, and project evaluation procedures.

V. Tests and Evaluation:

The course objective calls for production of an interactive tutorial program. This program will be evaluated according to the criteria included on the "Program Evaluation Sheet." Each student will receive a copy of the evaluation sheet at the beginning of the semester. The interactive tutorial program will count for two thirds of the semester grade. Other tests based on the unit goals and objectives will count for one third of the semester grade.

VI. Mediography:

> *Instructional Computing Fundamentals,* Culp and Nickles
> *Instructional Computing,* Dennis and Kansky
> *Microcomputer Applications in the Classroom,* Hofmeister
> *Understanding Computer Based Education,* Seigal and Davis,
> *Teaching Computers to Teach,* Steinberg

Appendix 2
Providing for Interactive Instruction in Correspondence School Materials

1. *Activity Reversal.*—For Example: Find what is *correct* in the following paragraph. Find what is *incorrect* in the following paragraph.

2. *Domain crossover.*—For example: In the case study below, list the violations of guidelines for Christian family living (cognitive domain). After reading the case study below (same as above) tell of a time in your own family life when you may have violated these guidelines for Christian family living (affective domain).

3. *Multiple sources.*—For example: Which verses in the following *Bible passage* deal with the nature of the church? Which phrases in the following *hymn* deal with the nature of the church?

4. *Elevation of learning level.*—For example: Quote the Beatitudes (knowledge-recall level). Which of the following best explains what *blessed* means? (comprehension level)

5. *Same level variation.*—For example: List the names of the books of the New Testament. Which of the names of the books of the New Testament is missing in the following list? (Both are knowledge level.)

6. *Single discrimination.*—For example: Is the following an example of *agape* love?(yes or no)

7. *Multiple discrimination.*—For example: In the following list of examples, check the two which are examples of . . .

8. *Item ordering.*—For example: Arrange in sequence the following events in the story of redemption:

_____ baptism of John	_____ crucifixion	
_____ resurrection of Jesus	_____ burial of Jesus	
_____ man's fall	_____ Jesus in Judea	
_____ creation of man	_____ the last supper	
_____ birth of Jesus	_____ ascension	

9. *Relative degree descrimination.*—For example: Which of the following comes closest to Baptists in church polity? Methodists? Presbyterians? Brethren?

10. *Graphic stimulus items.*—For example: Look at the following series of pictures. Make up a title for the series. Write the "title" in the blank.

TITLE:_____

11. *Graphic response items.*—For example: Which of the following shows the best way to arrange a room for preschoolers?

12. *Graphic ordering.*—For example: Number of the following pictures in the order in which the events occurred.

13. *Item matching.*—For example: Match the following names of books in the Bible with the authors to whom the books are generally attributed.

_____John	1. Acts
_____Luke	2. Hebrews
_____Paul	3. Philemon
	4. Revelation

14. *Item classification.*—For example: Classify the following names of the books of the Bible according to division.

Appendix 3
Guidelines for Teaching
for Knowledge, Understanding, Skills,
Attitudes, and Values

Knowledge

1. Involve learners in activities which call for active response.

2. Provide activities in which learners use more than one of the *senses* at the same time.

3. Provide activities in which learners use advance organizers. (They see in advance the total organization pattern of the information or establish in advance their learning intent.)

4. Provide for immediate knowledge of results.

5. Involve learners in numerous and varied activities related to the same goal.

6. Provide novel activities in regard to the information.

Skill

Demonstration:

1. Arrange for learners to see in advance the total organization of the process or product.

2. Arrange for learners to see a step-by-step demonstration.

Practice:

3. Ask learners to explain (say aloud) a set of instructions or a plan for carrying out a sequence of actions.

4. Guide learners in their first attempts.

5. Provide opportunities for learners to perform the activity repeatedly with little or no guidance.

6. Provide for practice under realistic conditions.

Understanding

1. Provide learning activities in which learners change (translate) ideas into new forms.

2. Use activities in which learners discover relationships between one idea and another.

3. Provide activities in which learners define and interpret ideas and concepts.

4. Involve learners in activities which call for them to use in practical ways what they have learned.

5. Provide learning activities in which the learners break material down into its parts.

6. Involve learners in activities in which they use a systematic approach to solving problems.

7. Use learning activities in which learners put together elements and parts to form a new creative "product."

8. Use learning activities in which learners judge the value or worth of something based on given standards.

Attitudes and Values

1. Arrange for learners to observe leaders and peers who set the right example and exemplify the attitude.

2. Provide opportunities for learners to read or hear about persons who exemplify the attitude.

3. Arrange for learners to confront sources which they consider authoritative.

4. Help learners identify and specify the attitude and learn what the attitude means.

5. Provide opportunities for learners to have meaningful emotional experiences.

6. Arrange for learners to take positive action in relation to the attitude and practice the attitude in situations which call for it.

7. Provide opportunities for learners to analyze their own values to practice making decisions on moral and ethical issues.

8. Provide activities in which learners reflect upon their own life experiences in the light of eternal truth.

9. Arrange for learners to share their insights with others in a climate of freedom.

> Elaborations of these four models appear in *Design for Teaching and Training: A Self-study Guide to Lesson Planning* by LeRoy Ford. The book consists of 232 practice cycles on the three elements of a lesson plan: goals and objectives, learning activities, and tests. It was validated on the basis of delayed posttests.

Appendix 4
List of Institutional Educational Goals
Winebrenner Theological Seminary[1]

As an institution of the Churches of God, General Conference, Winebrenner Theological Seminary is to provide theological education for men and women who are qualified candidates for the vocational ministries of the church; for those who desire to engage in theological studies as laypersons; and to give particular emphasis to programs preparing persons for leadership in the ministries of the local church. The following institutional educational goals have been identified because they refer to things the learner will do in a meaningful way during the entire course of her/his ministry. They serve as the Seminary's standard for preparing persons for the vocational ministries of the church and thus fulfilling the Seminary's mission. Not every student is expected to achieve all of the educational goals, rather students achieve that portion considered appropriate to the program in which they are enrolled.

Cognitive Domain

The learner demonstrates understanding of:

1. The background, history, contents, and major teachings of Scripture.

2. Methods and skills utilized in interpretation and application of Scripture.

3. The original languages of the Bible.

4. The broad outline of the history of Christian faith.

5. The nature of divine revelation and authority.

6. The essential doctrines of Christian theology.

---

1. Used by permission.

7. The application of the Christian faith to individual and corporate moral issues.

8. The integration of personal theological commitment and ministerial actions in light of Scripture, experience and context.

9. The ministry of the church as it is expressed in education, evangelism and the care and counsel of persons.

10. The mission of the church.

11. A basic grasp of the facts about the cultural, racial, ethnic and other special groups to/with whom they may minister.

12. Principles and processes of sermon preparation and delivery.

13. The nature, content and leadership of Christian worship.

14. Principles, approaches and skills utilized in leading and equipping persons for service in the church.

15. Denominational history and polity.

Affective Domain

The learner demonstrates:

1. Assurance of his/her call to vocational ministry.

2. Submission to God's leadership and to the leadership of spiritual authorities.

3. Commitment to the biblical models of servant leadership.

4. Faithfulness and dependability in the exercise of his/her gifts and assigned tasks for ministry.

5. Openness toward new ideas.

6. Commitment to personal wholeness: spiritually, physically, intellectually, emotionally and socially.

7. A positive attitude toward his/her own sexuality.

8. Commitment to assuming his/her own personal responsibility for the nurture and admonition of persons within his/her household.

9. Respect for the integrity, worth and uniqueness of all persons.

10. Commitment to ministry to the total person.

11. Commitment to acts of love and compassion for others which expresses a spirituality that is committed to obedience to Jesus Christ.

12. Commitment to the church's universal mission to take the message of the gospel of Jesus Christ to all peoples and nations.

13. Commitment to healthy, reproducing congregations.

14. Commitment to intentional ministry based on short- and long-range planning.

15. Persistence in working toward goals.
16. Commitment to equipping the saints for doing the work of ministry.
17. Loyalty to his/her church/denomination and its visions and traditions.
18. Respect for the value of ecumenical cooperation with other Christian denominations/traditions.
19. Commitment to lifelong learning.

Summary

This revised and expanded list of goals, in conjunction with the Mission Statement, Statement of Faith, Scope, and Educational Philosophy, represents clearly what the Seminary does and wants to accomplish. The Seminary believes that the educational goals lay the necessary foundation for integration of all the institution's educational processes, integration which leads to fulfillment of the Mission Statement.

Index